U.S.-EC Relations
in the Post–Cold War Era

U.S.-EC Relations
in the Post–Cold War Era

Conflict or Partnership?

René Schwok

Westview Press

BOULDER • SAN FRANCISCO • OXFORD

This study has been supported by a grant from the Swiss National Fund for Scientific Research.

This Westview softcover edition is printed on acid-free paper and bound in library-quality, coated covers that carry the highest rating of the National Association of State Textbook Administrators, in consultation with the Association of American Publishers and the Book Manufacturers' Institute.

Published in 1991 in the United States of America by Westview Press, Inc., 5500 Central Avenue, Boulder, Colorado 80301-2847, and in the United Kingdom by Westview Press, 36 Lonsdale Road, Summertown, Oxford OX2 7EW

Library of Congress Cataloging-in-Publication Data
Schwok, René
  U.S.-EC relations in the post–cold war era :
conflict or partnership? / René Schwok.
    p. cm.
  Includes bibliographical references and index.
  ISBN 0-8133-7998-9
  1. United States—Foreign economic relations—
European Economic Community Countries. 2. European
Economic Community Countries—Foreign economic relations—
United States. 3. Europe 1992. 4. European
Economic Community countries—Economic policy. 5.
United States—Economic policy—1981– 6. United
States—Economic conditions—1981– I.
Title. II. Title: US-EC relations in the post–cold
war era.
HF1456.5.E825S38   1991
337.7304—dc20   91-28294
                                                                        CIP

Printed and bound in the United States of America

The paper used in this publication meets the requirements
of the American National Standard for Permanence of Paper
for Printed Library Materials Z39.48-1984.

10   9   8   7   6   5   4   3   2   1

CONTENTS

PART THREE
POLITICAL AND STRATEGIC ASPECTS
OF U.S.-EC RELATIONS

ACKNOWLEDGMENTS

The research for this book could not have been completed without a three-year fellowship from the Swiss National Fund for Scientific Research. This generous financial assistance gave me time to research and assemble sufficient material in Boston, Washington, Brussels, and Geneva. I owe a particular debt to Professor Alois Riklin, who took the risk of accepting my project.

I would also like to acknowledge Professor Curt Gasteyger, who has supported this study from the beginning. Professors Lucius Caflish and Alexander Swoboda, as well as Mr. Jean-Claude Frachebourg, deserve particular thanks for having taken me on as Research Associate at the Geneva Graduate Institute of International Studies.

I also benefited from being a Fellow of the Center for European Studies at Harvard University during several stays between 1989 and 1991. The Center provided me the opportunity to benefit from unique intellectual stimulation and permitted me to take advantage of the convenient and well-organized Harvard libraries. For all of this support I am most grateful.

I especially owe an intellectual debt to Professors Stanley Hoffmann and Raymond Vernon, whose advice and ideas have influenced my approach to this topic, although responsibility for the content of this work rests with me alone.

During this research I have been especially impressed by the professional competence of all those "anonymous" persons involved in U.S.-EC relations. I therefore would like to acknowledge the staffs of the United States Commerce Department, State Department, Treasury Department, Defense Department, Offices of the Trade Representative, the Security Adviser, the Congress, the Senate, and the Library of Congress, who aided my efforts.

Special thanks also go to the National Association of Manufacturers and the U.S. Chamber of Commerce. I also would like to thank all the experts in the EC Commission, the EC Council Secretariat, and the GATT Secretariat.

I owe a particular debt of gratitude to my reviewers for their thoughtful reading: Gretchen Bouliane, Laurence Boisson de Chazourne, Diane Kent, Kalypso Nicolaïdis, and Eva Tanner. As for Claire-Lise, well, without her moral support, there would be no life, and certainly no book.

René Schwok

ACRONYMS

ACP	Africa, Caribbean, and Pacific
AMS	Aggregate Measure of Support
ANSI	American National Standards Institute
BC-NET	Business Cooperation Network
BENELUX	BElgium, NEtherlands, LUXembourg
BERD	European Bank of Reconstruction and Development (the acronym is based on the French title)
CAP	Common Agriculture Policy
CEN	European Committee for Standardization (the acronym is based on the French title)
CENELEC	European Committee for Electrotechnical Standardization (the acronym is based on the French title)
CEPT	Conference of European Postal and Telecommunications Administrations
CMEA or COMECON	Council for Mutual Economic Assistance
CNAD	Conference of National Armaments Directors
COCOM	Coordinating Committee on Multilateral Export Controls
COMETT	Community Program for Education and Training for Technology
COREPER	Committee of Permanent Representatives (the acronym is based on the French title)
CSCE	Conference on Security and Cooperation in Europe
DOD	Department of Defense
DG	Directorate General
EBRD	European Bank for Reconstruction and Development
EC	European Community
ECA	Economic Cooperation Administration
ECSC	European Coal and Steel Community
ECU	European Currency Unit
EDC	European Defence Community
EEA	European Economic Area
EEC	European Economic Community
EES	European Economic Space

EFTA	European Free Trade Association
EIA	Electronic Industries Association
EMS	European Monetary System
EMU	European Monetary Union
EOTC	European Organization for Testing and Certification
EPC	European Political Cooperation
ERASMUS	European Community Action Scheme for the Mobility of University Students
ERM	Exchange Rate Mechanism
ESCB	European System of Central Banks
ESPRIT	European Strategic Programme for Research and Development in Information Technology
ETSI	European Telecommunications Standards Institute
EURATOM	European Atomic Energy Community
FDIC	Federal Deposit Insurance Corporation
FRG	Federal Republic of Germany
GAO	General Accounting Office
GATS	General Agreement on Trade in Services
GATT	General Agreement on Tariffs and Trade
GDP	Gross Domestic Product
GNP	Gross National Product
G7	Group of the Seven most industrialized countries
G24	Group of Twenty-Four OECD countries
IEC	International Electrotechnical Commission
IEPG	Independent European Program Group
IGC	Inter-Governmental Conference
IMF	International Monetary Fund
ISO	International Standards Organization
ISDN	Integrated Services Digital Networks
MFN	Most-Favored Nation
MLF	Multilateral Force
MOU	Memorandum of Understanding
NAM	National Association of Manufacturers
NATO	North Atlantic Treaty Organization
NICs	Newly Industrialized Countries
NIST	National Institute of Standards and Technology
OECD	Organization for Economic Cooperation and Development
OEEC	Organization for European Economic Cooperation
PCBAs	Printed Circuit Board Assemblies
QR	Quantitative Restriction
RACE	Research and Development in Advanced Communications Technology for Europe
R&D	Research & Development

SDI	Strategic Defense Initiative
S&L	Savings and Loan
SEA	Single European Act
SME	Small and Medium-Sized Enterprise
SPRINT	Strategic Programme for Innovation and Technology Transfer
TEA	Trade Expansion Act
UK	United Kingdom
UL	Underwriters Laboratories
US	United States
USTR	United States Trade Representative
VAT	Value-Added Tax
VER	Voluntary Exports Restraints
WEU	Western European Union

INTRODUCTION

Relations between the European Community and the United States are gaining new momentum. The issue is whether there will be an evolution toward a U.S.-EC partnership or toward a series of conflicts. The dominating structure of this period called the post-Cold War (for lack of a better name) will partially depend upon the answer to this question.

A priori, there are as many convincing arguments for and against either assumption. The theory of partnership is attractive for converging reasons. At least three factors give it some legitimacy: the United States and the Community are the main economic blocs; they integrate two of the main military powers; and they affirm that they should be responsible for maintaining stability and prosperity in the world.

There are, moreover, three other converging factors between the United States and the European Community: common origins and values, comparable interests in the Third World, and quite similar attitudes toward the Soviet Union and Eastern Europe.

A contrario, one can observe more and more signs of possible conflicts between the two branches of the Atlantic Alliance. Among them one might mention: the implications of the EC-1992 internal market for the United States; the difficulties in the Uruguay Round GATT negotiations; and quite diverging strategic objectives.

Partnership or conflict? It is too early to answer this question definitively. Nevertheless, it is already possible to analyze the primary deep forces that will shape the future of U.S.-EC relations.

A multidisciplinary approach (historical, economic and political) is dictated by the nature of the relations between the

United States and the European Community. No one can understand this issue without having recourse to multiple instruments. There are, indeed, many existing strategic studies on U.S.-West European relations that underestimate the importance of the historical burdens and the economic dynamism. There are also too many business-oriented analyses that nearly ignore the underlying strategic dimension. Only a multidisciplinary approach allows an understanding of the nature of this relationship in all its components.

There are still many question marks on the future of the Soviet Union, on conflicts in the Third World, and on the final outcome of the Uruguay Round negotiations. Furthermore, in the European sphere, there is a lot of uncertainty about the final quantitative and qualitative reduction of American and Soviet military troops in Europe; the stability of Central and Eastern European states; and the solidity of the North African regimes. The main difficulty comes thus from the nature of this period that we call the "post-Cold War era" in default of clear structural characteristics.

This study is divided in the following way. The *first part* deals a conceptual reflection on the history of transatlantic relations in the realm of European integration. Such an analysis is necessary for two main reasons: first, American diplomatic documents on the creation of the European Community have recently been published. Second, a flexible conceptualization is needed for analy– zing contemporary history through the analytical tools shaped by numerous experts on U.S.-EC relations.

The *second part* deals with current economic problems between the United States and the European Community. Our attention focuses mainly on two aspects: the impact of the Community internal market (EC-1992) on the United States; and the deadlock in the Uruguay Round negotiations.

Concerning EC-1992, the main question is to determine whether the Americans are taking this challenge as an opportunity or as another form of discrimination. There are misinterpretations on both sides of the Atlantic Ocean. Many Europeans are convinced that American political and business leaders are ignorant of EC-

1992 and that their prejudice unjustly leads them to see a so-called Fortress Europe, whereas numerous Americans think that EC economic integration is directed against the United States and that the Community bears the whole responsibility for U.S.-EC clashes.

Despite the acrimony of the accusations, isn't it time to imagine in a constructive way the consequences of EC-1992? Is it still possible to avoid drawing conclusions from some dilemmas of the Uruguay Round Negotiations? Perhaps the moment is ripe to think about an integration of the U.S. and the EC markets through the creation of a common "Economic Area."

The *third part* deals with the political and strategic aspects, a domain also characterized by tenacious myths. In the view of many Europeans, the U.S. has always tried to destroy any velleity toward integration. Many Americans, however, are convinced that they have always supported European unification and they are even more europhile than many Europeans. It is, therefore, necessary to establish what the reality of both conceptions is in order to be able to determine what is truth and what is prejudice in both interpretations.

Naturally, the key question is to determine whether the European Community might be capable of developing a sufficient political and military dimension for questioning American strategic domination. In the beginning of the nineties, as in the five previous decades, numerous plans have been drafted for strengthening European identity in foreign, security, and defense affairs. It is now imperative to be able to judge what is rhetoric and what is serious. Only such analysis can give us the possibility of assessing future U.S.-EC relations.

PART ONE

THE UNITED STATES AND THE
HISTORY OF EUROPEAN INTEGRATION

CHAPTER 1

HISTORICAL OVERVIEW

Numerous good books and articles exist on U.S.-West European history but there is no comprehensive study dealing specifically with U.S.-EC relations in historical perspective. It is therefore important to establish our reflections on contemporary U.S.-EC relations on a solid background. Such an exercise is worthwhile for two other reasons: first, new historical documents have been published.[1] Second, the history of U.S.-EC relations should be analyzed within the new context created by the post-Cold War period.

This last point is the most important. There are indeed many interesting historical studies on the U.S.-EC issue – and we make a large use of them – but one should never forget that they have been influenced by the historical perspectives of their conception. Therefore, they sometimes stress too much points more relevant in the past than today.

The Period Until 1945

After the First World War, the U.S. was not enthusiastic about the different pan-Europeanist plans. The most often-heard position was that a unified Europe would create trade discrimination against the United States. In fact, when the German and French foreign ministers, Gustav Stresemann and Aristide Briand, proposed in the late twenties using the League of Nations for promoting European unification, Washington gave the proposal only a lukewarm reception.

During the Second World War, more voices were heard in the U.S. in favor of the unification of Europe. The Americans supported a unified Europe for two main reasons: (1) they hoped to avoid new conflicts in Europe through a reconciliation among the different states; and (2) they were convinced that the Second World War had been partly caused by the international economic crisis which was itself generated by too much protectionism.

For example, a study done in 1942 by the Council on Foreign Relations at the request of the U.S. Department of State revealed:

> The United States would favor economic unification of Europe only if steps were taken to avoid the creation of an autarkic continental economy. Positive American policy should aim at the interpenetration of Europe's economy with the rest of the world, as well as a lowering of barriers within Europe. To be successful in this course, the United States must work for the reduction of trade barriers against European goods throughout the world, including the United States.[2]

The End of the Second World War

In the period just after the Second World War, the United States was *not* inclined to launch or support proposals for a unified Europe, fearing that the USSR would interpret it as being directed against it. Most American leaders believed that a victory against Germany, and later international stability and prosperity, depended upon good relations with Moscow. They were anxious to avoid any clash with the Soviet Union, and President Roosevelt was convinced that the American people would not tolerate keeping American troops in Europe too long.

As President Roosevelt was ready to accept the idea of a Soviet sphere of influence in Eastern Europe, it is therefore no accident that he rejected recommendations for a European Federation as proposed by Richard Coudenhove-Kalergi and the Pan-European Union,[3] and that the U.S. draft of the United Nations Charter made no provision for regional organizations.

The U.S. Congress was more favorable than the administration toward the drafts proposed by the advocates of a European

Federation. It is interesting to analyze the arguments which were put forward because they anticipate many theses heard later. On the one hand, the idea that Europe would be modelled on a federal system, similar to the American one, pleased many representatives. Therefore, some Congressmen (pre-burden-sharing) advocated the idea of European unity in order to diminish the costs of a U.S. presence outside the territory. On the other hand, many representatives feared that a unified Europe would weaken the newborn U.N. and that the American economy would suffer economic discrimination.

The Marshall Plan and the First Attempts to Unify Europe Economically

By 1946, tensions with the Soviet Union led to a reevaluation of the main objectives of American international policy. Washington had to focus more on a regional than on an international perspective. The Marshall Plan marks the cornerstone of this shift. It was not only an economic package but also a stage toward European political and economic unification. American leaders were among the first to realize that cohesion was a prerequisite condition for any economic recovery. The Americans did not want to repeat the mistakes of the twenties when financing the reconstruction of Europe. They tried to avoid the fragmentation of the European economy and promoted instead a unified market which, like that of the U.S., could foster economies of scale and greater specialization.

For example, in July 1947, Under-Secretary of State William Clayton supported the proposal to create a European customs union, but Britain remained hostile to this project despite Italian and French sympathy for the scheme. Washington also encouraged other regional attempts at creating customs unions, such as Francita between France and Italy, Fritalux (or Finebel) between France, Italy and the Benelux, Uniscan between the United Kingdom and some Scandinavian countries. However, those proposals failed and only the Benelux was a success.

In another interesting symbolic gesture, resolutions were also .
introduced in 1947 in both Houses of Congress advocating a
United States of Europe. Against the will of a more prudent
Truman administration, there were many attempts to insert amend-
ments assuring that the policy of the U.S. was to encourage the
political unification of Europe. Since 1948, American policy has
favored economic integration in Western Europe "as a means of
building strength, establishing security, and preserving peace
and of cementing Germany to the West by organic bonds of common
interest."[4]

For example, in 1948, the Select Congressional Committee on
Foreign Aid affirmed:

> The solution to the problem of preventing the resurgence of
> aggressive German nationalism is to be found within the
> pattern of European federation, of which a democratic Ger-
> many will be an integral but not dominating part.[5]

In 1949, the reconstruction of Europe was well on track. Production levels of the European states surpassed levels of the
pre-war period. However, the volume of intra-European trade was
still low, diminishing the beneficial effects of the Marshall
Plan. If the European countries were unable to boost their
exchanges among themselves, they could not sufficiently reduce
their imports in dollars and would, in turn, need American help
for a longer time period. Therefore, the Congress – where the
American taxpayers are represented – was eager to see progress
in the European integration process.

In the Fall of 1949, the Economic Cooperation Administration
(ECA) – the agency devoted to shipping and administering American aid to Europe – insisted that all members of the Organization for European Economic Cooperation (OEEC) multiply their
exchanges by banning quantitative restrictions. But to achieve
this objective, as there was no convertibility of the different
currencies, it was necessary to establish a multilateral system
of clearing.

The European Payments Union (September 1950) was built on this
system, thanks to basic funding by the ECA. The Americans were
ready to accept this discrepancy with their conception of the

World Economic Order based mainly on the IMF and GATT, and to be discriminated against temporarily in order to boost trade in Europe.

Paul Hoffman, the Administrator of the Economic Cooperation Administration (ECA), forecast the European Common Market of a decade later:

> The substance of such integration would be the formation of a single large market within which quantitative restrictions on the movements of goods, monetary barriers to the flow of payments, and eventually all tariffs are permanently swept away.[6]

Hoffman also remarked that U.S. interest in European recovery was interrelated with progress toward more economic unity, and saw economic integration as essential to obtaining an end to Europe's recurring economic crises.

The European Coal and Steel Community (ECSC)

The Cold War, especially after the beginning of the Korean War, increased American interest in developing European integration as a tool against the Soviet Union. America worried about a fragmented Western Europe which could be a prey for the Soviet Union. The anti-Communist motive was the decisive factor for most American decision-makers.

Therefore, the United States welcomed and fostered the French proposition, launched by the French Foreign Minister Robert Schuman in 1950, for an European Coal and Steel Community (ECSC) that would pool under a supranational authority the coal and steel economies of France, Germany, and any other democratic European nation.[7] One should, nevertheless, be aware that the idea of the ECSC preceded the Korean War.

In America, the ECSC was welcomed as the first stage toward a *United States of Europe*. Robert Schuman's plan came at the same moment that Secretary of State Dean Acheson was searching for a way to anchor the Federal Republic of Germany into the Atlantic security framework. Schuman's timing and the concentration on coal and steel took the United States by surprise, however. American heavy industry was especially dissatisfied and feared a revival of a modern, disguised European cartel.

U.S. support was, nevertheless, firm. Washington encouraged European unification along a Franco-German axis. Behind the curtain Washington played an advisory role and the project received a lot of encouragement. The American government accepted the ECSC into the OEEC and GATT despite its discriminatory character,[8] and in Congress, it was considered not only as a hopeful promise of Franco-German reconciliation but also as the beginning of diminished American economic support for Europe.

The European Defence Community (EDC)

By 1950 and the Korean war, the Eisenhower administration applied pressure for German rearmament. French leaders were, however, opposed to a German army within the NATO framework. They were ready to accept the involvement of German soldiers but were refusing participation by Germany. Paris thus proposed a plan for rearming Germany within a supranational European Defence Community (EDC) on the ECSC's model. The EDC was viewed with some doubt in Washington because Bonn could not accept an unequal status allowing other European states to keep their own national armies outside the new European army.

After some hesitation, President Eisenhower supported the French proposal for a European army when Paris accepted dropping the principle of unequal status for Germany.[9] The American administration was deeply involved in the difficult negotiations for an EDC Treaty that started in June 1951. It saw in the EDC not only a solution to the question of defending Europe but also a way to permit U.S. forces to come home.[10]

After the signing of the EDC Treaty in May 1952 and its acceptance by Italy, Germany, Belgium, the Netherlands and Luxembourg, Congress included in the Mutual Security Act of 1952 a provision authorizing direct military assistance to the Defense Community when it should come into being. But in August 1954, the French National Assembly rejected the EDC Treaty and dashed American hopes.

Therefore, American Secretary of State John Foster Dulles decided to adopt the British proposal for achieving German rearmament by expanding the Brussels Treaty of 1948 between France, Great Britain, Belgium, the Netherlands and Luxembourg to include the Federal Republic of Germany in a broadened Western European Union (WEU). This was the Treaty of Paris, whose chief purpose was the control and monitoring of West German rearmament. It remains important to this day because it solved the military question. Without this settlement of strategic relations between the United States and Western Europe, progress toward other aspects of European integration would have been very difficult. Questions of security had a priority over any other aspect of the U.S.-West European relationship. With the Treaty of Paris, the military question was solved, making it easier to go in the direction of economic integration.[11]

Toward the Creation of the European Economic Community

After the failure of the EDC, Washington still warmly supported European unification, while keeping a much lower profile. The United States welcomed the *relance* of the European integration process, the so-called Messina negotiations among the six members of the ECSC concerning the creation of a European Economic Community (EEC) and a European Atomic Energy Community (EURATOM).

By 1955-1956, Secretary of State John Foster Dulles no longer feared that the Soviet Union would launch a general war, but nevertheless remained cautious about the Soviet Union's attempts to achieve its objectives through other means. In this context, his main priority was to avoid any German temptation to advance reunification through neutralization or alignment with the USSR:

The best means of doing this, in my judgment, is to so tie Germany into the whole complex of Western institutions – military, political and economic – and to so command her loyalties that neutrality or orientation to the East will be commonly accepted as unthinkable.[12]

On December 10, 1955, Secretary of State Dulles repeated in a letter to British Foreign Secretary Harold Macmillan that the Eisenhower administration would support the Six although their project could generate protectionist measures:

It may well be that a Six-nation community will evolve protectionist tendencies. It may well be that it will show a trend towards greater independence. In the long run, however, I cannot but feel that the resultant increased unity would bring in its wake greater responsibility and devotion to the common welfare of Western Europe.[13]

In January 1956, Secretary of State John Foster Dulles summed up in his own words the most serious problems in Europe:

a. Problem of tying Germany organically into Western Community so as to diminish danger that over time a resurgent German nationalism might trade neutrality for reunification with view seizing controlling position between East and West.
b. The weakness of France and need to provide positive alternative to neutralism and "defeatism" in that country.
c. The solidifying of new relationship between France and Germany which has been developing since 1950 through integration movement.[14]

Many American leaders shared the viewpoints of their administration. Yet did they support European integration out of anticommunist feeling or more for pro-European reasons? The debate on this issue seems very artificial. Many Americans were indeed deeply and emotionally attached to the idea of a united Europe out of idealistic motives but this fact does not contradict the view that a stronger Europe would be more capable of resisting the Soviet Union, and, eventually, of being a magnet for the countries of Central and Eastern Europe. Right or wrong, the American conviction that the USSR threatened Western Europe was without doubt a fundamental factor in gaining American support for European integration.

The Role Played by Jean Monnet

The history of American policy toward the European unification process cannot be understood without taking into account the role played by Jean Monnet.[15] He influenced decisively the most important American statesmen and officials, and gained incomparable prestige in the United States. Many Americans leaders were deeply committed to the concept of European unity and became fascinated with the process. His relations with people like Dwight Eisenhower, John Foster Dulles, John McCloy,[16] Douglas Dillon, Robert Bowie, George Ball, and Robert Schaetzel were unique.[17]

For example, Jean Monnet played a major role in convincing the American leaders, first very reluctant, of the importance of a European army. Eisenhower was particularly hostile to the EDC. However, after one meeting with Monnet, by 21 June 1951 he had changed his mind. From then on, the entire support of American diplomacy, the Congress and the mass media was behind the EDC. Ironically, the Americans were still ardent advocates of the project when the French became hostile and finally rejected it!

Rare are comparable cases in history of an individual from a foreign country who had such capacity to influence leaders and officials of another nation. Monnet's attitude toward the United States was based on two main ideas: first, the European states would not accept, without being compelled, any real form of integration. Second, only the United States could give the necessary impetus on the condition that an integrated Europe would not jeopardize the *Pax Americana.*

Moreover, Monnet knew how to speak to the "American mind." He stressed four elements especially that fit the American psychology: (1) a pragmatic approach to problems, (2) the importance of economic well-being in promoting political stability, (3) a federalist solution which naturally appeals to Americans because of their own experience with such a system, and (4) the role of a united Europe in sharing America's burdens.[18]

The main tool of Monnet's action was personal contact and nongovernmental groups. For instance, in 1955, Monnet created the Action Committee for the United States of Europe. What gave the Committee impetus was his unparalleled access to America's leading personalities and his ability to influence them. Many Americans were fascinated by his arguments, which appeared to require only political determination and American support for their success.

To be sure, Jean Monnet was inspiring in two directions: from Europe to the United States and vice versa. As an ironic consequence, on the one hand, some European governments (Benelux) became more integrationist because they were prodded by the American government, especially on the issue of the EDC. On the other hand, the Eisenhower administration was more interested in EURATOM than most European governments and the "Spaak Committee" set up to shape the future Economic Community. As a matter of fact, there was strong American pressure to create the EDC and EURATOM but not so much for the Common Market.

EURATOM

To be sure, the Eisenhower administration followed Monnet's concepts because of his force of conviction. But the American massive support for EURATOM was also due to other motives. First, American enthusiasm for EURATOM coincided with the peak of popularity for nuclear energy, considered at that time as having almost no vices. Moreover, one should not forget that in 1956 the closure of the Suez Canal emphasized the dependence of the European economy on oil and the necessity of finding alternative sources of energy.

One should also realize that EURATOM fits well into the American tradition, reconciling ideal and interest.[19] Ideal because EURATOM was a peaceful program and did not contradict traditional American fears of a world of nuclear powers. Ideal also, because an organization such as EURATOM made the problem of control easier by creating a system of mutual supervision. Interest, because the United States could find profitable markets and expected a lot from this market of the Six (France, Germany, Italy, Belgium, the Netherlands, and Luxembourg), which could offer interesting outlets.

The American vision of EURATOM was essentially peaceful. It was symptomatic that the Americans encouraged the Six by promising to sell uranium at a very low price. But did Washington want only a pacific collaboration in the framework of EURATOM? According to most documents, it also seems that Washington wanted to extend this collaboration to the security field. The archives show an intention to create a strong European technology which could be of dual use.[20] One must always take into account the American obsession with strategic aspects. The Americans established a direct link between civil cooperation in nuclear matters and the necessity of boosting European cooperation in weaponry. As Secretary of State Foster Dulles wrote in a secret telegram in January 1956:

> Six-country supranational EURATOM would be a powerful means of binding Germany to West and may be most feasible means for achieving effective control over *weapons-quality* material. States does not attach to common market proposals same immediate *security and political* significance as we do to EURATOM.[21]

Indirect American Contribution to the Creation of the EEC

Washington also contributed to the creation of the EEC in a paradoxical way: European perceptions of American lack of reliability reinforced the Europeans' conviction that they should take responsibility for their fate and not rely solely upon Washington.

The first example concerns a relatively forgotten event, the July 1956 proposal by the American General Radford for a drastic withdrawal of 800,000 American soldiers from Europe. West German Chancellor Adenauer was then inclined to think that the United States was trying to make a deal with the Soviet Union which would be at the expense of the Federal Republic. He feared that the Western allies would dissociate the question of German reunification from the initiatives on disarmament.[22]

This situation helped Adenauer to overcome the hesitation in his own party of those who were opposed, like his Minister of Economy Ludwig Erhard, to a too protectionist and centrally-administered Community.

The American attitude in the Suez affair – against France and the UK – also played an important role, especially in France, and to a lesser extent in Germany. It convinced Paris that France could not always count on Washington and that Europe should be united if it hoped to play any further role at a global level.[23] The American attitude in the Suez affair led many Europeans to think that the U.S. would always favor American interests at their expense.

Finally, the Soviet invasion of Hungary in 1956 showed the Europeans their weakness in comparison to the superpowers. The defeat of the Hungarian Revolution reminded the Six of the need for unity to survive Soviet expansionism.

The treaties for the European Economic Community (EEC) and for the European Atomic Energy Community (EURATOM) went into effect on January 1, 1958. Throughout the gestation of the Common Market and EURATOM, the American government kept a low profile. Moreover, there is no mention in State Department archives of any direct involvement in the creation of the EEC or any American influence on the "Spaak Committee."[24]

Although America did not participate in the negotiations of the Treaty establishing the "European Economic Community," the Treaty was examined by the United States at various stages of its preparation. One should nevertheless note one American mark, the fact that the Treaty negotiators recognized the interests of third countries, i.e., the Treaty has provisions saying that it does not affect obligations under other international agreements (GATT and IMF).

EEC Treaty Reception in the United States

America welcomed the Treaty of Rome which founded the European Economic Community but was not satisfied with a number of points in this treaty: (1) Treaty provisions relating to agriculture; (2) the establishment of new tariff preferences favoring the Community members as a result of the arrangements affecting the overseas territories; and (3) the level of the external tariff of the Community, particularly with respect to agricultural products.[25]

But the United States was conscious that, in 1957, it was impracticable to obtain changes in the EEC Treaty without jeopardizing chances for the establishment of the Community. Therefore, Washington decided to discuss the commercial problems posed by the EEC Treaty within the framework of the GATT.

It is interesting, in this context, to note that the American business community played a minor role in the U.S. support for the creation of the EEC. There were no economic pressures on President Eisenhower and the State Department advocating an American contribution to the EEC in order to boost U.S. exports in goods and services.

On the contrary, the U.S. business community was fearing discrimination coming from the Common Market. The Department of State's files reveal that, in a closed round-table of forty major American companies (the Chase Manhattan Bank, Dupont, Ford, Standard Oil, Westinghouse), the main conclusion was that the short and long-run impact of the Common Market would discourage U.S. exports of manufactured products. This analysis was based both on the expectation of an impetus for European productivity and on fear of discrimination against U.S. companies. One should nevertheless note that these big companies already foresaw that a high income market unimpeded by internal trade barriers was "a juicy opportunity for direct investment."[26]

The U.S. Attitude Toward the UK Opposition to the EEC

Washington wanted the United Kingdom, first, not to hinder the Six, and, second, to join the EEC as quickly as possible. Without the UK as an active associate, the United States feared a reappearance of political rivalries between France and Germany that have proved so disruptive in past European history:

> It is in the U.S. interest not only that the two current projects, the Common Market and EURATOM, be carried through, but – of far greater importance – that the momentum be maintained until a political and economic community has been developed in Europe which will enable that area to play the important role in world affairs for which it is so well equipped by its talents and resources. The attainment of this goal depends in large measures upon the British outlook. Without the United Kingdom as an active associate, there might be a reappearance of political rivalries among the major Continental participants – particularly between France and Germany – that have proved so disruptive in past European history.[27]

The Americans were reticent toward their traditional British allies and their project of a big free-trade area. The British proposal to create an association between the EC and the other Western European countries under the OECE framework could not be supported by the Americans. They argued that such an area might have maintained discrimination against the United States without promoting European construction. For example, the United States firmly supported the Common Market when the British and the Scandinavians tried to attack the Treaty of Rome at the GATT level. They also "protected" the EEC at the 1957 and 1958 ses – sions. In short, the U.S was ready to pay economic price for European political unity but not for nothing. They supported European integration in the hopes that these developments represented steps toward increasing political union, which would further contribute greatly to the strength and cohesion of the Atlantic area as a whole.

Moreover, the Americans were suspicious about the British will to maintain the imperial preferences. Finally Washington was sure that the British made the proposal for a large European trade area in order to jeopardize the European Community. Thus, the Americans did not wish any lowering of tariffs between the EC and the future European Free Trade Association (EFTA) from which they could not profit.[28] They wanted a general reduction of tariffs within the framework of GATT. This explains the proposals of American Under-Secretary Douglas Dillon, in November 1958, to open multilateral negotiations in order to diminish tariffs by 20 percent. This would have the double advantage of avoiding a division of Europe and of maintaining profits for American exports. One should remember that in 1958 the U.S. had a deficit in its balance of payments and was inclined to lower its economic and military aid to Europe.

At the same time, however, the Americans were preferring cooperation with the UK at the defense level. This had a lot of repercussions later. In March 1957, President Eisenhower and Prime Minister Macmillan met in the Bermudas and decided to strengthen U.S.-UK relations in the nuclear field. England received American support to guarantee its nuclear advantage over its European competitors. This was a terrible blow for the future of European unity. France interpreted this as a manifestation of ostracism. By helping England to overcome its deep financial difficulties and by guaranteeing artificially its military superiority, the Americans killed French confidence in a "truly European United Kingdom."

The policy led to the following consequences: first, the United Kingdom was less interested than ever in any European integration; second, American-British military cooperation was strengthened after the Suez Crisis; third, the Americans increased support for British production of nuclear weapons (refused to the French and the Germans). These were the factors demonstrating that relations involving military strategy, the evolution of the Cold War, and European integration were far from being linear.

The de Gaulle-Kennedy Period (1960-1964)

The period 1960-1964 is certainly one of the most complex in U.S.-West European relations. One cannot understand this epoch without taking into consideration two elements: (1) the French policy under *General de Gaulle;* and (2) the *ambivalence of the American attitude* toward European integration.

France under General de Gaulle

It is difficult to sum up the European political vision and actions of General de Gaulle. There are two main difficulties: first, General de Gaulle was the main saboteur of the Community, and, at the same time, the most audacious proponent of an European Political Union. Second, external circumstances led him to pursue several different policies.

General de Gaulle was a supporter of an inter-state confederal Europe dominated by France. He had been opposed to Jean Monnet's idea of leading Europe to political federation through economic integration.[29] General de Gaulle did not want to weaken the sovereignty of France. He was a high-level officer and the hero of the resistance against Nazi Germany. In short, General de Gaulle was a strong nationalist who did not want to give up France's independence to Brussels.

Although General de Gaulle did not like the idea of supranationality and strongly opposed it when he was in the opposition, he nevertheless accepted, and even supported, the EEC (i.e., a customs union, a common external tariff, a common agricultural policy). From 1958 until 1964, France under General de Gaulle appeared as one of the most important motors of EEC integration.

General de Gaulle, nevertheless, played finally a very negative role and carried the main responsibility for the deadlock of the Community. As a matter of fact, after 1965 he started a policy of systematic obstruction which led to the so-called Compromise of Luxembourg (1966) – i.e., to the paralysis of the Community through a unanimity decision-making mechanism instead of majority rule. One had to wait until the Single European Act (1986) to see the Community again able to overcome vetoes or threats of vetoes. Moreover, General de Gaulle, instead of welcoming the UK into the Community in order to avoid a division of Western Europe, twice refused the British candidacy and triggered anxiety among its EEC partners, causing further paralysis of the Community.

At the same time, however – and this is what makes the whole story difficult – General de Gaulle was also one of the leading precursors of the idea of an European Political Union. Indeed, he promoted the idea of a Confederation of European states from the Atlantic to the Urals. He saw such a confederation as an association of sovereign states without any kind of supranationality. General de Gaulle was convinced that the "Yalta division" should be phased out (i.e., that the Atlantic Alliance and the Warsaw Pact should be replaced by a reunited Europe). He was sure that Europe's future necessitated more distance from the United States but, paradoxically, assumed a total solidarity between France and the United States. He was a kind of prophet of a Europe based on a Franco-German axis, beyond East-West divisions, which would be allied on an egalitarian basis with the United States.

In 1960, General de Gaulle proposed the following plan for a Political Union: (1) a confederal organization of Europe based on regular meetings between Chiefs of State and Governments; (2) the creation of a Secretariat to assist the organization; and (3) the establishment of an Assembly reserved for delegates nominated by each Parliament.

In early 1961, a Political Union Commission was set up under the presidency of Christian Fouchet, and in June 1961, the EEC partners approved the plan and were said to be determined to give form to the will of Political Union already expressed in the Treaties which instituted the European Communities. A Political Union seemed to have been born but it was soon to be buried.

Two main factors explain the failure of the Fouchet Plan. First, the candidacy of the UK to join the EEC, announced in July 1961, seen by France as a risk, introduced a strong ally of the United States into the Community. Second, there was fear of the Benelux countries becoming too dependent upon the Franco-Germans and losing their privileged relationships with the United States. The Dutch, especially, set as a condition for their approval of the Political Union that it would be truly supranational (to protect the small countries) and remain open to the

UK. For the first time, European construction and Atlantic solidarity were antithetic.

The Kennedy Period

American policy toward European integration was almost as complicated as the one practiced by General de Gaulle. Here the difficulty comes from the fact that the United States was a strong supporter of the EEC but at the same time contributed a lot to torpedoing it.

First, American support for Europe's unification was clearly reaffirmed by all American administrations during this period. At the beginning of the 1960s, with the resurgence of the Cold War, Western Europe again began to appear like a strong ally in the global confrontation against the Soviet Union. In December 1961, American Secretary of State Dean Rusk spoke of a "Grand Design"[30] of constructive association between the United States and a uniting Europe. President Kennedy developed the concept of an "Atlantic partnership", and in his Independence Day speech in Philadelphia in 1962, he said:

> The United States will be ready for a *Declaration of Interdependence*. . . . We will be prepared to discuss with a united Europe the ways and means of forming a *concrete Atlantic partnership,* a mutually beneficial partnership between *the new union now emerging* in Europe and the old American Union founded here 175 years ago.[31]

This declaration seemed utopian, since the very condition of its realization would be the unification of the Europeans. To give the objective more substance, President Kennedy received approval from the Congress for the Trade Expansion Act (TEA, 1962), which envisaged free trade for most industrial goods between the United States and the European Community.

The Trade Expansion Act was designed to provide an economic basis for a *political partnership* between the United States and a uniting Europe. Kennedy said that "a freer flow of trade across the Atlantic will enable the two giant markets on either side of the ocean to impart strength and vigor to each other and to combine their resources and momentum to undertake the many enterprises which the security of free peoples demands."[32] Kennedy's policy seemed marked by one main idea: to realize a progressive integration of the non-Communist world around concentric circles. The Kennedy administration wanted to establish a strong link between the richest states, and from this basis, to help the less-developed countries of the South and to protect their independence.

This view reflected Kennedy's awareness that the United States was unable to support its responsibilities alone. His main priority was "burden sharing": a particular effort to reabsorb the deficit in the balance of payments and the monetary consequences of it. Already in 1961, the OEEC, the old organization of the Marshall Plan, was transformed into the OECD. The direct participation of the Canadians and the Americans (and from 1964, the Japanese) was an attempt to move toward a non-Communist world dominated by the most highly industrialized countries.

Economic frictions, nevertheless, arose with Western Europe. The Kennedy administration expressed concern over the implications of the EC customs union on the U.S. economy if the common external tariff remained high. To be sure, in 1962, the Dillon Round was successful in a 10 percent lowering of the Community's Common External Tariff, but this was not sufficient. Therefore, one has to understand that the Trade Expansion Act was a tool of the Kennedy administration for obtaining the competence to negotiate on tariff barriers, and to rally the Congress in convincing the Europeans to accept negotiations toward allowing more concessions.

American fear was aggravated by deterioration of the U.S. balance of payments. Yet trade worries did not dilute U.S. support for European integration. Washington encouraged the UK's decision to apply for EC membership in 1961. The objective was, indeed, to guarantee the Community's Atlantic orientation. Again, Washington lacked enthusiasm for the European Free Trade Association, the organization founded by the British to balance the European Community.

The GATT negotiations were the major elements in the U.S.-EC relationship. The process started with Congressional enactment of the Trade Expansion Act of 1962 and ended when the negotiations were brought to a successful conclusion in the fall of 1968. It should be pointed out that President Kennedy would never have sought such far-reaching authority from the Congress had British entry into an expanded Community not been its goal.

After 1962 trade conflicts with the EC erupted. The first one, the "chicken war," was due to the EC's decision to impose new charges on imported frozen chicken. In 1963 the United States retaliated by raising duties on several European products. This was the first of a series of frictions over the EC Common agriculture policy, considered by Washington to be too protectionist. The Kennedy Round went from crisis to crisis. Announced first as a formidable step toward Atlantic partnership, the negotiations turned into an endless discussion between the United States and the European Community.[33]

The Evolution of the American Strategic Concept

The evolution of the American economic situation explains the many difficulties which occurred with the EEC, but the main indirect American contribution to the deadlock of the Community is linked to the evolution of the American strategic concept. Broadly speaking, the United States tried during this period to strengthen its leadership over the Atlantic Alliance, partly because it was afraid of nuclear proliferation and total war.

The Americans perceived an atomic deadlock in the Soviet development of satellites (sputniks) and nuclear rockets. This led the U.S. to control NATO more and to develop a stronger classical defense. As early as May 1962, Secretary of Defense Mc Namara stressed that the Atlantic Alliance should avoid using nuclear weapons except in the case of general attack by the Soviet Union. The main consequence of this concept of "gradual retaliation" was to control more strictly the nuclear weapons of the other members of the Atlantic Alliance.[34]

Instead, France's major aim, under General de Gaulle, was to keep and develop its independent *force de frappe.* Paris wanted to avoid to give any suggestion to Moscow that the USSR could attack without any risk of systematic nuclear retaliation by the United States. France's concept of deterrence was based on the destruction of the enemy's cities.[35] For the U.S., however, it was not possible that one part of the Alliance (France) would attack the Soviet urban zones while another avoided this type of war altogether. In this context, the interest of the United States was to assure total control of the nuclear weapons within the Atlantic Alliance, possibly under a symbolic "multilateral force" (MLF) concept, in order to avoid nuclear dissemination and contradiction among different strategic concepts.[36]

Therefore, at the end of 1962, President Kennedy concluded the following agreement with British Prime Minister Macmillan: the United States would deliver Polaris rockets in exchange for British acceptance of placing its nuclear submarines under a *de facto* American command. To be sure, the offer was extended to France, but General de Gaulle refused any plan for reinforcing American control over the nuclear strategy of its partners.

In January 1963, General de Gaulle rejected both the American offer and the British candidacy to the Community.[37] He was upset by what he considered British perfidy. As a matter of fact, he proposed to Prime Minister Macmillan in the summer of 1962 developing a close nuclear cooperation with Britain and Germany, but the UK preferred the American proposal and gave priority to its Atlantic partnership at the expense of European solidarity. Therefore, General de Gaulle shut the door on the UK's accession to the Community as a kind of measure of retaliation, leading to an open crisis between Washington and Paris. For President Kennedy, this meant the end to his "Grand Design."

On January 22, 1963, a Franco-German Treaty was signed but the German Parliament insisted that the preamble include the need for close cooperation between the United States and Europe, and that common defense was part of NATO and of the Western European Union (UK included).[38] Wedged between Atlantic solidarity and their European idealism, the other European members refused to choose between the security shield given by the Americans and the European idea proposed by France.

The Johnson Administration

America's positive attitude toward Europe gradually changed.
The 1960s showed an important shift in the relative economic
strength of the United States and Europe, with the "Common
Market" becoming an economic challenge to the United States
and Western Europe's usual balance-of-payment deficits evolving
in surpluses. The American government was also disillusioned by
numerous intra-EC conflicts over institutions, budget, and
agriculture. At stake were not only commercial conflicts but also
political divergence of views. Relations between the United
States and Europe were not badly jeopardized by the Kennedy
Round, but, in a somewhat unconscious way, U.S. feeling toward
the EC had changed.

The American government was especially upset by the two ve-
tos General de Gaulle gave to British membership in the Community. Moreover, the advocacy of Paris for gold (against the
dollar) as the main international currency was taken as another
proof of what could be a Community dominated by France. The
Johnson administration was also disappointed by the lack of
French solidarity in the Vietnam War and De Gaulle's support
for Quebec's freedom. Washington was dismayed by the perspective of a Western Europe dominated in one way or another by
Gaullism. Anti-Gaullism became a professional attitude in some
Washington circles.

Slowly the objective of a political union which gave the main
impetus to American faith evaporated. EC pragmatic construction
through the "Common Market" disenchanted Americans, especially
academics, whose sympathy was based on a belief in a scientific
evolution from economics to politics. As the political objective
disappeared, the issue of economic unity was no longer appealing
if not threatening.

The erosion of American interest in the Community should be
seen in this context. Many Americans took the EC attitude as a
kind of betrayal. They were dreaming of some kind of idealistic
United States of Europe (the American political system + European culture) and they were observing a simple Common Market

difficult in negotiations – without long-term objectives. American disappointment was proportional to the irrational enthusiasm of the 1950s. As the dream of a united Europe was slowly transformed into the more prosaic reality of a simple customs union without long-term vision, most Americans lost interest in the Community.

The Nixon-Kissinger Period

During Richard Nixon's first term, his administration did not give a lot of attention to improving relations with Western Europe. Richard Nixon and Henry Kissinger (Security Adviser and later Secretary of State) were busy much more with Vietnam, the Middle East, China and the Soviet Union. President Nixon, like his predecessors, nevertheless, stressed the primary importance of the U.S.-West European partnership. Nixon reaffirmed American support for the EC despite the economic discrimination the United States would have to endure. In one of his first speeches to the House of Representatives in 1970, he declared: "We consider that the possible economic price of a truly unified Europe is outweighed by the gain in the political vitality of the West as a whole."[39]

In 1971, the Communitys' office in Washington was elevated to the diplomatic level of a "delegation." On the whole, however, Washington did not try to enhance the status of the EC Commission. Washington always searched for ways to deal directly with the member states, by-passing the Commission. Relations with France had priority, as France was at the heart of American problems with Western Europe; relations with Paris were assiduously cultivated to support the broader Western European agenda. The Nixon administration was aware of Gaullist antipathy to the pretensions of the EC Commission and was more keen to avoid offending Paris sensibilities than to establish a relationship with the Community.

Kissinger's conception of international relations also played a key role. The idea of European integration did not appeal to him with his knowledge of nineteenth-century diplomacy. According to the then American Ambassador to the European Community Robert Schaetzel, Henry Kissinger did not want to support a Community which could be a rival to the United States:

> What greater folly than for the major power to assist in the organization of what could become an independent coalition of otherwise subordinate European states? Contributing to this bias was Kissinger's ignorance of economics, shared by Nixon.[40]

After the successful completion of the Kennedy Round (GATT), attention was devoted especially to agriculture. The Common Agriculture Policy (CAP), which until 1970 had been only a prospective menace, began to have specific adverse effects on American exports. For a few crops – but important ones such as wheat and feed grains – the agricultural levy system turned out to be too restrictive. Furthermore, as the Nixon administration concentrated on the critical farm vote in the 1970 elections, Washington's aversion to the Community's agricultural policies became an obsession.

As the United States was less ready to suffer some economic discrimination in the interest of long-term political benefits, the EC member states began to disagree with more elements of American policy, in particular with the U.S. war in Vietnam, and the manner in which the United States destroyed the Bretton Woods System (15 August 1971). Clashes occurred between the United States and Western Europe after the monetary crisis of August 1971, when the United States decided to suspend convertibility of the dollar into gold and to impose a 10 percent temporary surcharge on imports.

Here one has to avoid a common misinterpretation. It was not the monetary crisis that triggered the Community's decision to create a monetary union. The objective of a monetary union can be traced to the general philosophy of the Treaty of Rome, and significant attempts to restart the concept of a monetary union were tried during the 1960s. For example, the most important study done by the Commission was the so-called Plan Barre, already presented in February 1969.

After the The Hague Summit (1969), a committee of experts was set up and chaired by the Luxembourgian Minister Pierre Werner. This committee wrote a report (the Werner Report) which was the first political engagement of the Community toward the creation of a genuine monetary and economic union. One should be aware that this report was already adopted in March 1971, that is, before the announcement of the American abandonment of the Bretton Woods system (August 1971). This shows that the relaunching of monetary integration was not directly linked to American monetary policy. On the contrary, American policy jeopardized the so-called European monetary snake because instability of the dollar made it impossible to keep stability of exchange rates within the "snake."

1973, The "Year of Europe"

The political initiative known as the "Year of Europe" was launched by Henry Kissinger on April 23, 1973. Ironically, it led to the most bitter clashes to date between the United States and Western Europe. Henry Kissinger proposed a new "Atlantic Charter" which would define a new kind of relationship within the Atlantic Alliance. Although he strongly emphasized U.S. support for European integration, the West Europeans did not like the following paragraph:

> Diplomacy is the subject of frequent consultations but is essentially being conducted by traditional nation-states. The United States has global interests and responsibilities. Our European allies have *regional interests.*[41]

Henry Kissinger seemed to be saying that the Europeans should maintain only a regional role, whereas for the Americans there was the responsibility of the world. The Europeans did not like what they perceived as a condescending tone and reacted to the initiative of Dear Henry with a remarkable lack of enthusiasm. Moreover, they feared that the main objective of the new charter was to contribute to the American budget deficit shaken by the Vietnam War.

This led to endless discussions between the Nixon administration and the European states, in particular with the French Foreign Minister Michel Jobert on the question of who would be the right European interlocutor for economic, political and defense matters. Furthermore, setting of rather different policies during the Kippur War (October 1973) led to more tensions between the partners of the Atlantic Alliance.

Both camps shared responsibility in this controversy. When the French complained about American action, they forgot their lack of will to take risks anywhere. When the Americans criticized the Europeans for having regional preoccupations, they forgot that they were indeed greatly satisfied not to be hindered by a strong and organized Europe.[42]

Ironically, these difficult relations helped the EC member states to define their identity with respect to the United States. On December 14, 1973, they adopted a document which said:

> The close ties between the United States and Europe of the Nine – we share values and aspirations based on a common heritage – are mutually beneficial and must be preserved. These ties do not conflict with the determination of the Nine to establish themselves as *a distinct and original entity.* The Nine intend to maintain their constructive dialogue and to develop their cooperation with the United States on the basis of equality and in a spirit of friendship.[43]

The difficulties encountered by Kissinger's "Year of Europe" proved the need for more foreign policy-oriented consultations between the United States and the European Community. Nineteen seventy-four marked the beginning of regular but pragmatic consultations with the United States.

In 1976, the Nine (the Six plus Britain, Denmark, and Ireland) decided that the head of state or government chairing the European Council would meet with the American president once during his six-month term of office. Furthermore, it was agreed that the country holding the Presidency of the Community would inform the U.S. Embassy in its capital before and after a Political Committee meeting about the agenda and the results. The United States also wished to establish similar relations at the European

Political Cooperation (EPC) Working Group level, which was not well received by the EC.

The Carter and Reagan Periods

The Carter administration's approach to European integration was quite different from the previous one. It assumed that the Europeans had been pointedly insulted by Henry Kissinger's patronizing proclamation of the "Year of Europe." President Carter himself visited the EC in January 1978, the first such visit by a President of the United States. He declared that the United States would give its "unqualified support" for what the Nine were doing to strengthen European cooperation.[44] He also welcomed the participation of the President of the European Commission at the annual Western Summits. Carter also instructed the American agricultural bureaucracy to accept the Common Agriculture Policy (CAP) as a *fait accompli.*[45]

A new phase of U.S.-EPC dialogue began in 1982 after the EC Venice Declaration on the Middle East (June 1980)[46] and the Gas Pipeline Dispute (summer 1982).[47] In this latter case, the EC chose to move away from the Reagan administration line and toward the Soviet Union. The Community refused to take punitive measures against the Soviet-supported suppression of Solidarity in Poland by banning the supply of equipment from European subsidiaries of American firms to the Soviet-European gas pipeline. This caused unprecedented damage to European-U.S. relations.[48]

Since then, to avoid further clashes, the level of consultations has been gradually upgraded although the EC has always been keen on avoiding any form of quasi-official U.S. interference in its own affairs. First, there have been irregular Troika meetings at the political director level with the Americans. The Troika consists of three foreign ministers of the EC member states: (1), the foreign minister of the state who heads the Community in one semester; (2) the foreign minister of the country who occupied this position in the previous semester; and

(3) the foreign minister of the country who will occupy the position in the next semester.

Then, in 1983, the Political Directors' Troika meeting with the U.S. assistant secretary of state for European affairs became a regular annual arrangement on the fringes of the UN General Assembly. In September 1986, it was agreed that: (1) at the beginning of each year there would be a visit to the United States by the Foreign Minister of the country holding the EC presidency; and (2) there would be a meeting of the Political Directors' Troika with their respective American counterpart during each Presidency.

In the 1980s, the West European states once again saw the need for further unification in the strategic area. The so-called Genscher/Colombo Initiative originally included defense provisions. This aim turned out to be impossible due to Danish, Greek, and especially Irish reservations. Consequently, the security policy cooperation in the Stuttgart Declaration was limited to "political and economic" aspects. This formula was taken up in the Single European Act (SEA), (Article 30 (6a).[49] The SEA states that nothing should "impede closer cooperation in the field of security between certain of the High Contracting Parties within the framework of the Western European Union or the Atlantic Alliance."[50]

Finally, it was the Western European Union (WEU) which was seen as the expression of a European defense identity.[51] One of the most important WEU documents, the Platform on European Security Interests, adopted by the Council of Ministers in The Hague on October 27, 1987, emphasized this fact:

> We recall our commitment to build a European Union in accordance with the Single European Act which we all signed as members of the European Community. We are convinced that the construction of an integrated Europe will remain incomplete as long it does not include security and defence. . . . We intend therefore to develop a more cohesive European defence identity which will translate more effectively into practice the obligations of solidarity to which we are all committed through the modified Brussels and North Atlantic Treaties.[52]

The Reagan administration was first reluctant to support this WEU initiative. It considered NATO to be the only genuine institutional framework for the transatlantic defense dialogue. However, the American attitude has evolved because the WEU members provided a contribution to mine-sweeping operations in the Persian Gulf.

As for commercial relations, clashes arose particularly concerning European subsidies to Airbus, and the EC's ban on hormones in beef and numerous other minor products. As analyzed in later chapters (part II), the most salient events of this period have been the launching of the Uruguay Round negotiations in 1986 and the negative reception of EC-1992 by the Reagan administration which developed the concept of "Fortress Europe."

Conclusions

Our analysis has already brought to light one element in the study of the history of the Community's construction: the importance of the American factor in explaining both successes and failures of the Community's integration. This remark might seem obvious to any observer of U.S.-West European relations. It is, however, less obvious to experts who are strictly specialized on the Community and who sometimes have a tendency to stress the domestic West European evolution and the Community's bureaucratic process at the expense of elements linked to international relations.

Another observation should be made, the epistemological remark that the notion itself of integration is ambiguous. Integration can indeed be limited to interstate cooperation like that in the Council of Europe, or a more supranational aspect like that of the Common Agricultural Policy (CAP). The concept of integration can designate all possibilities of cooperation from the simplest to the most complex.

The European Community embodies intergovernmental features like the European Political Cooperation (EPC) as well as supranational elements like the Commission when controlling rules of competition. The Community is more than an *international regime* but less than a federal state.[53] It will remain a single political construction which cannot be compared to any other. Let us call it an "Unidentified Political Object" (UPO).

One should also make a distinction between "intention of integration" and fulfillment of those projects. There have been hundreds of schemes for European integration which have been forgotten. Moreover, between the time a project of integration is proposed and the moment it is realized, there might be a long period, giving a false historical perspective.

At a theoretical level, since 1946-1947, the United States has been sympathetic to West European integration. To be sure, this American support came from the hope of strengthening the Atlantic Alliance, of having a continental counter-weight to the USSR and of alleviating the American burden.

Here let us recall that European integration can work with or without any direct American link. For example, the European Economic Community (EEC) does not have any organic link with the U.S., but the European Defense Community (EDC) should have been a part of the Atlantic Alliance and dependent upon the United States. One can also find this link in the Western European Union and in the Independent European Program Group (IEPG). These are organizations of European integration closely linked to the United States.

The most surprising observation is the constancy of the American attitude toward European construction. Statements by John Foster Dulles, John Kennedy, and Henry Kissinger are still valid today. Indeed, one might find the same objectives: (1) to strengthen the European pillar of the Atlantic Alliance; (2) to anchor Germany organically to the Western world; (3) to reconcile definitively France and Germany; (4) to foster prosperity in Western Europe as a means of avoiding destabilization by communism and the Soviet Union; and (5) to create trade and wealth for the United States and the world economy.

Another American pattern of attitude toward European integration is the following: the United States often sacrificed its fundamental interests for the sake of Europe's integration. First, its own economic studies demonstrate that the advantages of *trade creation* triggered by European integration could over-come the disadvantages from *trade diversion*.[54] Second, superior imperatives of global strategy led the United States to soften its criticism of the EC. For example, John Foster Dulles was fully aware of the economic discrimination brought forward by the Community, but he was nevertheless ready to make some sacri-fices for the sake of European integration. Later chapters will show that the Bush administration has been tempted several times to follow similar patterns of attitudes.[55]

It is therefore reasonable to argue that all American adminis-trations were, in theory, sympathetic toward European integra-tion. But that is not the whole story because they have had, as previously shown, negative impact on various aspects of the praxis of the Community's integration. This was particularly true when Washington developed the strategic concepts of limitation of nuclear proliferation, of gradual retaliation and of centra-lization of decision within NATO. This led to the French refusal to welcome the UK into the Community and, finally, to deep tensions within the EEC.

One can mention numerous other examples, such as the aban-donment of the Bretton Woods system by the United States, which led to monetary instability and the rapid death of the "European Monetary Snake."

It is not possible to draw one single conclusion on the ques-tion of American attitudes vis-à-vis European construction of unity. Although there is a general American sympathy toward European integration, it is nevertheless true that some American action has had a reverse impact. Observations made by Stanley Hoffmann in 1964 are still valid in the post-Cold War period:

> America's relationship to Europe has been and remains dual. On the one hand it is the relation of the leader in a hege-monial alliance to the lesser states. . . . On the other hand there is a relation of adviser to client: the United States has supported the kind of supranational integration that Monnet advocates. . . . The combination of these two rela-tions has inhibited in three ways the emergence of a new European sense of identity.

First, America's relationship of domination has undermined the policy promoted in its capacity as an adviser. . . . Second, America's advice and promotion of supranationality have also had divisive and delaying effects on Europe's search for a new mission.

Finally, America's impact on Europe has been inhibiting because of the ways in which the United States reacted when it discovered – in the areas of tariffs, agriculture, and strategy – that European unification could lead to conflict, not harmony, in the Atlantic world.[56]

Notes

1. Especially, Foreign Relations of the United States (FRUS) *1955-57, Western European Security and Integration* (Washington, D.C.: United States Government Printing Office, 1986), Volume IV.

2. Quoted by Boyd France, *A Short Chronicle of United States-European Community Relations* (Washington, D.C.: European Community Information Service, 1973), p. 6.

3. Arnold Zurcher, "Coudenhove-Kalergi et les Etats-Unis," in Henri Rieben (cd.), *Coudenhove-Kalergi. Le Pionnier de l'Europe Unie* (Lausanne: Centre de recherches européennes, 1971), pp. 83-90.

4. FRUS, "Report by the Subcommittee on Regional Economic Integration of the Council on Foreign Economic Policy to the Council," *1955-57, Western European Security and Integration,* 15 November 1956, p. 483.

5. Quoted by Boyd France, *A Short Chronicle of United States-European Community Relations,* p. 10.

6. Ibid., p. 9.

7. Thomas Alan Schwartz, *America's Germany: John J. McCloy and the Federal Republic of Germany* (Cambridge: Harvard University Press, 1991), pp. 104-105.

8. The ECSC has a discriminatory character but is nevertheless legal according to Article XXIV of GATT.

9. Initially, the United States had doubts about the EDC Plan. The Spofford Plan was proposed to permit German participation in NATO without waiting for a European army. In June 1951, however, Jean Monnet convinced Eisenhower of the French plan's value and thus shifted the U.S. position toward EDC. Richard Mayne, *Postwar: The Dawn of Today's Europe* (New York: Schocken Books, 1983), pp. 311-316.

10. Schwartz, *America's Germany,* pp. 232-234.

11. Hanns Jürgen Küsters, *Fondements de la Communauté économique européenne* (Luxembourg/Brussels: Office des publications officielles des Communautés européennes/Editions Labor, 1990), p. 355.

12. FRUS, *1955-1957, Western European Security and Integration,* volume IV, p. 363.

13. Ibid., Letter from the Secretary of State to Foreign Secretary Macmillan, 10 December 1955, pp. 362-364.

14. Ibid., pp. 399-400. "Telegram From the Secretary of State to the Embassy in Belgium."
For the whole text, see document 1.

15. See, Jean Monnet, *La Communauté européenne et l'unité de l'Occident* (Lausanne: Centre de recherches européennes, 1961); 10 p.

And also, Jean Monnet, *Europe-Amérique. Relations de partenaires nécessaires à la paix* (Lausanne: Centre de recherches européennes, 1963); 13 p.

16. Schwartz, *America's Germany,* p. 98.

17. Alfred Grosser, *Les Occidentaux. Les pays d'Europe et les Etats-Unis depuis la guerre* (Paris: Fayard, 1981), p. 36.

18. Henry Kissinger, *Years of Upheaval* (Boston/Toronto: Little, Brown & Co., 1982), pp. 137-138.

19. Pierre Melandri, *Les Etats-Unis et le "défi" européen* (Paris: Presses universitaires de France, 1975), pp. 79-81.

20. Enrico Di nolfo, "Gli Stati Uniti e le origini della Comunita economica europea," in Enrico Serra (ed). *Il rilancio dell'Europa e i trattati di Roma, actes du colloque de Rome, 25-28 March 1987* (Milano: Giuffrè, 1989), p. 388.

21. "Telegram From the Secretary of State to the Embassy in Belgium," FRUS, *1955-1957, Western European Security and Integration,* volume IV, pp. 399-400. (My emphasis.)

22. Konrad Adenauer, *Erinnerungen, 1955-1959* (Stuttgart: Deutsche Verlags-Anstalt, 1967), pp. 197-214.

23. Michael M. Harrison, *The Reluctant Ally: France and Atlantic Security* (Baltimore: Johns Hopkins University Press, 1981), pp. 34-35.

24. See FRUS, *1955-1957,* volume IV and Paul-Henri Spaak, *Combats inachevés* (Paris: Fayard, 1969), Volume 2, pp. 84-100.

25. FRUS, *1955-57,* Volume IV, "Report to the Council on Foreign Economic Policy Regarding the European Common Market," pp. 550-553.

26. Ibid., pp. 555-556.

27. Ibid., "Western European Chiefs of Mission Conference, Paris, May 6-8, 1957: Summary Conclusions and Recommendation," *1955-1957, Western European Security and Integration,* p. 605.

28. Lawrence B. Krause, *European Economic Integration and the United States* (Washington, D.C.: the Brookings Institution, 1967), p. 27.

29. Jean-Baptiste Duroselle, *Deux types de grands hommes. Le général de Gaulle et Jean Monnet* (Geneva: Institut Universitaire de Hautes Etudes Internationales, 1977), pp. 17-22.

30. David P. Calleo, *The Imperious Economy* (Cambridge: Harvard University Press, 1982), pp. 9-24.

31. John F. Kennedy, "Address at Independence Hall, Philadelphia, July 4, 1962," *Public Papers of the Presidents of the United States, John F. Kennedy* (Washington, D.C.: United States Government Printing Office) PUB 18, 1962, [278], pp. 538-539. (My emphasis.)
For the whole text, see document 2.

32. Quoted by Boyd France, *A Short Chronicle of United States-European Community Relations,* p. 24.

33. Romain Yaremtchouk, "L'Europe face aux Etats-Unis," *Studia Diplomatica.* 29/1986, No 4-5, pp. 456 and 468.

34. Pierre Melandri, *Une incertaine alliance. Les Etats-Unis et l'Europe, 1973-1983* (Paris: Publications de la Sorbonne, 1988), p. 41.

35. The U.S. adopted flexible response in 1962 but it was not formally accepted by the rest of the alliance until 1967. William Kaufman, *The McNamara Strategy* (New York: Harper and Row, 1964), pp. 102-134.

36. For European resistance to the concept of flexible response, see Lawrence Freedman, *Evolution of Nuclear Strategy* (London: Macmillan Press, 1981), pp. 293-302.

37. See abtracts from de Gaulle's press conference in Henri Brugmans, *L'idée européenne 1918-1965* (Bruges: Tempelhof, 1965), pp. 282-288.

38. "Der deutsch-französische Vertrag vom 22 Januar 1963" in Curt Gasteyger, *Europa zwischen Spaltung und Einigung 1945-1990* (Bonn: Bundeszentrale für politische Bildung, 1990), pp. 230-234.

39. Boyd France, *United States-European Community Relations,* p. 28.

40. Schaetzel, *The Unhinged Alliance, America and the European Community,* 1975, pp. 51-52.

41. Kissinger, *Years of Upheaval,* p. 153. (My emphasis.) Source: "Fourth Annual Report to the Congress on United States Foreign Policy, May 3, 1973," *Public Papers of the Presidents, Richard Nixon,* PUB 29(Washington, D.C.: United States Government Printing Office, 1973), [141], pp. 402-405. See also in appendix, document 3.

42. André Fontaine, *Un seul lit pour deux rêves. Histoire de la "détente" 1962-1981* (Paris: Fayard, 1981), pp. 531-535.

43. Horst Krenzler, "The Dialogue Between the European Community and the United States of America: Present Form and Future Prospects" in Jürgen Schwarze (ed.), *The External Relations of the European Community* (Baden-Baden: Nomos Verlag, 1989), p. 96. (My emphasis.) "Dokument über die europäische Identität" in Gasteyger, *Europa zwischen Spaltung und Einigung 1945-1990,* pp. 302-305.

44. See "Address by the President before the Commission of the European Communities, 6 January 1978," in U.S. State Department, *American Foreign Policy: Basic Documents, 1977-1980* (Washington, D.C.: 1981), Document 209.

45. Zbigniew Brzezinski, *Power and Principle: Memoirs of the National Security Adviser, 1977-1981* (New York: Farrar, Straus, Giroux, 1983), p. 289.

46. Claude Imperiali, "Coopération politique et conflit du Moyen-Orient. Divergences Europe-Etats-Unis" in Jacques Bourrinet, (ed.) *Les relations Communauté européenne-Etats-Unis* (Paris:

Economica, 1987), pp. 511-514.

47. Karsten D. Geier, *The European Community in the 1982 Siberian Gas Pipeline Conflict* (Washington, D.C.: George Mason University, 24-25 May 1989), pp. 12-30. Draft presented at the Conference of the European Community Studies Association.

Julie E. Katzman, "The Euro-Siberian Pipeline Row: A Study in Community Development," *Millennium* 17, 1988, pp. 25-40.

48. Roy H. Ginsberg, *Foreign Policy Actions of the European Community: The Politics of Scale* (Boulder: Lynne Rienner), 1989, pp. 146-147.

49. The Single European Act, *Bulletin of the European Communities,* Supplement 2/86, p. 18, Article 30 (6a).

50. Ibid., Article 30 (6c).

51. Michèle Bacot and Marie-Claude Plantin, "La réactivation de l'UEO: éléments d'un rééquilibrage dans les rapports Communauté européenne Etats-Unis" in Bourrinet, *Les relations Communauté européenne-Etats-Unis,* pp. 579-592.

52. Western European Union, *Platform on European Security Interests,* The Hague, 27 October 1987.

53. Robert O. Keohane and Stanley Hoffmann, "Community Politics and Institutional Change" in William Wallace (ed.) *The Dynamics of European Integration* (London: Pinter Publishers, 1990), pp. 276-300.

54. Part Two of this book is entirely devoted to those economic questions, especially Chapter 3 .

55. See Chapter 12 of this book.

56. Stanley Hoffmann, *Gulliver's Troubles, or the Setting of American Foreign Policy* (New York: McGraw-Hill, 1968), pp. 447-449.

See also the original article, "Europe's Identity Crisis," in *Daedalus* (Fall 1964), pp. 1279-1282.

CHAPTER 2

IMPACT OF THE COLD WAR

Did East-West *tensions* lead to more European integration or, in contrast, to stagnation or even to a set-back of European integration. In other words, did periods of *detente* foster European integration or block it? To answer those questions, one should first define what were the periods of *tension* and *detente* during the Cold War. There is indeed an important literature on this issue but opinions are still diverging. For example, should one remember 1956 for the denunciation of Stalin's crimes in the 20th Congress of the Soviet Union Community Party and the Soviet-American connivance in the Suez Crisis? Or, on the contrary, should one remember 1956 for the crushing of the Hungarian Revolution?

The question is fundamental if one knows that the Treaty of Rome was signed in March 1957, just three months after the above mentioned events. Despite these epistemological uncertainties, we will try to answer the question of the impact of the Cold War on European integration. First, with the *tensions,* two clearest examples concern the years 1948 and 1950. In 1948, the *Coup of Prague* of February 24 led to the Brussels Treaty, signed on March 17 between France, the United Kingdom, and the Benelux nations. This was the first foundation of the Western European Union. Soviet domination in Eastern Europe also had an important impact on the Congress of The Hague, in May 1948, and on the creation of the Council of Europe the following year.

One should note, however, that the United States was not officially connected to the Treaty of Brussels, because Washington was not authorized in 1948 to be a part of military alliances in peacetime outside the American continent. The so-called Vandenberg resolution removed this obstacle and the way became free to the creation of the Atlantic Alliance. Since then, every European attempt for more military integration has been linked to the United States in one way or another.

As for the Congress of The Hague and the creation of the Council of Europe, one should also be careful about linking it to the Cold War. First, the idea of the Congress preceded the *Coup of Prague*. Second, the Council of Europe can be seen more as a failure of European integration than the contrary. Instead of supranationalism as promoted by the Federalists, and instead of political integration among the governments, the Council of Europe has been limited to the establishment of an Assembly designated by the national Parliaments and without genuine legislative competences.

The year 1950 is interesting because it corresponds to the Korean War, and also to the proposals of the Schuman and Pleven plans. The Schuman Plan led to the creation of the European Coal and Steel Community (ECSC) and the Pleven Plan was an appeal to establish an European Defence Community (EDC). Once again, the background constituted by East-West *tension* is important for explaining the origin of both initiatives. One should, nevertheless, point out that the idea of the ECSC preceded the Korean War. As for the EDC, it was planned as a pillar of NATO.

The year 1956 is fundamental in the context of the creation of the European Community. The double character of this period comes from the fact that it was at the same time a period of *detente* (20th Congress, success of destalinization) and *tension* with the crumbling of the Hungarian Revolution. It is precisely this contradiction which strengthened the dynamics leading to the signing of the Treaty of Rome. The German case is a very good one. Chancellor Adenauer was especially afraid of the detente side in 1956. He feared that the United States would conclude an agreement with the Soviet Union at the expense of Germany. Adenauer particularly worried about General Radford's proposal to withdraw 800,000 American soldiers from Europe. By strengthening its integration with France, Italy, and the Benelux countries, Adenauer viewed the Community as a way of avoiding any initiatives on disarmament without taking into account German reunification. This political element was fundamental in Adenauer's decision to support the creation of the EC against the opinion of people like his economic minister, Ludwig Erhard, who at that time judged the EC to be a centralist, protectionist, and socialist-oriented organization.

As for France, it was mainly the anti-French American policy in the Suez Crisis that was the determinant in lifting the last hesitation of a nationalistic country which did not hesitate a few years earlier to reject the European Defence Community. But so-called American connivance with the Soviet Union convinced Paris that France should not only be dependent upon the Americans, but that Europe should unify in order to play a more substantial role at the world level.

However, it is interesting to note that the United Kingdom, also a "victim" of American policy during the Suez Crisis, did not draw the same conclusions that France did. London tried in this period to torpedo the Community by using all sorts of stratagems such as the Maudling Committee, proposals for reshaping the OEEC, and, finally, the creation of EFTA. Without any doubt, *tension* or *detente,* the UK did not at that time like the idea of European integration.

In 1957-1958, Washington supported EURATOM much more than the European Economic Community. As it has been shown in the previous chapter, one of the reasons for the American relative lack of enthusiasm for the EEC can be partly explained by the influence of Jean Monnet. Studies by scholars like Ernst Haas and Karl Deutsch reflected and influenced the views of many American leaders.[1] Those theories assumed that a gradual functional integration, sector by sector, would lead finally to European unity. Theorizing from Jean Monnet's analysis (ironically, a pragmatist *par excellence),* they wanted to avoid too fast integration in delicate political areas. According to this approach, the European Defence Community failed because it lacked progessiveness in its development. Therefore, most Americans were skeptical about *big leaps forward* and rather supported specialized forms of integration like EURATOM, hoping that a *spillover* effect would lead later to more European integration.

American interest in EURATOM (more than in the EEC) had especially something to do with the strategic component of nuclear energy. The American attitude was nevertheless ambiguous. The United States supported EURATOM as a kind of compensation for the failure of the EDC, but at the same time the United States was interested in this organization because it wanted to control it and to avoid any nuclear proliferation, i.e., to avoid the Community's becoming a military power.

One should also mention the dualist American attitude toward the United Kingdom in the context of European integration. On the one hand, Washington always pressed London to take part in all operations of European integration, before and after the Treaty of Rome. For example, the Americans were never enthusiastic about EFTA, because this system would have maintained discrimination against trade in dollars without contributing to European construction. In addition, they opposed EFTA because they viewed it as a purely commercial arrangement without political perspectives, especially given the presence of so many neutral countries.

But, on the other hand, the American policy was not coherent, because the U.S. special partnership with the UK contributed greatly to the difficulties of the Community. Its first effect was to deter the United Kingdom from looking for more integration with the old continent and to foster its anti-European convictions. Moreover, the increased Anglo-American military cooperation after the Suez Crisis, and the American contribution of British nuclear weapons (refused to the French and the Germans), showed once again that relations among military strategy, the evolution of the Cold War, and European integration were far from linear.

The events of 1973 offer another illustration of the complexity of the relations between the Community and the United States in the context of the Cold War. The year started in a period of *detente,* as President Nixon signed the SALT 1 Treaty with the Soviet leader Leonid Brezhnev in May 1972. At the same time we also saw Kissinger's *Year of Europe.* According to the American professor Richard Ullman,[2] it was also in 1973 that the French started their secret program of nuclear military cooperation.

This means that, despite *detente,* Paris was more interested in benefiting from American nuclear technology than in trying to restart the Western European Union (despite one speech by French Foreign Minister Michel Jobert).

The year 1973 finished, however, with one of the deepest crises between Western Europe and the United States. This has to do with a series of different factors, such as the blunders of Kissinger, the visceral anti-Americanism of Michel Jobert, and European lack of will to resist the Arab oil blackmail. The Yom Kippur War led to one of the deepest crises between the United States and the Soviet Union, as Kissinger had been obliged to put the American nuclear forces on alert No 3, sign of a terrible escalation. This *tension,* however, did not lead to strengthening of the Atlantic Alliance at the expense of European integration, but, on the contrary, led to progress in the Community's definition of its identity and to an improvement in European political cooperation.

Let us mention a final example of misinterpretation. This one concerns the revival of the Community in the mid-1980s, thanks to the adoption of the EC Commission's White Paper and of the Single European Act.[3] Many American observers, fascinated by Soviet-American relations, see wrongly in the re-launching of the Community's integration in the mid-1980s a reaction to East-West *tension* and link it to the Afghanistan war,[4] the Pershing II and Cruise Missile crises,[5] the Strategic Defense Initiative (SDI),[6] and Reagan's tough policy.

To be sure, such strategic elements explain attempts to revive the Western European Union (WEU) and the development of some extra-Community technological cooperation programs such as EUREKA. But the EC's boost in the mid-1980s had nothing to do with these elements. The origins of the Single European Act should be traced to an internal EC development: (1) Gaston Thorn's Propositions of June 1981; (2) the European Act of German and Italian Foreign Ministers Genscher and Colombo (November 1981); (3) the Stuttgart Declaration (1983); and (4) the *Crocodile* and Spinelli Resolutions (1981-1983); which are un-related to the Cold War.[7]

Other specialists, on the contrary, have maintained that the revival of the EC in the mid-1980s was due to the Gorbachavian *detente*. They point out, thus, the importance of Gorbachev's accession to power, of the *double-zero option* on short and long-range intermediate nuclear missiles, and of the Reykjavik Summit (1986) which raised anxiety among the Europeans of a Soviet-American partnership at their expense. Once again, the explanation is anachronistic because very different dynamic trends were involved.

***

It is almost impossible to draw theoretical conclusions from the impact of the evolution of the Cold War on European integration.[8] There are as many arguments for, and against, every interpretation. Thus, East-West *tensions* of the years 1948-1950 led to a dynamic of integration, marked by the creation of the Council of Europe, the European Steel and Coal Community, and the European Defence Community. But East-West *tensions* in 1962 contributed to the paralysis of the Community's integration (French refusal of the UK membership), at the same time that President Kennedy was proposing his concept of a new *Atlantic partnership*.

The same obstacles arise when analyzing periods of *detente*. On the one hand, at the beginning of 1973, there was a process of European integration directed against the United States. On the other hand, the period of *detente* linked to Gorbachev did not contribute to European Community integration, as the EC-1992 process was not triggered by any East-West context.

It is very difficult to draw lessons from the past, even from a well structured period such as the Cold War. *A fortiori*, in this current period without clear characteristics beyond the Cold War, it is even more difficult to predict the future by observing the past.

Notes

1. Ernst Haas, *The Uniting of Europe: Political, Social and Economic Forces: 1950-1957* (Stanford: Stanford University Press, 1958).

Karl Deutsch, *Political Community in the North Atlantic Area: International Organization in the Light of Historical Experience* (Princeton: Princeton University Press, 1957).

For an overview, see Panayotis Soldatos, *Le système institutionnel et politique des Communautés européennes dans un monde en mutation* (Brussels: Bruylant, 1989), pp. 33-85.

2. Richard Ullman, "The Covert French Connection," *Foreign Policy* (Summer 1989), pp. 3-33.

3. See Chapter 3 of this book.

4. Anastasia Pardalis, "European Political Cooperation and the United States," *Journal of Common Market Studies* XXV, No. 4 (June 1987), p. 278.

5. John Palmer, *Europe without America? The Crisis in Atlantic Relations* (Oxford: Oxford University Press, 1988), p. 50.

6. Jean Charpentier, "L'Europe face à la proposition américaine de participation à l'IDS" in Jacques Bourrinet (ed.), *Les relations Communauté européenne-Etats-Unis* (Paris: Economica, 1987); pp. 527-529.

7. Jean De Ruyt, *L'Acte unique européen* (Brussels: Université de Bruxelles, 1987), pp. 25-45.

8. We do not agree with David Calleo's simplistic affirmation: "In short, European reactions almost inevitably counterbalance American oscillations." David P. Calleo, *Beyond American Hegemony* (New York: Basic Books, 1987), p. 6.

PART TWO

ECONOMIC ASPECTS OF
U.S.-EC RELATIONS

CHAPTER 3

ECONOMIC IMPACT OF EC-1992 ON THE U.S.

The EC-1992 internal[1] market program was initiated in 1985 with the publication of an EC Commission White Paper entitled, "Completing the internal market."[2] This program is part of a much longer historical process aimed at creating a free-border economy among the members of the European Community. The foundation for this historical process lies in the Treaty of Rome. The White Paper is a detailed plan for the removal of all obstacles to the four freedoms of movement by 1992: free movement of goods, people, services, and capital. It presents a specific timetable (not legally binding) for around 300 directives (legislative measures) that would abolish all physical, technical, and fiscal barriers to trade.

Vital to the success of the 1992 project was the passage of the Single European Act,[3] which changed voting procedures. Instead of unanimity in Council voting, the Single Act allows certain decisions relating to the internal market exercise to be made by a qualified and weighted majority. Approximately two-thirds of the internal market directives are included, with the exceptions falling in the areas of taxation, professional qualifications, and the rights and interests of employees. The act became effective on July 1, 1987, and represented the final critical step in the launching of the EC internal market program.

Background

It was not until 1988 that the United States grasped the importance of the European Community project. There are three main reasons for this: (1) the Americans were disillusioned by 30 years of Community slogans which did not lead to spectacular success; (2) the Reagan era coincided with isolationist tendencies and exaggerated obsession with the confrontation with the USSR and Japan; (3) the success of EC-1992 was dubious before the Irish ratification of the Single European Act and the adoption of a compromise on the reform of the the Community budget which gave some credibility to EC-1992 (Brussels, March 1988).

The surge of momentum toward an EC internal market was clearly underestimated by most American observers of Europe. Not much attention was paid in 1985-1987, when the Commission published its White Paper and when the Council of Ministers had adopted the Single European Act.

Americans grew disheartened with the European Community especially because they were disappointed by the failure of the EC to fulfill the dream of the 1950s, the one of a "United States of Europe." Years of so-called European malaise gave the impression to many Americans that the EC had lost its sense of purpose. Common wisdom held that Europe did not have the political will to accomplish such a complex task. The Community seemed immobilized by debates over the budget and agricultural subsidies, and it had broadened its membership to include Greece, Portugal and Spain, instead of deepening and strengthening its bonds.

However, as soon as the Americans took EC-1992 seriously, they took it too seriously. They suddenly considered themselves confronted by the terrible danger of a so-called "Fortress Europe." War was launched against the Community because the first draft (at the level of the Commission) of the Second Banking Directive contained a reciprocity provision that appeared potentially to apply a mirror-image standard.[4] Significant modifications were later made in response to concerns expressed by the United States – and by some EC member states –leading America to stop its attacks against the Community.

Since this modification took place in April 1989, Washington has shifted to a much more positive attitude towards EC-1992. This American moderation has a lot to do with Bush administration

and geostrategic considerations, but it would be wrong to attribute this shift of policy only to political factors. The Bush
administration takes a positive view of the Community for the
simple reason that serious studies have reached relatively
positive conclusions about the implications of the EC internal
market for America.

Numerous systematic and comprehensive reports have been published by different ministries, professional associations, and
consultants. Almost all vested professional associations, big
enterprises, the administration, and the Congress have published
detailed studies of the impact of EC-1992 on the U.S. economy and
have concluded that there are no reasons to fear the EC internal
market.[5]

All of the Community's directives have been carefully screened,
and almost all imaginable theses have been tested. Conclusion:
EC-1992 is seen as good news for the U.S. economy. The Americans
see the following advantages:

A Unified Market

A unified market gives American firms the opportunity to work
in more than the three or four major states where they had
previously concentrated, as they have tended to overlook other
markets because the results were not worth the effort. EC-1992
will lower the costs and difficulties of selling in the EC, and
will make the European market more attractive to a larger range
of U.S. companies. An integrated common market is a good means of
saving costs, thanks to more efficient administration, simplified
shipping, cheaper and quicker transportation.

One Set of Standards[6]

The replacement of twelve standards by one will ease the circulation of American products on the Community's market. As soon
as a product is put on "free practice," twelve differing national
standards will be considered functionally equivalent as long as
they contain certain agreed-upon essential ingredients. U.S.
corporations would, even be able to pick the most convenient of

twelve member states' standards and be assured of free entry in all twelve member states. It is important to stress that the EC is willing to accept not only products meeting EC standards, but also those produced by different standards if the manufacturer can demonstrate that the product meets the EC's "essential requirements."

Less Testing and Certification[7]

This could be an interesting benefit to U.S. companies. They wouldn't have to worry about meeting different requirements within each EC country. Major opportunities will exist especially for smaller U.S. firms which have shied away from exporting in the past because they lacked the resources to service twelve national member state markets.

Opening of Public Procurement[8]

EC government purchases are roughly equal to 15 percent of the EC's total gross domestic product (or about $600 billion per year). Unfortunately, 85 percent of those markets are closed. With EC-1992, EC member states governments will buy more from all over the world, especially from American firms.

Liberalization of Services[9]

American financial sectors are optimistic about the perspective of benefiting from new opportunities in areas such as banking, investment, and insurance. Cross-bordering in services will reduce costs for American firms which are not always able to settle in all EC states. It is the same with the principle of free establishment of persons, which eases hiring of qualified personnel in American multinational companies.

End of Quantitative Restrictions

The completion of the EC internal market forces member states such as France or Italy to suppress their previous quantitative restrictions on the import of foreign goods such as automobiles.

As a matter of fact, in a free-border market, it is very difficult to control diversion of traffic. This perspective could help to promote export of American goods to some restrictive countries.

Improvement of Competition Policy

Establishment of EC level control over mergers and acquisitions involving large-scale multinational conglomerates is potentially of major importance for U.S. businesses in the EC. Such a policy, if it allows for a quick and exclusive ruling by the EC on proposed mergers, could reduce the obstructive or delaying effect of approvals by multiple national jurisdictions.

Monetary Integration[10]

Most American financial sectors support EC progress made on free circulation of capital, extension of the EMS to more countries (UK, Portugal), and success in monetary coordination, less uncertainty on inflation and exchange rates. The Bush administration views trends toward the creation of a EuroFed independent from political authorities and devoted to fighting inflation positively.[11]

A monetary union may have micro- and macroeconomic impact, creating "static" and "dynamic" gains by (1) eliminating nominal exchange rate variability; (2) banning the transaction costs of exchanging currencies; (3) strengthening price stability; (4) fostering fiscal policy consistency; and (5) outlawing devaluations.

For example, the Commission has predicted that direct savings in transactions costs of ECU 13-19 billion (approximately $18-24 billion) a year would result from a genuine European monetary union.[12] This should lead to less need for external currency reserves, more ECU denominated financial issues managed by European banks, lower transaction costs in international trade, and also some financial gains (seigniorage, or the international use of the ECU).

At the political level, a monetary union could facilitate international coordination through establishment of a balanced multi-polar regime of ECU, dollar, and yen, and thus contribute to international stability.[13] But since the dollar ceases to be the reference currency in a trilateral system, the United States will lose a privilege it enjoyed in the Group of Seven. The implication for America is that the Community and Japan will become more formidable negotiators in international policy coordination.[14]

Comparative Advantages of American Businesses[15]

American enterprises are often more oriented to a whole European perspective than their European competitors. American firms were never psychologically limited by the more nationalist and fragmented approach of European firms. Furthermore, one must point out that many small U.S. companies sell their products in the EC through their inclusion as components of products sold by larger companies with investments in Europe. About 34 percent of all U.S. exports to the EC go directly to the affiliates of U.S. companies with direct investments here.

Improvement of the American Balance of Payments

In 1990, the U.S. exported $98 billion of goods into the EC, against $49 billion in 1985, which contributed to an important lowering of the American trade deficit.[16] For the first time in years, the U.S. was running a trade surplus with the EC. The EC is the world's biggest market for American export; therefore, a prosperous EC contributes to a stable market. According to the U.S. National Association of Manufacturers, "this strong investment growth has been directly stimulated by the EC-92 program and industrial restructuring in anticipation of its impact."[17] Thus, expected implications of EC-1992 can help to ease some American economic difficulties. The significance of EC-1992 is underlined when it is compared to the less glamorous U.S. trade performance with Japan.

U.S.-EC Trade, 1985-1990

	U.S. Exports		U.S. Imports		Balance
	$ bns	% chg.	$ bns	% chg.	$ bns
1985	49.0	-3	67.8	13	-18.8
1986	53.2	9	75.7	12	-22.6
1987	60.6	14	81.2	7	-20.6
1988	75.9	25	84.9	5	- 9.0
1989	86.6	14	85.1	0	1.5
1990	98.0	13.5	92.0	8	6.0

Sources: Stephen Cooney, *Update on EC-92. An NAM Report on Developments in the European Community's Internal Market Program and the Effects on U.S. Manufacturers* (Washington, D.C.,: National Association of Manufacturers Publications, April 1990), p. 8. Stephen Cooney, *EC-92: New Issues and New Developments. NAM's Third Report on the European Community's Internal Market Program and the Effects on U.S. Manufacturers* (Washington, D.C.,: National Association of Manufacturers Publications, April 1991), p. 22.

A Stronger Economic Partner

The EC economies are now less dependent than they were on the U.S. business cycle due to the intensification of intra-European commerce and strong incentives for investment in preparation for the EC internal market. Furthermore, as a strong trading partner, the EC could serve as a cushion when things go wrong in another part of the global trading system: it has already been proven that the EC market can act as a shock absorber for the world economy. From 1970 until 1988, U.S. direct investment in Europe jumped from 15 percent to 40 percent of overall U.S. direct investment abroad. Sales of U.S. subsidiaries in the Community exceed $300 billion annually.[18] The internal market is creating a second continent-wide economic target for U.S. companies.

***

The question of the implications of EC-1992 is vast and complex. Nevertheless, despite some initial worries, the Americans look with optimism at the economic advantages brought by the EC internal market. They see in EC-1992 outlets for their products, a credible partner, and a pole of stability.

In the following chapters, we will analyze more in detail some specific questions such as standards, certifications, public procurements, rules of origin, and financial services.

Notes

1. We never use the expression "single market" because the 1992 program does not aim at harmonizing completely the EC markets as within France or even the U.S.

2. Commission of the European Communities, *Completing the Internal Market [the White Paper]* (Luxembourg/Brussels: Office for official publications of the European Communities, 14 June 1985), COM(85)310.

3. Commission of the European Communities, "Single European Act," *Bulletin of the European Communities,* effective July 1, 1987, reprinted at 1986 EC Bulletin supp. No.2.; 26 p.

The Single European Act, as an amendment of the Treaty of Rome, is now integrated in any new version of the Treaty.

Be aware that the expression "Single European Act" has nothing to do with the nature of the EC market. It is called "single" because it joins in one single document economic and political elements such as the European Political Cooperation.

4. See chapter 8 of this book.

5. See the selected bibliography and especially:

Business Roundtable, "The United States and the European Community's Single Market Initiative: An Analytical Framework," in U.S. Congress, *Europe 1992: Economic Integration Plan.* Hearing. 101 Cong. 1 sess. (Washington, D.C.: Government Printing Office, February-May 1989), pp. 425-436.

Stephen Cooney, *Update on EC-92. An NAM Report on Developments in the European Community's Internal Market Program and the Effects on U.S. Manufacturers* (Washington, D.C.,: National Association of Manufacturers Publications, April 1990), pp. 8-11.

U.S. Chamber of Commerce, *Europe 1992. A Practical Guide for American Business* (Washington, D.C.: Publications of the U.S. Chamber of Commerce, 1989); 143 p.

U.S. Chamber of Commerce, *Europe 1992. A Practical Guide for American Business #2* (Washington, D.C.: Publications of the U.S. Chamber of Commerce, 1990); 56 p.

U.S. Department of Commerce, *EC 1992: A Commerce Department Analysis of European Community Directives* (Washington D.C.: U.S. Government Printing Office, 1989/90); 3 volumes.

U.S. General Accounting Office, *European Single Market. Issues of Concern to U.S. Exporters* (Washington, D.C.: Publications of the General Accounting Office, February 1990); 46 p.

U.S. General Accounting Office, *U.S. Financial Services' competitiveness Under the Single Market Program* (Washington, D.C,: Publications of the General Accounting Office, May 1990); 72 p.

U.S. Government Task Force on the EC Internal Market, *An Assessment of Economic Policy Issues Raised by the European Community's Single Market Program* (Washington, D.C.: U.S. Government Printing Office, 1990); 31 p.

U.S. International Trade Commission, *The Effects of Greater Economic Integration Within the European Community on the United States.* Report to the Committee on Ways and Means of the United States House of Representatives and the Committee on Finance of the Senate (Washington, D.C.: USITC Publication, July 1989); 310 p.

Jorge Pérez-Lopez, Gregory K. Schoepfle, John Yochelson and the U.S. Department of Labor (ed), *EC 1992: Implications for U.S. Workers* (Washington, D.C.: Center for Strategic and International Studies, 1990); X-149 p.

6. U.S. Chamber of Commerce, *Europe 1992. A Practical Guide for American Business #2*, pp. 22-23.

U.S. General Accounting Office, *European Single Market*, pp. 14-27.

U.S. Government Task Force on the EC Internal Market, *An Assessment*, pp. 11-12.

U.S. International Trade Commission, *The Effects of Greater Economic Integration*, 6-7 to 6-35.

7. U.S. Chamber of Commerce, *Europe 1992. A Practical Guide for American Business #2*, pp. 23-25.

U.S. General Accounting Office, *European Single Market*, pp. 14-27.

U.S. Government Task Force on the EC Internal Market, *An Assessment*, pp. 13-14.

U.S. International Trade Commission, *The Effects of Greater Economic Integration*, 6-14 to 6-15.

8. U.S. Chamber of Commerce, *Europe 1992. A Practical Guide for American Business #2*, pp. 37-39.

U.S. General Accounting Office, *European Single Market*, pp. 39-45.

U.S. Government Task Force on the EC Internal Market, *An Assessment*, pp. 19-21.

U.S. International Trade Commission, *The Effects of Greater Economic Integration*, 4-7 to 4-10.

9. U.S. Chamber of Commerce, *Europe 1992. A Practical Guide for American Business #2*, pp. 40-42.

U.S. General Accounting Office, *U.S. Financial Services' Competitiveness Under the Single Market Program* (Washington, D.C,: Publications of the General Accounting Office, May 1990), pp. 34-53.

U.S. International Trade Commission, *The Effects of Greater Economic Integration*, 5-5 to 5-8.

10. For more details on the European Monetary Union, see Chapter 13 of this book.

11. Arlene Wilson, "Prospects for a Central Bank and for Monetary Union," in Glennon J. Harrison (ed.), *European Community:*

Issues Raised by 1992 Integration (Washington D.C.: Congressional Research Service Report, 1989), pp. 85-88.

12. Commission of the European Communities, "One Market, One Money," *Information of the Spokesman's Service,* (Brussels: 19 October 1990), P(90) 78, p. 2.

See also U.S. Chamber of Commerce, *Europe 1992. A Practical Guide for American Business #2* (Washington, D.C.: Publications of the U.S. Chamber of Commerce, 1990) p. 16.

13. U.S. Chamber of Commerce, *Europe 1992. A Practical Guide for American Business #2,* p. 16.

14. Walter W. Eubanks, "The European Central Banking System and the 1992 Monetary Union," *Congressional Research Service Report for Congress,* 10 January 1990, pp. 16-17.

15. Stephen Cooney, "EC-92 and U.S. Industry," in Joint Economic Committee. *Europe 1992: Long-Term Implications for the U.S. Economy* (Washington, D.C.: Government Printing Office, 26 April 1989), p. 28.

16. U.S. International Trade Commission, *The Effects of Greater Economic Integration Within the European Community on the United States,* pp. 3-5 to 3-7.

17. Stephen Cooney, *Update on EC-92. An NAM Report on Developments in the European Community's Internal Market Program and the Effects on U.S. Manufacturers* (Washington, D.C.: National Association of Manufacturers Publications, April 1990); p. 8.

18. James K. Jackson, "U.S. Direct Investment in the EC," in Glennon J. Harrison (ed.), *European Community: Issues Raised by 1992 Integration* (Washington D.C.: Congressional Research Service Report, 1989), pp. 18-25.

CHAPTER 4

STANDARDS

The European Community might adopt standards which are not used in the United States or at an international level. This situation could put some American firms outside the European market. Other forms of discrimination are possible, such as: lack of first notification, harmonizing-up, and abuse of specific norms. For these reasons, the United States demands the right to get "a seat at the table" of the European standardization organizations.

This chapter introduces first the notion of standards and the so-called new approach of the European Community. In a second part, there will be a discussion of what the main problems for the United States are. Finally, we will try to make an assessment of the EC and U.S. positions. For instance, is the EC position so unfair? Are the Americans not themselves "sinners"? Is it so strange that the EC does not authorize the whole world to take part in its decision-making process?

Background

An exporter faces a technical barrier to trade if he has to modify his products to comply with the standards of the country in which he wants to sell. The removal of such barriers is one of the main objectives of EC-1992.[1] Of the 300 or so directives programmed in the 1985 White Paper, more than half are standard-related.

Technical barriers lead to extra costs for consumers and producers. They multiply the cost of storing products; they make large-scale production more difficult; they reduce the competitiveness of industry, and they diminish competition. There are two types of legal regulations and standards: the first are the different national regulations. These regulations are enacted in order to protect safety, the environment, health, and the like. For example, the composition of most EC pharmaceutical products is strictly regulated and it is not possible to sell medicines which do not conform to different national legislations.

The second type of barrier is due to differences between national industrial standards (Afnor in France, BSI in the UK, DIN in Germany, etc.), which must be fulfilled in order to be able to import a product. Such standards for quality, form, and functioning are not legally binding. They are set forth by private organizations,

Between 1960 and 1985, the Community adopted some 300 directives on standardization. However, the overall result has been modest because in certain product sectors such as foods, the Commission used to incorporate mandatory technical standards into directives. Therefore, paradoxically, national rules were being implemented more rapidly than existing ones were being harmonized at an EC level.

Since 1985, the Community has been forced to change its strategy and decided to try a "new approach." It means that any product legally marketable in one member state must also be admitted to markets of all other member states. The Commission came to the conclusion that directives could be limited to reaching the equivalence of objectives.

The "new approach" has given an important impetus to the process of integration. The EC makes a distinction between the *standards* themselves and the *general requirements. General requirements,* usually for the safe and environmentally-sound use of products, are issued in broad and general terms. They are adopted by a vote within the EC.

Standards are far more specific than *general requirements.* However, the EC does not develop standards; they are drafted by three extra-EC European standards organizations: the European Committee for Standardization (CEN), the European Committee for

Electrotechnical Standardization (CENELEC), and the European Telecommunications Standards Institute (ETSI).[2] Those committees take the broad requirements and write the standards insuring that the requirements for each product are met.

The governments of most of the Western European countries, including the ones of the European Free Trade Association, have voting representatives in the CEN/CENELEC working groups. The status of standards is private. They are not binding, but codify the "state of art" at a given time.

The Issue for the United States

The important deals in standards setting are usually made by the time a draft standard is agreed upon, but companies or trade associations without a European presence do not have direct contact with the European standards bodies during the all-important drafting stages of standard-setting by CEN, CENELEC, and ETSI. It is therefore difficult for American enterprises to acquire information on new standards.

At stake are the following issues for the United States:

1. CEN, CENELEC, or ETSI might adopt standards that are not used in the United States or at an international level by organizations such as ISO and IEC.[3] This might hinder or exclude U.S. goods, or necessitate costly modification to U.S. products.[4]
2. Significant advanced notice might be given to EC firms to change their products to meet new standards, while U.S. firms wait for word. If American companies are unaware of the specifications of a new standard until it is released in its draft form, there may not be sufficient time for the U.S. firm to adapt its product to meet the new regulation. For instance, in medical technology, it can take six months to two years to change the design of a product.[5]
3. Some Americans fear a "harmonizing up" process of key EC product standards.[6] For certain branches, firms set their own standards that, in turn, become the national standards.

Concerns exist in the United States that the EC firm with the most stringent standard may make it an EC-wide standard to protect their EC market position. For example, a U.S. telecommunications firm which previously was denied access to the West German market because of a tough standard could now be excluded from the entire European market.[7]

4. Specific national rules can be used to keep out American products. Although an American product might meet all requirements for commercial sale in any EC member state, it might not meet some national requirements. For example, an electrical product fitting all EC legal requirements for sale in the Community might not be able to get insurance in France.[8]

As a consequence, many Americans fear that their products may be banned or discriminated against, thus reducing the competitiveness of American products. This is especially a concern among small-and medium-sized enterprises (SMEs) based outside Europe. They may face standards which have been specifically designed to benefit EC industry. Two-thirds of American electronics industries, medical technology, and forest products originate in small-and medium-sized companies not based in Europe.[9]

There are several examples of discrimination against the United States. In 1988, the CEN introduced a standard on battery cables for forklift trucks.[10] Only European-manufactured cables were able to conform to standards. It took American producers more than a year to be able to adapt their products.

Another example of discrimination: the EC has proposed the use of a particular test to measure the emission of automobiles that the United States long ago abandoned in favor of a more sophisticated test.[11] This could force American manufacturers to use two different sets of testing procedures to demonstrate compliance with EC standards.

The standard for a high-tech medical device could specify that it had to be sterilized with a sterilization method utilized only by European firms, but not in line with an equally effective method utilized in the United States. The U.S. forest products industry fears that the EC could set standards that are tied to specific material properties of European forests that are not found in American forests.

To set most product standards, the U.S. government relies upon private organizations, mainly trade associations and standards organizations. Therefore, European companies interested in American standards, even if they do not produce in the United States, have the opportunity to make known their views on a particular standard. For example, the Electronic Industries Association (EIA) has many standards committees that have European members: Thompson-SGS, Ericsson Philips, Siemens. These firms may attend EIA meetings and take part in votes on standards.

Assessment

The issue of standards does not evolve into big clashes between the United States and the EC for three main reasons: First, the EC position is not so unjust; second, EC standardization creates advantages for U.S. companies; and third, the EC has made a lot of concessions.

The EC Position

The European position is not so unjust. One has to understand it completely before accepting the severe American criticism. Moreover, the American system itself cannot be taken as a good model:

1. Standards enacted by the European standards organizations are not compulsory. There are other ways to show conformity to the Community's essential requirements. U.S. companies might follow other paths.
2. CEN and CENELEC do not let third country experts take part in their meetings in order to avoid any duplication of existing international standards organizations such as ISO and IEC, which already serve in this capacity.
3. The risks of harmonizing-up should not be exaggerated. Experience teaches that the need to achieve consensus within

the CEN/CENELEC mitigates the risk that European companies with rigid standards could seek to protect their EC market position by having their national standard adopted on an EC-wide basis.

4. The United States is not well placed to criticize other countries as its own record is not glittering. The United States does not place a lot of emphasis on international solutions. For instance, in 1989, "out of 89,000 standards used in the United States, only 17 were directly taken from ISO."[12] No IEC standards have been followed. As the American General Accounting Office observes: "Less than half of 1 percent of ISO and IEC standards have been formally adopted as American National Standards."[13] By contrast, the EC seems to be much more committed to the implementation of international standards.

5. No more than 50 percent of the technical regulations enacted by the American Federal Government (mandatory) are international standards. This is in contradiction to the GATT Standards Code.

6. The U.S. federal administration does not take serious measures to ensure that states and private standardizing bodies use international standards. States and other local government bodies often have additional legal requirements of their own.

7. There isn't any central standardization organism in the United States covering the whole country (such as it exists in Canada). There are more than six hundred private bodies engaged in standardizing activities. There is therefore no assurance, that by following one particular standard, a product will be accepted throughout the whole territory.

Advantages Created by EC Standardization

Progress in standardization in the Community presents more advantages than disadvantages for the United States. For the moment, divergent standards among the EC member states have held back the competitive potential of U.S. suppliers. American exporters have sometimes had difficulties in meeting the requirements of each of the EC states. Although the EC countries have been moving closer to harmonization of requirements, there are still many situations in which requirements for products and specific standards are different.[14]

However, under EC 1992, a U.S. exporter will have to meet only one standard to sell throughout the EC. After the completion of the Single Market, if a product exported to the EC meets the standards of the member states, as well as the minimum EC requirements established by the White Paper process, it is theoretically freely circulated in any EC country.

Twelve differing national standards would be considered functionally equivalent as long as they contain certain agreed-upon essential ingredients. The EC is willing to accept not only products meeting EC standards, but also those produced to different standards if the manufacturer can demonstrate that the product meets the EC's "essential requirements."

U.S. corporations will be able to pick the most convenient of twelve member states standards and be assured of free entry to all twelve member states.

Some U.S. industries, such as telecommunications and pharmaceuticals, expect to benefit as a result of the EC's actions. Moreover, large U.S. firms established in Europe might enjoy a competitive advantage under harmonized conditions, since they are accustomed to operating on a continental scale. This is particularly true of automobile, telecommunications, and pharmaceutical firms.

Removal of technical barriers by adoption of unified standards, could prove a boon to U.S. firms. Scale economies gained by the acceptability of a single product throughout the EC and reduced inventory storage costs could provide an immediate, positive boost to these U.S. firms.

All U.S. firms would enjoy cost savings, because they could now market their products throughout Europe by meeting one set of standards rather than twelve. American exporters would not be any worse off than they are under the current system and could be much better off.

The EC Concessions

The Community has accepted making some concessions and efforts to lend more clarity to standardization:

(1) Since 1989 CEN and CENELEC provide a monthly report on European standards under development and those planned for the future.[15]

(2) This report is available through the American National Standards Institute (ANSI).

(3) CEN and CENELEC have implemented a mechanism allowing non-members to provide comments to European technical committees through the relevant ISO and IEC contact points and to accept requests for non-members to make oral presentations to representatives of the relevant technical committees on an ad-hoc basis.[16]

***

Fearing discrimination on the European market, the United States asked for a right to be directly involved in the European standardization organizations. This request has been refused to the United States, but Washington has the assurance of more transparency in CEN, CENELEC, and ETSI. In our opinion, the EC position is quite justified: standards proposed by European organizations are not compulsory; it is normal that the EC not authorize the whole world to take part in its decision-making process; risks of harmonizing-up should not be overstressed.

Morover, the United States respects international norms even less than the EC: the American administration does not take serious measures to make sure that international norms are respected by the states of the Union and private organizations; and the United States lacks homogeneity and a central body (as in Canada) for elaborating new norms. The United States is no less a "sinner" than the European Community.

Notes

1. U.S. International Trade Commission. *The Effects of Greater Economic Integration Within the European Community on the United States. Report to the Committee on Ways and Means of the United States House of Representatives and the Committee on Finance of the Senate* (Washington, D.C.: USITC Publication, July 1989), pp. 6-8 to 6-11.

2. ETSI is an autonomous body set up in 1988 to develop telecommunications in Europe. Membership in ETSI is open to non-governmental bodies. Unlike CEN/CENELEC, ETSI allows non-member organizations to obtain oberver status, allowing the possibility to speak but not to vote.

3. ISO means International Standards Organization. It is the world's largest international standards body, covering all fields. As of 1991, ISO had published over 7,000 standards.

IEC means International Electrotechnical Commission. This body deals exclusively with electrical and electronics standards. As of 1991, IEC had published over 2,500 standards. The majority of ISO and IEC member bodies are governmental institutions.

4. Stephen Cooney and the National Association of Manufacturers, "EC-92 and U.S. Industry," in U.S. Congress. Joint Economic Committee. *Europe 1992: Long-Term Implications for the U.S. Economy.* Hearing. 101 Cong. 1 sess. (Washington, D.C.: Government Printing Office, 26 April 1989), pp. 36-37.

5. Richard W. Young, "Statement" in U.S. Congress. House Committee on Foreign Affairs. Subcommittee on Europe and the Middle East, *Europe 1992: Economic Integration Plan.* Hearing. 101 Cong. 1 sess. (Washington, D.C.: Government Printing Office, February-May 1989), pp. 225-230.

6. The Business Roundtable Task Force on International Trade and Investment, "The United States and the European Community's Single Market Initiative" in *Europe 1992: Economic Integration Plan,* ibid, p. 433.

7. Peter F. Cowhey, "Telecommunications" in Gary C. Hufbauer (ed.), *Europe 1992. An American Perspective* (Washington, D.C.: The Brookings Institution, 1990), pp. 208-212.

8. Michael C. Maibach, "The Implications of EC 1992 for U.S. Electronics Companies and Workers," in Jorge Pérez-Lopez, Gregory K. Schoepfle and John Yochelson (ed), *EC 1992: Implications for U.S. Workers* (Washington, D.C.: Center for Strategic an International Studies, 1990), pp. 66-67.

9. U.S. General Accounting Office. *European Single Market. Issues of Concern to U.S. Exporters* (Washington, D.C.: Publications of the General Accounting Office, February 1990), p. 16.

10. U.S. International Trade Commission, *The Effects of Greater Economic Integration,* pp. 6-26 and 6-27.

11. "Emission of Gaseous Pollutants from Diesel Engines," and Air Pollution by Gases from Motor Vehicles Engines" in U.S. Department of Commerce, *EC 1992: A Commerce Department Analysis of European Community Directives* (Washington D.C.: U.S. Government Printing Office, 1990), volume 3, pp. 5 and 15.

12. Commission of the European Communities, *Report on United States. Trade Barriers and Unfair Trade Practices* (Brussels: Services of the Commission of the European Communities, 1990), p. 15.

Commission of the European Communities, *Report on United States. Trade Barriers and Unfair Trade Practices* (Brussels: Services of the Commission of the European Communities, 1991), p. 40.

Original Source: Congress Research Service, *Report on International Standardization: The Federal Role,* April 1989, p. 16.

13. GAO adds "but this is not representative bacause many ISO and IEC standards are based on U.S. technology".

U.S. General Accounting Office. European Single Market. Issues of Concern to U.S. Exporters (Washington, D.C.: Publications of the General Accounting Office, February 1990), p. 18.

14. U.S. Chamber of Commerce, *Europe 1992. A Practical Guide for American Business* (Washington, D.C.: Publications of the U.S. Chamber of Commerce, 1989), p. 45.

15. U.S. Government Task Force on the EC Internal Market, *An Assessment of Economic Policy Issues Raised by the European Community's Single Market Program* (Washington, D.C.: U.S. Government Printing Office, 1990), p. 12.

16. Stephen Cooney, *Update on EC-92. An NAM Report on Developments in the European Community's Internal Market Program and the Effects on U.S. Manufacturers* (Washington, D.C.: National Association of Manufacturers Publications, April 1990), p. 15.

CHAPTER 5

TESTING AND CERTIFICATION

American worries about EC tests and certification concern the following issues: the future of existing bilateral agreements; necessity of tests in the EC and not in the United States; extension of the Community's principle of mutual recognition to American products; conformity of American laboratories' procedures required for EC certification; and the necessity of an insurance of quality. As for standards, the question is to determine what is the issue and whether American grievances are well founded.

Background

There exists a dialectical link between the issue of standards and the one of testing and certification. These two questions, however, do not lead necessarily to the same kind of problems. Therefore, the two issues will not be dealt with in the same chapter, as is generally found in the specialized literature.

Testing and certification procedures are the means of ensuring the conformity of a product to a set of standards. These procedures might become technical barriers each time an importing country requires certification in addition to what is required by the country of origin.[1]

In the sectors which require *harmonization* of standards, national authorities require certification to control application of common rules. They have to recognize the validity of checks already carried out in other member countries so that they do not have to be repeated. Such recognition is made obligatory and is the subject of very specific procedures. The mutual recognition of certificates of conformity standards is a prerequisite condition for the free movement of goods.

The question of testing and certification applies *a fortiori* to sectors which *do not require harmonization*. One should be aware that the "new approach" and the principle of mutual recognition of standards make the whole more difficult. Let's assume that one does not need any more harmonization of the ingredients put in a product such as ham. It means that any EC country will accept any ham already on the market in other EC countries without demanding any prior harmonization of the ingredients. As a consequence, in such cases, testing and certification by the country of origin will acquire an even greater significance, as an unique means of guaranteeing the safety, security, and health of a product. The Community is therefore confronted with the delicate question of trust between the different EC bodies of testing and certification.

One way of solving this dilemma is to extend the principle of mutual recognition to certificates of conformity issued by the controlling authorities. This could be a solution in some cases where problems of safety, security, and health are not important and for sectors without overly strong protectionist pressures.

However, for other products, according to the Commission, the national governments, laboratories, and certification bodies, there is a need for a *European testing and certification council*. This autononomous body, independent of the Community, would be given the means to promote the negotiation and conclusion of mutual recognition agreements among all the European laboratories. In addition, this Council would have to guarantee the transparency of agreements and respect for the interests of all the parties involved.

Issues

Testing and certification procedures could lead to direct and indirect costs for third-country products. Different means could be used in EC countries – such as insurance requirements or delays in certification – to try to keep non-national products out of EC national markets.

Such technical barriers could reduce the overall competitiveness of American industry by market expansion, diminish competition, make large-scale production more difficult, and increase the cost of storing products. The resulting extra costs are well known, especially in such sectors as pharmaceuticals, where delays in certification could last three or more years.

It is still not yet clear how the Europeans will assess the conformity of U.S.-made products to the European standards of the EC essential requirements. More specifically, there exist six different types of problems for American enterprises due to the development of an EC testing and certification system:

Future of the Old Arrangements?

Presently, most EC nations have bilateral arrangements with U.S. laboratories, certification bodies, and accreditation bodies to test products for compliance with European standards so that they may be sold without additional tests in Europe. There are concerns regarding how these arrangements will be affected by EC-1992.[2]

The directive on how U.S. products should be tested has yet to be released by the EC Commission. Should the Commission not allow for mutual recognition of testing, it could constitute a major unfair barrier to the free flow of goods to the EC from the United States.

Tests Required in the EC and not in the U.S.

Some product tests are being required in the EC that are not normally conducted by U.S. companies, and, in some cases, it appears the only way to certify an American product for sale in the EC may be to do it on European soil, by an EC-recognized testing facility.[3]

The certification systems in the EC and the United States are very different. The EC's global approach to testing and certification calls for reciprocal access to markets in any agreements negotiated with non-member countries. Because the EC is opening its market completely, this requirement means the United States would have to do the same.[4]

In America, Underwriters Laboratory, the largest product safety testing and certification organization in the world, accepts European participants in its meetings.[5] The Americans, in turn, demand reciprocity from the future European testing and certification council.

Extension of the Principle of Mutual Recognition?

Will the U.S. exporter enjoy the same benefits of mutual recognition, i.e., the principle that products manufactured to acceptable standards in any one EC country can be sold in all? In other words, will an exporter to the EC find Europe to be the same unified market that is available to a European-based competitor?

"Euro-worthiness" of American Laboratories

Will American laboratories be accepted to certify the "Euroworthiness" of American exports? The Community has said yes in principle, but it could take many years for American laboratories to qualify. The EC will need to prove to the United States that the certification bodies in the other EC countries are competent before the agreements are extended EC-wide.[6]

Treatment of U.S. Declarations of Conformity

Will the declarations of conformity by U.S. manufacturers be accorded the same treatment as those by European manufacturers? A producer's declaration of conformity is sometimes demanded. It is a means of proving that a product complies with the specified requirements. This is a condition where the manufacturer is granted the right to put an EC mark on a product. There is a concern that the use of the EC mark by U.S. manufacturers may be restricted because declarations of conformity from U.S. companies may not be considered to be at the same level as those coming from European manufacturers.[7]

Assessment

The issue of testing and certification should be assessed in all its complexity.

U.S. System of Testing is No Model

It is important to point out that the U.S. system of testing and certification is far from perfect. It cannot be taken as a model and is even criticized by many U.S. laboratories. EC exporters also have problems due to the lack of American centralization. There is, for example, no guarantee that getting a certification from one laboratory or from one American state will grant it access to the whole country.[8]

With regard to terminal equipment in telecommunications, according to the EC Commission, the costs of adapting European-based products to U.S. specifications are much higher than the costs for the necessary adaptation work required for other countries.[9] In practice, foreigners have to comply with a number of voluntary standards, set by industrial organizations in order to ensure compatibility and safety. For example, Los Angeles and Chicago require that terminal equipment be manufactured according to Underwriters Laboratories (UL) standards and that it be tested by UL.

For electrical products and components, there are at least 2,700 divergent safety certifications, due to the large number of state, city, and municipal governments. These requirements are far from being consistent with one another. Moreover, sometimes there exists no national standard.[10]

There are also a lot of questions as to whether the U.S. private sector wants mutual recognition of laboratories. Industry and business associations officials have expressed concern over whether the United States can or would want to provide reciprocal access. It is far from sure that the United States is ready to extend bilateral agreements currently in place with one member state to the other eleven member states.[11]

Both the American Council of Independent Laboratories and the Underwriters Laboratories (UL) fear that U.S. local government bodies, such as states and municipalities, would have to accept foreign-made products built in accordance with standards that do not necessarily take U.S. codes into consideration.[12]

In addition, because most testing and certification is done privately in the United States, it is doubtful that the U.S. government could negotiate an agreement covering U.S. private sector testing and certification.

Advantages of Simplifying Formalities

It is important to remember that American businesses will continue to profit from advantages due to the simplification of the formalities within the EC. Progress in testing and certification in the EC could be a interesting benefit to U.S. companies. They would not have to worry about meeting different requirements within each EC country. For example, at present there is no guarantee that an American manufactured product that is tested and accepted for certification in one EC state would be accepted in other countries, even though the standards for the categories may be the same.

However, after the completion of the internal market, it will be enough to meet one European test and certification in order to be able to sell a product throughout the whole Community. Twelve differing national tests and certifications would be considered as compatible.[13]

Currently, bilateral agreements exist for testing only a few of the U.S.-made products sold in Europe. Even if the EC continues to require most products to be tested in Europe, the fact that European certification enables a product to move freely throughout the EC should save U.S. exporters the cost of getting products tested in each country. Moreover, American firms might have the possibility of choosing the most attractive of twelve states' tests and certifications.

Large American multinationals with a European foothold might benefit from less certification red tape as they will not have to multiply their industries in the twelve different countries.[14] Major opportunities will also be present for smaller U.S. firms which have shied away from exporting to Europe in the past because they lacked the resources to service twelve national member state markets.[15]

EC Cooperation Mood

It is fair to say that a lot of progress has already been accomplished with regard to greater European cohesion and collaboration with the United States. American industry bodies and testing laboratories will be able to participate in the European Organization for Testing and Certification (EOTC). The EOTC has three levels:

The first is made up of committees on calibration testing and quality assurance. The second consists of sectoral committees which represent such sectors as aerospace, steel, electrical equipment, medical technology, machine products, information technology, building materials, gas, and chemicals. The third level is made up of agreement groups formed among laboratories supported by the sectoral bodies.

The proposed structure of the EOTC will allow access for U.S. involvement into only two tiers of its organization: (1) its industry sectoral committees, where there will be a forum for dialogue with U.S. industry groups; and (2) in the agreements established among laboratories through a "memorandum of understanding" between American and European laboratories.[16]

Pending Problems

However, many of the above mentioned problems are still pending. This explains the aggressiveness of some Congressmen like Sam Gejdenson. In April 1990, he proposed with Congressman John Miller legislation denying EC companies the right to "self-certify" compliance with standards set by the five governmental agencies: the Federal Communications Commission, the Environmental Protection Agency, the Food and Drug Administration, the Energy Department, and the Labor Department.

The requirements would remain in effect until the U.S. Commerce Secretary certifies that the EC is setting product standards and requirements in an open and fair manner and has established equitable rules for testing and certifying products for compliance with product standards and requirements."[17]

This bill is not very popular among the American laboratories and testing bodies[18] for the following reasons:

1. It is seen as disproportionate to the objective. This would have no leverage on the EC and many small- and medium-sized laboratories would be at a serious competitive disadvantage.

2. The main victims would be the numerous joint ventures between U.S. and EC enterprises. There are many American firms or partly American firms which self-certify in Europe in order to reexport into the U.S. Their part of the market is very important. They could be the main hostages of the Gejdenson's bill.

3. There are official negotiations between the U.S. administration and the Community that should not be jeopardized. Protectionist or retaliatory measures can backfire. The American motto is that general sectoral reciprocity is not a good idea. The proper basis for determining data acceptability is laboratory competence, not geography. One should not confuse standards issues and testing and certification. It is in not the American interest to link the progress on standards clarification with mutual acceptance of test data. In sum, the chances of the Gejdenson's bill being successful are weak, but it is, nevertheless, a reflection of American uneasiness.

***

One should observe first that the EC has shown its good will by opening the future EOTC to the American companies at its second and third stages. It is also important to remember that American businesses will continue to profit from advantages due to the simplification of the formalities in the EC. It is fair to assess that a lot of progress has already been made on the way to greater European clarification and collaboration with the United States.

Moreover, as for standards, the Community is far from being the sole "sinner." Weaknesses in the American system are obvious: lack of a centralized system of testing and certification; absence of mutual recognition among laboratories. To be sure, the American system of testing and certification cannot be taken as a model and is even criticized by many U.S. laboratories.

But problems linked to tests and certification, as well – although in a lesser measure to standards – explain the aggressiveness of some Congressmen such as Sam Gejdenson and John Miller who proposed in April 1990 to ban EC companies for continuing to proceed toward self-certification of their own products in some areas. Such measures of retaliation against the Community are extreme and not supported by the American administration nor by most laboratories and roof organizations. These bills are, nevertheless, a mirror of the bitterness felt by many Americans, and they represent a foretaste of future clashes between the Community and the United States.

Notes

1. U.S. International Trade Commission, *The Effects of Greater Economic Integration Within the European Community on the United States. Report to the Committee on Ways and Means of the United States House of Representatives and the Committee on Finance of the Senate* (Washington, D.C.: USITC Publication, July 1989), pp. 6-14 and 6-15.

2. Stephen Cooney and the National Association of Manufacturers, "EC-92 and U.S. Industry," in U.S. Congress. Joint Economic Committee, *Europe 1992: Long-Term Implications for the U.S. Economy.* Hearing. 101 Cong. 1 sess. (Washington, D.C.: Government Printing Office, 26 April 1989), p. 39.

3. U.S. Chamber of Commerce, *Europe 1992. A Practical Guide for American Business* (Washington, D.C.: Publications of the U.S. Chamber of Commerce, 1989), p. 50.

4. Ibid., p. 50.

5. Joe Bahtia and the Underwriters Laboratories, "Europe-1992: Product Standards and Testing" in U.S. Congress. House Committee on Foreign Affairs. Subcommittee on Europe and the Middle East, *Europe 1992: Economic Integration Plan.* Hearing. 101 Cong. 1 sess. (Washington, D.C.: Government Printing Office, February-May 1989), p. 306.

6. Joe Bahtia, "Testimony" in U.S. Congress. Subcommittee on Exports, Tax Policy, and Special Problems, *European Community Approach to Testing and Certification: Should the U.S. Government Play a Role?* Hearing, 101 Cong. 2nd sess. (Washington, D.C.: Government Printing Office, 30 April 1990), p. 21.

7. Ibid., p. 20, and Joe Bahtia, "The European Community's Approach to Testing and Certification: Should the U.S. Government Play a Role," Ibid., p. 85.

8. Commission of the European Communities, *Report on United States. Trade Barriers and Unfair Trade Practices* (Brussels: Service of the Commission of the European Communities, 1990), p. 15.

Commission of the European Communities. *Report on United States. Trade Barriers and Unfair Trade Practices* (Brussels: Services of the Commission of the European Communities, 1991), pp. 42-44.

9. *Report on United States,* 1990, Ibid., p. 17. or *Report on United States,* 1991, Ibid., p. 40.

10. *Report on United States,* 1990, Ibid., p. 18. or *Report on United States,* 1991, Ibid., p. 41.

11. Milton Bush and the American Council of Independent Laboratories, "Testimony," in *European Community Approach to Testing and Certification,* p. 104-105.

12. Ibid., pp. 90 and 104.

13. Charles Ludolph and the Department of Commerce, "State of the International Trade Administration," in ibid., pp. 62-63.

14. U.S. Chamber of Commerce, *Europe 1992. A Practical Guide for American Business* (Washington, D.C.: Publications of the U.S. Chamber of Commerce, 1989), p. 50.

15. U.S. General Accounting Office, *European Single Market. Issues of Concern to U.S. Exporters.* (Washington, D.C.: Publications of the General Accounting Office, February 1990), pp. 22-23.

16. Bureau of National Affairs, "Testing and Certification. U.S. Industry Representatives Upbeat on Access after Visit," *1992-The External Impact of European Unification,* 23 March 1990, pp. 2-3.

17. Congressman Sam Gejdenson, *Five Bills,* presented at the 101st Congress, 2nd Session, No 4471-4474 and 4476, 14 April 1990, (not published).

See also, Congressman Sam Gejdenson, *Extension of Remarks,* 14 April 1990, 2 p. (not published).

18. Bureau of National Affairs, "More Reservations Expressed Over 'Retaliatory' Measures", *1992 – The External Impact of European Unification,* 4 May 1990, p. 3.

CHAPTER 6

PUBLIC PROCUREMENT

The Community directive concerning the so-called "excluded sectors" adopted in September 1990 discriminates against third countries. It has a "Buy European" clause which authorizes the EC to reject proposals which contain less than fifty percent of Community content and which proposes a preference of price of three percent for all Community companies.

The issue of public procurements is still a question being dealt with at the GATT level. What are the probabilities of agreement if one knows that the United States also has a discriminatory system in its states and local communities which protect public markets by so-called "Buy American" clauses?

Background

Opening up government procurements is one of the main objectives of EC-1992. Simply stated, government departments, public utilities, and local authorities in EC countries buy too much from local suppliers. EC government purchases are roughly equal to 9 percent of national Gross Domestic Product (GDP) if only contracts placed by central and local government are considered, and as much as 15 percent of GDP if nationalized industries are included.[1] Seventy-five percent of government needs are awarded to "national champions" for whom the tenders are tailor-made.

The failure to open public-sector purchasing and construction markets to EC-wide competition costs a lot of money, roughly half the total EC budget. However, more competition in procurements should lead to: (1) pressure on EC industry toward more rationalization, (2) opportunities for companies to scale up to international competition, and (3) budget savings.[2]

EC legislation requiring public contracts to be opened to competition dates back to the 1970s. Since then, the EC has tried to open public procurements with two directives: (1) the "works" directive to liberalize bidding on public works projects, and (2) the "supplies" directive which requires open, non-discriminatory consideration of suppliers' bids.

These measures have been widely ignored. The failure of the opening of the public procurements in the EC is generally attributed to the following factors:[3]

1. Too many differences in the various definitions of public procurements. For example, some EC states are centralized, but others are decentralized.
2. Administrative tricks to empty the aims of the directives. To mention a few: arbitrary definition of the thresholds, incapacity to inform potential foreign bidders, addition of technical requirements that favor "local champions," and abuse of administrative discretion.
3. Incapacity to implement most directives. Some states simply never incorporated the directives in their national legislation.
4. Deficiency of the enforcement mechanisms. It depends from one state to the other but even if the judicial system works, it is too slow and too "soft" most of the time.

To reverse this negative tendency, the EC has developed initiatives focusing on the following measures: harmonization of the different EC practices, increased clarification, fewer exceptions to competitive tendering, and more effective procedures for addressing nonnational grievances. In 1980, the EC procurements legislation was amended to adapt EC law to the GATT Procurements Code. This extended nondiscrimination principles to all code signatories for procurements by specific government agencies.

The GATT Government Procurements Code requires signatories to allow suppliers of products for other signatories to compete for government contracts in sectors covered by the code that meet specified criteria. It also establishes common and more trans-parent procedures for providing information on proposed pur-chases, open bids and awarding contracts, and settling disputes.

The "Excluded Sectors"

Certain very important purchasing entities and public authority construction projects were excluded from the GATT Code: water, energy, transport, and telecommunications sectors. In September 1990, the Council of Ministers adopted a directive to open up intra-EC competition in the so-called excluded sectors. The measures will cover both public and private companies, including water companies, gas and electric utilities, gas and oil explorers,[4] rail transport companies, airports, maritime ports, postal services, and telephone and telegraph monopolies. The directive will go into effect on January, 1 1993.

Issues

The most controversial EC procurements directive affects the so-called excluded sectors. The directive provides that EC governments or purchasing entities in the excluded sectors would be permitted (but not required) to discriminate against suppliers of non-EC products:[5]

1. They may exclude from consideration offers containing less than 50 percent EC content;
2. If they do consider bids with less than 50 percent EC content, they must grant a 3 percent price preference to equivalent offers with 50 percent EC content.

The local content rules governing the "excluded sectors" make it possible for the EC to exclude from consideration certain U.S. bids. Even if U.S. bids receive consideration, they will be disadvantaged by mandatory price preferences favoring EC suppliers. So, if an American-based producer's offer contains more than 50 percent EC content, it must also undercut an EC bidder's price by more than 3 percent to win a contract.

American suppliers fear the way in which EC content will be calculated.[6] There may be differences between contract price and contract value. It seems that the 50 percent content requirement, unlike that of the "Buy American" Act, will be based on the value of both goods and services in the contract, including research and development.

Moreover, American exporters using U.S.-sourced components face uncertainty in both their production decisions and in market access. U.S. exporters will be in a quite unpredictable market access situation because EC procuring entities are under no obligation to consider offers of non-EC products nor to inform their suppliers of the possible status of their bids prior to submission.

As a result of this situation, suppliers of non-EC products may be discouraged from making long-term plans and from dedicating the financial resources necessary to prepare bids for procurements because they do not know how open the market will be.[7]

Alternatively, American exporters may feel compelled to increase the EC content of their bids to more than 50 percent in order to ensure that their bids are considered by procuring entities. U.S. companies may put their money into preparing bids that may never be seriously considered.[8]

Most American officials recognize that the directive on "excluded sectors" was influenced by the U.S. "Buy American" Act.[9] They argue, however, that American companies bidding for contracts with EC public procurements would be treated less favorably than the American government treats EC firms. There is a substantial difference between the two systems. Unlike the U.S. Buy American provisions, where third country bidders can evaluate before applying whether they would be competitive with American enterprises or not, procuring entities in the Community are allowed to reject any foreign proposal that does not contain 50 percent EC-content.

In other words, under the American system, almost all products coming from countries that have signed the GATT Government Procurement Code are allowed to bid. However, the EC directive does not require the extension of competitive rights to non-EC products, even when third country products cost less than 3 percent of the equivalent EC products.[10]

Another difference, the EC's 50 percent content requirement, unlike that of the "Buy American" Act, will be based on the value of both goods and services in the contract, including research and development. This policy could lead American firms to divert their research & development to the EC. Also dissimilar is the possibility left by the Community to exclude private entities when they are subject to government control. For example, the EC directive would include private entities such as British Telecom.[11]

Public purchasers in the European Community account for 90 percent of U.S. telecommunications equipment sales in the EC and up to one-third of the sales by major U.S. computer and office machine manufacturers. EC governments are also significant purchasers of data processing services.[12]

U.S. telecommunications industry officials are concerned that the 3 percent price preference for products and services, applied in conjunction with EC content rules, may restrict the sales of telecommunications equipment in the EC.

According to representatives of the heavy electrical equipment industry, meeting the EC content requirement would necessitate substantial financial investment in Europe.[13] Because the majority of these manufacturers are small business, few have the resources to open a European plan. Thus, sales of U.S. heavy electrical equipment to EC government entities are unlikely to increase in the near future.

In defense procurements, there is a concern about squeezing out U.S. exports or joint-production agreements, especially as European firms begin to work more closely together across national lines.[14] The extension of newly tightened EC government rules to the generally excluded sector of defense procurement could create a systematically protected and favored EC-based defense industry.

The U.S. Department of Defense maintains a series of memoranda of understanding (MOUs) with European nations governing the purchase of defense articles. These MOU's give EC companies non-discriminatory access to a greater percentage of the U.S. government procurements budget than U.S. firms receive access to in Europe.

It appears that, without code coverage of these currently excluded sectors to gain nondiscriminatory bidding opportunities in these sectors, U.S. business will have to increase the value of EC parts, labor, and incentive for the growth of U.S. investment, joint ventures, and licensing agreements in the EC. There is debate, however, as to whether U.S. investment will come as a result of economic opportunity or as a result of fear of exclusion from the EC market.

Opportunities for American Business

Opening the Community public sector markets to non-EC suppliers will provide additional export opportunities for U.S. firms. Actual levels of procurements from nonnational suppliers remain low in all EC member states.[15] Harmonizing the various member-state public procurements laws, regulations, and practices, and introducing formal procedures could make it easier for foreign suppliers to compete for EC public sector contracts, because the same fundamental principles and procedural ground rules will be in effect in all twelve member states.

Rules that were previously vague and loosely worded will be more specific and detailed, making them easier to interpret and less likely to be circumvented. Member-state obligations and rights will be more clearly defined, and enforcement of such rights made tougher, both at the national and at the EC level.

Greater harmonization of EC government procurements policies and practices could significantly improve market access for U.S. suppliers by breaking down long-standing barriers at the EC-nation level. Other benefits could also include: greater predictability, simplicity of design and performance standards, and greater uniformity in price-setting.

There will be increased market opportunities for American subsidiaries located within the Community.[16] These companies will be accorded treatment equivalent to that accorded to EC companies. They will be able to bid on any contract covered by the EC measures, and they will benefit from the requirements for broader coverage and increased transparency. They will also be protected by the 3 percent "Community preference" provision in bidding on public sector contracts.

Liberalization of EC government procurements in the excluded sectors is also of particular interest to the U.S. telecommunications and heavy electrical equipment sectors. The United States exported $1.3 billion of telecommunications apparatus to the EC, compared with $0.6 billion to Japan and $0.8 billion to Canada.[17] But U.S. exports to Europe could be far larger. The EC telecommunications equipment market is expected to grow 67 percent by 1995. Even more dramatic is the prospective growth in telecommunications services, an area of decided U.S. strength.

American Discrimination in Public Procurements

The United States often criticizes the EC without being aware of its own discriminatory policy. We will first give a brief description of the "Buy American" provisions in general, and, second, give examples of U.S. procurement restrictions which violate the existing GATT Code.

The "Buy American" restriction is a preference given to domestic products over third country goods. It means that products with 50 percent American content (sometimes 65 percent) will be supported by a privilege which can range from 6 percent to 50 percent. There are numerous "Buy American" legal instruments: around forty at the Federal level, thirty-seven at the state level, and innumerable ones at the local government level.[18]

The acknowledged aim of "Buy American" restrictions is to maintain an American industrial base by protecting domestic enterprises. This policy has led to a decline in the value of the procurements covered by the GATT Code (from $19 bn in 1982 to $15 bn in 1986) and a shift in procuring responsibilities from the federal government to the state and local governments.[19] U.S. procurement at the federal level totaled approximately \$200 billion in 1988. However, through "Buy American" provisions, procurement worth \$180 bn was reserved for American enterprises.[20] To be sure, these "Buy American" provisions can be waived by bilateral reciprocal defense procurements (MOU). However, as mentioned earlier, these MOUs can be unilaterally modified by the United States.

Most types of discrimination involve the Department of Defense because it tends to abuse in its interpretation of the GATT Code on Government Procurement. Article VIII.1 of the GATT Code allows parties to make exceptions to the general rules of the Code for products considered indispensable for national security or defense. But article IX.5 (a) provides that exceptions may be made only in exceptional circumstances and must be negotiated with the other parties.

However there is a clear tendency in the United States to extend unilaterally and exaggeratedly the list of exceptions. The American abuses of exceptions are numerous. By way of example, two specific restrictions are examined below.[21]

A first example concerns *synthetic fibers*. This is a market estimated to be worth \$200 million a year.[22] The American exception is based on the so-called Berry Amendment, which prohibits any use of foreign synthetic fibers as long as they are available domestically. As a consequence, European firms are not allowed to sell non-American fibers to the Department of Defense. To be sure, this exception does not correspond to the general spirit of the exceptions authorized by the GATT Code for national security reasons.

A second example concerns *machine tools* acquired by the Department of Defense. This is a market estimated at \$1 billion a year.[23] According to the GATT Code on Government Procurement, the Department of Defense can not make any discrimination against the acquisition of foreign machine tools. However, since 1981, the U.S. has unilaterally decided to exclude most of these machine tools for security reasons. And, in 1986, the discriminatory Mattingly Amendment was adopted by Congress. This Mattingly Amendment allows only American (and Canadian) bidders to supply the Federal Supply Classes of machine tools used in Department of Defense facilities.

Furthermore, since 1989, a change has been made in the rule of origin of machine tools. Previously, the rule allowed assembly in a foreign country. Now, the so-called Department of Defense Appropriation Act requires that assembly also take place on American (or Canadian) territory. This means that, to sell machine tools to Department of Defense, EC enterprises are forced to invest in the United States.

There are other U.S. discriminations in areas covered by the GATT Code. First, Americans tend to abuse the exception for small business. As a matter of fact, there is an American reservation in the GATT Code to exclude U.S. small or disadvantaged businesses because there is legislation in the U.S. requiring procurement from small and minority enterprises. Federal agencies are required to award contracts to certain small businesses in accordance with different rules. Furthermore, legally established preferences for small business exist in eighteen states and practices having similar effects are found in a larger number of states.

The definition of a small or disadvantaged business is based on the annual turnover or on the number of employees (from 500 to 1,500). However, there has been abusive definition of a small or disadvantaged enterprise. Therefore, according to official American statistics, small or disadvantaged businesses are currently obtaining between 20 and 30 percent of total federal procurement. In practice, these preference mechanisms do substantially reduce the scope of application of the GATT Code.

A second abuse concerns state and local entities' restrictions. States and local governments cover around 70 percent of the U.S. public procurements. Discriminations against foreign suppliers are numerous. For example, in Massachusetts, there is a difference between in-state and out-of-state products. Massachusetts's goods get a preference first, then U.S. products, and third country goods are third on the list of priority. In California, the legislation requires an exclusively domestic supply. As regards public works, a price preference of ten percent is used for goods and services. In New York City there are value-added conditions such as use of the local workforce and the location of the enterprise in New York.

It is important to note that the federal government can not disengage from its responsibility in case of discriminations made by states and local governments. The administration has the authority to use sanctions such as refunding the federal money in case of abuse by states or local purchasing entities. Federal funding to these entities represents 16 percent of their expenditures.

Finally, there is another American abuse, consisting of unilateral interpretation of violations of the GATT Code on procurements. As a matter of fact, the U.S Trade Act of 1988 (title VII) authorizes banning certain countries from access to U.S. procurement if they are "not in good standing" with the GATT Code. This is contrary to the GATT Code, which requires raising any issue to the relevant GATT committees and passing through a process of institutionalized dispute settlement.

Prospects for a GATT Agreement

The EC's integration procurement policies have already affected the GATT procurement code negotiations. Negotiations to expand the code stagnated for several years, primarily because the Community had no jurisdiction over the procurement markets of the member states in the "excluded sectors."[24] The momentum of EC 1992 gave the Commission the possibility of gaining the authority to help push international negotiations forward. Now the EC is capable of offering an opening of its public procurement market in return for reciprocal treatment from foreign bidders. In essence the EC is proposing to extend its own legislation to the rest of the industrialized world.

At present, the GATT codes exclude numerous goods, as well as virtually all services, from the non-discrimination tenets of the code. Liberalization of government procurement has been negotiated on a reciprocal basis, that is, the right of competitive treatment is only extended to those countries that have provided comparable rights in return: the EC, the U.S., Japan, Canada, five of the six EFTA countries (excluding Iceland), Hong Kong, Singapore and Israel. In other words, discriminatory treatment is retained for products from countries that have not done so.

***

The EC wants not only to open the "excluded sectors" but also suggests that new rules should apply to "works" –building and construction – as well as to "supplies."[25] It has offered to negotiate a similar deal on purchases of services by public entities. Under the EC proposal the code's rules on open tendering and non-discrimination in granting contracts would also be extended to state, regional, and local government bodies. The EC also calls for the introduction of a "bid challenge" system under which firms discriminated against in the awarding of contracts would be able to secure rapid redress.

Will the United States override its "Buy American" provisions, both at the federal and at the state and local levels, by subjecting a wide range of public purchases to the GATT Code on Government Procurement, in order to gain access to the EC market?

Notes

1. Paolo Cecchini, *The European Challenge 1992: The Benefits of a Single Market* (Aldershot: Gower, 1988), p. 16.

2. For a good overview, see Commission of the European Communities, *Public Procurements and Construction – Towards an Integrated Market* (Brussels: European Documentation, 1988); 107 p.

3. U.S. International Trade Commission, *The Effects of Greater Economic Integration Within the European Community on the United States. Report to the Committee on Ways and Means of the United States House of Representatives and the Committee on Finance of the Senate* (Washington, D.C.: USITC Publication, July 1989), pp. 4-13 and 4-14.

4. The directive on the excluded sectors was combined in 1989 and subsequently renamed the "Utilities Directive." The directive also covers products previously not considered part of the excluded sectors, such as oil and gas and coal mining equipment.

5. U.S. Department of Commerce, *EC 1992: A Commerce Department Analysis of European Community Directives* (Washington, D.C.: U.S. Government Printing Office, 1990), volume 3, pp. 111-116.

6. Stephen Cooney and National Association of Manufacturers," EC-92 and U.S. Industry," in U.S. Congress. Joint Economic Committee, *Europe 1992: Long-Term Implications for the U.S. Economy.* Hearing. 101 Cong. 1 sess. (Washington, D.C.: Government Printing Office, 26 April 1989), pp. 20-21.

7. U.S. General Accounting Office, *European Single Market. Issues of Concern to U.S. Exporters* (Washington, D.C.: Publications of the General Accounting Office, February 1990), p. 44.

8. U.S. Department of Commerce, *EC 1992: A Commerce Department Analysis of European Community Directives* (Washington, D.C.: U.S. Government Printing Office, 1990), volume 3, p. XXI.

9. James M. Murphy, "European Economic Integration" in U.S. Congress. Committee on Foreign Affairs, *The European Community's Plan to Integrate Its Economy by 1992,* p. 337. James M. Murphy is Assistant U.S. Trade Representative for Europe and the Mediterranean.

10. U.S. Department of Commerce, *EC 1992: A Commerce Department Analysis of European Community Directives,* Volume 3, p. XXI. One should nevertheless remember that the Community allows procuring entities to accept foreign bids according to their goodwill.

11. Ibid., p. XXI.

12. Peter F. Cowhey, "Telecommunications," in Gary C. Hufbauer (ed.), *Europe 1992. An American Perspective* (Washington, D.C.: The Brookings Institution, 1990), pp. 197-200.

13. U.S. International Trade Commission, *The Effects of*

Greater Economic Integration Within the European Community on the United States, pp. 4-32 and 4-33.

14. Michael Moodie, *Defense Implications of Europe 92* (Washington, D.C.: The Center for Strategic and International Studies, 1990), pp. 17-19.

15. U.S. Chamber of Commerce, *Europe 1992. A Practical Guide for American Business* (Washington, D.C.: Publications of the U.S. Chamber of Commerce, 1989), p. 85.

16. Ibid., p. 85.

17. Gary Hufbauer, *Europe 1992,* p. 43.

18. Commission of the European Communities, *Report on United States. Trade Barriers and Unfair Trade Practices* (Brussels: Service of the Commission of the European Communities, 1990), pp. 20-21.
Commission of the European Communities, *Report on United States. Trade Barriers and Unfair Trade Practices* (Brussels: Services of the Commission of the European Communities, 1991), pp. 45-62.

19. *Report on United States,* 1990, Ibid., p. 23.
Report on United States, 1991, Ibid., p. 48.

20. *Report on United States,* 1990, Ibid., p. 23.
Report on United States, 1991, Ibid., p. 48.

21. The following procurements restrictions were also adopted on "national security" grounds: telecommunications; coal and coke for the American forces in Europe; supercomputers for the U.S. Army; coastguard vessels and naval vessels; equipment for the "Voice of America," etc.

22. *Report on United States,* 1990, Ibid., p. 26.
Report on United States, 1991, Ibid., p. 51.

23. *Report on United States,* 1990, Ibid., pp. 26-27.

24. U.S. International Trade Commission, *The Effects of Greater Economic Integration Within the European Community on the United States,* pp. 14-15 and 14-16.

25. William Dullforce, "EC Offers Big Opening in Public Procurement Market," *Financial Times,* 3 August 1990.

CHAPTER 7

RULES OF ORIGIN AND LOCAL CONTENT

Rules of origin requirements, local content rules and quantitative restrictions: those extremely technical questions come back with regularity in the external relations of the EC. Although those problems are not specifically and officially an EC-1992 policy, it was issued by the Community in the heat of the economic integration process.

In broad terms, the EC is afraid that Japan and the New Industrialized Countries (NICs) could flood its market by dumping products. To avoid what the EC considers unfair competition, the Community uses anti-dumping measures like taxes to ban foreign products. Sometimes it also exercises pressure on foreign countries to limit their exports (Voluntary Export Restrictions, VERs).

During the last several years, there have been problems, especially on two questions: semiconductors and the future of VERs. The question of semiconductors is linked to the EC's lack of competitiveness in electronics and its desire to create a modern Community industry. Therefore, the EC wants the so-called silicon chips to be made entirely in the EC rather than simply assembled or tested in the EC.

The second problem concerns the future of VERs. What will be the outcome of the VERs concluded by France, Italy, and the United Kingdom with Japan in the 1992 free-border market? Countries without VERs do not want to adopt them just to contribute to the homogeneity of the EC market. This also worries the Americans as a commercial principle and because many Japanese enterprises export to the EC from the American territory.

Background

Local content and *rules of origin* are two concepts that, when linked in certain ways, can create trade barriers. *Local content* refers to the percentage of value embodied in a good or service made within a geographic area.[1]

Rules of origin define the patrimony of individual components. There are laws, regulations, and administrative practices that are applied to ascribe a country of origin to goods in international trade.

No internationally accepted definition of rules of origin exists among the GATT signatories nor is there a uniform set of procedures for applying them. However, the application of many of GATT's provisions recognizes the need for a determination of origin, and a GATT article contains guidelines on origin marking require–ments.[2]

The basis for the application of recent EC rules of origin included several existing agreements and regulations, such as the 1973 Kyoto Customs Convention, the 1968 EC Council Regulation 803/68, and the GATT Antidumping Code of 1979. In practice, both the United States and the EC have complex and sometimes unpredictable processes for determining the origin of different products.

The Kyoto Customs Convention Annex D.1 –which became effective in 1977 – defines two criteria in determining rules of origin: (1) whether the goods have been wholly produced in one country; and (2) whether substantial transformation involving two or more countries has occurred. America signed the Kyoto Convention but did not ratify Annex D.1 because the American government considered that it more closely reflected the European system for determining origin than the U.S. system.[3]

Issues

A state sets a local-content requirement when it wants to force foreign firms to use domestic producers. For example, if the local-content level is not met, the product is not considered as domestic but as imported. Therefore, it can be slapped with import quotas as well as with import and anti-dumping duties.

The coupling of stringent local content requirements with tight rules of origin can essentially exclude products made outside the Community. "The local content issue has for example created a transatlantic melodrama in television programming, where the EC Broadcast Directive gives national authorities permission to require a 50 percent European content."[4]

The U.S. government and industry officials worry that the EC may manipulate rules of origin in some sectors for trade and industrial policy purposes. Because rules of origin are applied on a product-by-product basis, the EC could also yield to political pressures to protect certain industries during the transition to 1992. The lack of transparency, the unpredictability, and the arbitrary nature of EC rules of origin could discourage U.S. companies from exporting to Europe.

The United States has expressed concern that similar policies will be adopted with respect to (1) products subject to EC anti-dumping circumvention investigations, as well as (2) those, such as automobiles, which are subject to quantitative restrictions, voluntary restraint agreements, or monitoring arrangements.[5]

Semiconductors[6]

The February 1989 EC regulation on determining the origin of integrated circuits and assembly provisions poses a potential threat to U.S semiconductor manufacturers. The new rule of origin for integrated circuits states that the criterion for the origin of semiconductors is no longer the *assembly* process but the *diffusion* or wafer fabrication process.

To obtain EC-origin, semiconductors will now have to contain silicon chips that are diffused in the EC; otherwise, they will be subject to a 14 percent tariff. This change makes it more difficult for foreign-based companies to obtain EC origin for their semiconductors.

Integrated and Printed Circuits

In the case of *integrated* circuits, the EC has changed its rules of origin interpretation so that origin is assigned to the country in which the capital-intensive process of diffusion takes place. Previously, *assembly* and testing of an integrated circuit in an EC country had been sufficient to confer origin. This has placed pressure on U.S. and other semiconductor producers to open diffusion facilities in the EC in order to supply semiconductors to customers who seek certain levels of EC content.

The EC has also used a value added rule of origin for *printed* circuit board assemblies (PCBAs), in antidumping circumvention cases. This has resulted in the substitution of EC components for U.S. components on the printed circuit board assemblies. The EC is now considering what origin rule interpretation to adopt for PCBAs for customs purposes. If a value added PCBA rule of origin is adopted, this same problem likely would arise in other circumstances in which there is an incentive to have the PCBA be considered "European."

Certain EC rule of origin interpretations, in particular those applied to integrated circuits and PCBAs, when combined with measures to prevent dumping, have had the effect of encouraging increased EC content in certain electronics products. This has caused U.S. and other non-EC firms to lose sales in the European Community, has encouraged investment in otherwise economically unjustified manufacturing facilities in the EC, and has induced manufacturers to shift to EC sources for components.

The "Screwdriver" Rule

Another EC regulation, known as the "screwdriver assembly rule," states that antidumping duties may be imposed on certain imported products assembled and sold in the EC that have been considered to have been dumped in the past, unless at least 40 percent of their parts and materials was obtained outside of the dumping country. No more than 60 percent of the value of a product's parts and materials may originate in the dumping country. The provision also states that the EC will take into account, on a case-by-case basis, the variable costs incurred in the operation and the research and development carried out and applied within the EC.

According to U.S. government and industry representatives, EC rules of origin, coupled with screwdriver assembly measures, create a strong influence on foreign firms to use components from an EC member state rather than from another country to avoid dumping duties and may constitute nontariff barriers to trade in semiconductors.

For example, although the EC guidance calls for 45 percent non-Japanese value in printed circuit boards, semiconductor industry representatives claim that Japanese manufacturers are apparently being told that the circuit board component of their computer printers must contain at least 45 percent EC value for the printer to obtain EC origin. Only by obtaining EC origin for the boards can Japanese manufacturers assure at least 40 percent non-Japanese value in the finished printer and avoid dumping duties under the screwdriver assembly rule. The Japanese are reportedly attempting to insure the European origin of their circuit boards by replacing U.S. semiconductors with European semiconductors, thus avoiding dumping duties without reducing the level of Japanese content in their printers. At the same time, the EC succeeds in increasing the market for its own semiconductors. American commerce and industry officials believe this is one example of an EC-origin decision with local content implications that, taken together with other rules of origin, compels local investment.

Photocopiers

A case involving a Japanese manufacturer of photocopiers assembled in the United States also illustrates how the EC rules of origin, combined with EC antidumping policies, might affect U.S. economic interests.

The details are the following: the Japanese firm was assembling photocopiers in its California plant, then shipping them to the

EC as products of U.S. origin, thus avoiding 20 percent dumping duties on photocopiers exported directly from Japan. In early 1989, the EC questioned the origin of these U.S.-assembled copiers. When EC officials visited the plant in California to determine whether it should be considered a substantial operation, they found that U.S. assembly and manufacturing fell below the 45-percent value-added requirement and therefore decided to apply 20 percent antidumping duties unless the firm increased the non-Japanese content of these copiers. The firm subsequently increased its U.S. operations to the point where dumping duties no longer apply.

American officials fear a possible loss of Japanese investment in the United States due to stricter EC origin rules for photocopiers and other Japanese products manufactured or assembled there.

Within the last two years, EC antidumping duties have been levied against Japanese typewriters, electronic scales, and photocopiers assembled in the EC. Other EC antidumping investigations are currently in progress for certain Japanese computer printers. Since the imposition of these duties, most of the affected Japanese firms have undertaken to raise the EC content of their products progressively.

Automobiles[7]

Italy, Spain, France, Portugal, and Britain have bilateral import quotas on Japanese automobiles and would like to extend them to the whole EC. This has resulted in a certain number of "national champions," such as Peugeot/Citroën, Renault, and Fiat, putting pressure on the EC to maintain some form of protection.

As borders open among EC member states, enforcement of the approximate import restrictions maintained by individual member states will become impossible. Consequently, the EC faces a choice between either phasing out these restrictions after 1992 or transforming them into EC-wide restrictions.

As a compromise, the EC will likely maintain some transitional rules restricting imports in an effort to protect automobiles.

Although these measures will be directed at the Japanese, American officials are not sure how the EC will define "transitional" and how these measures will affect U.S. trade. There are many different propositions: either that Japanese car imports be "stabilized" at their current 9 percent share of the EC market, or that, after 1993, the EC should impose a temporary EC quota and that only Japanese cars made in Europe with 80 percent local content be considered of European origin.

The U.S. "may pay for the Japanese," if the EC decides that cars assembled in the U.S. by "transplant" manufacturers – Toyota, Mazda, Nissan, Subaru, Isuzu and Mitsubishi – be considered Japanese automobiles instead of American cars. It also puts into question the origin of cars constructed in the U. S. under joint ventures between an American manufacturer and a Japanese manufacturer, such as the GM-Toyota plant in California. (Only between 20,000 and 30,000 Americans are working in those plants.) If these cars were considered Japanese, they would be subject to the tough import quota against Japanese automobiles.

One should nevertheless not forget that U.S. companies have about a quarter of the EC market in automobiles. Attempts to gently coerce the EC into policy positions they would rather not take could result in damage to U.S. interests already firmly established in Europe. Firms like General Motors (GM) and Ford are concerned about an increased Japanese presence in Europe. Here is the dilemma U.S. government and industries faced by. On balance, the fundamental choice for GM and Ford is to privilege their European companies against the Japanese cars.

***

This chapter identified only a few examples of how changing EC rules of origin and application of antidumping regulations could affect American industry. Whether the regulations affecting semiconductors and automobiles will become part of a more general trend is not clear. The problems surrounding the EC's application of origin rules are not new, and resolution will likely be a gradual process.

To be sure, the EC's abuse of quantitative restrictions is a good indicator of its industrial difficulties. Internally, the Community is eliminating discrimination. It is creating a market quite opened to third countries. Externally, in contrast, the Community has been pursuing highly discriminating practices.

The observation that the EC is pursuing a mostly protectionist policy in advanced-technology industries contradicts some theories. As a matter of fact, some political scientists argue that the Community's success in the mid-eighties was mainly due to an incentive of responding in a liberal way to the Japanese challenge, particularly in the electronics sector.

Ironically, the EC-1992 internal market is a success and is relatively opened to third countries' companies but the European electronics industry was successful enough to protect itself against foreign competition through an arsenal of quantitative restrictions.

Notes

1. U.S. International Trade Commission, *The Effects of Greater Economic Integration Within the European Community on the United States. Report to the Committee on Ways and Means of the United States House of Representatives and the Committee on Finance of the Senate* (Washington, D.C.: USITC Publication, July 1989), pp. 11-5 and 11-6.

2. U.S. General Accounting Office, *European Single Market. Issues of Concern to U.S. Exporters* (Washington, D.C.: Publications of the General Accounting Office, February 1990), p. 30.

3. Ibid., p. 30.

4. Gary C. Hufbauer (ed.), *Europe 1992. An American Perspective* (Washington, D.C.: The Brookings Institution, 1990), p. 40.

5. Eugene J. McAllister, "Testimony" in U.S. Congress. House Committee on Foreign Affairs. Subcommittee on Europe and the Middle East, *Europe 1992: Economic Integration Plan.* Hearing. 101 Cong. 1 sess. (Washington, D.C.: Government Printing Office, February-May 1989), pp. 349-350.

Eugen McAllister is Assistant Secretary for Economic and Business Affairs, Department of State.

6. There is already an enormous body of literature on the semiconductors issue and there is no reason for duplicating it here. Any reader interested in more details should consult:

Business Roundtable, "The United States and the European Community's Single Market Initiative: An Analytical Framework" in U.S. Congress, *Europe 1992: Economic Integration Plan.* Hearing. 101 Cong. 1 sess. (Washington, D.C.: Government Printing Office, February-May 1989), p. 430.

Robert E. Hunter and John Yochelson, *Beyond 1992: U.S. Strategy Toward the European Community* (Washington, D.C.: The Center for Strategic and International Studies, September 1990), pp. 24-25.

Gary C. Hufbauer (ed.), *Europe 1992. An American Perspective* (Washington, D.C.: The Brookings Institution, 1990), pp. 40-41.

Kenneth Flamm, "Semiconductors" in Gary C. Hufbauer (ed.), *Europe 1992,* Ibid., pp. 225-292. (Very comprehensive.)

Michael C. Maibach, "The Implications of EC 1992 for U.S. Electronics Companies and Workers," in Jorge Pérez-Lopez, Gregory K. Schoepfle and John Yochelson (ed.), *EC 1992: Implications for U.S. Workers* (Washington, D.C.: Center for Strategic an International Studies, 1990), pp. 56-71

U.S. General Accounting Office, *European Single Market. Issues of Concern to U.S. Exporters* (Washington, D.C.: Publications of the General Accounting Office, February 1990), pp. 28-38.

U.S. Government Task Force on the EC Internal Market, *An Assessment of Economic Policy Issues Raised by the European Community's Single Market Program* (Washington, D.C.: U.S. Government Printing Office, 1990), pp. 15-18.

7. There is also an abundant literature on the automobile issue. See especially:

Christopher E. Bates, "The Impact of Europe 1992 on the Motor Vehicle Parts Manufacturing Industry," in U.S. Congress, *Europe 1992: Economic Integration Plan.* Ibid., pp. 57-61.

Thomas L. Brewer, "EC 1992 and the U.S. Automotive Industry: Shifting Pattern of Trade and Investment" in Jorge Pérez-Lopez (ed.), *EC 1992: Implications for U.S. Workers,* Ibid., pp. 33-51.

Michael Calingaert, *The 1992 Challenge From Europe* (Washington, D.C.: National Planning Association, 1988), pp. 102-104.

John Krafcik and the Motor Vehicle Program, "Prepared Statement," in U.S. Congress, *Europe 1992: Economic Integration Plan.* Ibid., pp. 66-75.

Alasdair Smith and Anthony J. Venables, "Automobiles" in Gary C. Hufbauer (ed.), *Europe 1992,* Ibid., pp. 119-158.

CHAPTER 8

FINANCIAL SERVICES

American financial firms have long been active in European financial markets and have established networks of institutions throughout the EC. American banks hold 5 percent of the EC's banking assets, U.S. securities firms are leaders in a number of European investment markets, and insurance companies are increasing their presence in the EC in anticipation of new opportunities. Therefore, these firms have a keen interest in the internal market and how it will affect their operations.

In the first part of this chapter we will introduce the EC-1992 program in financial services. Then we will focus on the notion of reciprocity. Finally, we will deal with the American financial system in order to show how the EC-1992 program has forced the United States to adapt its own service industry.

The EC-1992 Program in Financial Services

The EC-1992 program in financial services emphasizes (1) the *free movement of capital* among the Twelve; and (2) the objective of freedom for financial firms to operate throughout the EC under the same set of regulations, a *single license.*

Free Movement of Capital[1]

A free-barrier financial market is not possible without the unrestricted flow of capital among nations. Free capital movement means that a resident of one EC member state can use the financial services of any other member state, including banking, real estate markets, and stock exchange. This freedom allows capital to move to the most competitive marketplace.

Two EC directives have been key to the market integration process: (1) a 1986 directive ensuring free capital movement for long-term commercial transactions, bond issues, and unquoted securities; and (2) a 1988 directive eliminating all restrictions on short-term and long-term transfer of capital, by removing currency exchange, and eliminating other discriminatory measures, such as certain taxes on investments. The latter proposal went into effect for most countries on July 1, 1990. Thus, a resident of one EC member state will have unrestricted access to banking services, stock exchanges, real estate markets, and other financial services in all EC countries.

Single License[2]

The concept of a single banking passport or single license allows any bank authorized in one member state to provide a broad array of financial services, similar to those conducted by universal banks, in any other member states. In turn, consumers of financial services will be able to select the institutions offering the lowest cost and best service regardless of where they live.

The EC has specified a minimum level of regulation, beyond which countries are free to regulate their markets as they see fit. Known as *mutual recognition,* this element requires a minimum level of harmonization, or essential equivalence, to ensure the safety and soundness of the financial system. For instance, the Second Banking Directive requires all EC banks to have a minimum capital base, a minimum level of shareholder disclosure, and a maximum limit on the degree of equity participation in nonfinancial firms.

Investment Services Directives[3]

The proposed *Investment Services directive* is structured very similarly to the *Second Banking Directive,* but applies to nonbank financial firms not covered by the banking directive. The directive is based on the same principles as the *Second Banking Directive* regarding a single passport, mutual recognition, and home country control.

This directive will introduce a single license for such activities as brokerage services, portfolio management, arranging or offering underwriting services, or giving professional investment advice. With this license, investment firms incorporated in any member state will be free to open branches or to offer their services across borders to any other member state, subject to the same set of regulations as they would be under home country control.

Insurance Market[4]

The liberalization in the *insurance market* follows a different path from either banking or investment services. There are several reasons for this. The insurance industry is still one of the most strictly regulated segments of the economy in many member states. In contrast to the banking and investment services directives, the insurance directives allow the "host" country to retain much greater authority.

Insurance directives distinguish between "large risks" (250 employees and an annual turnover of at least ECU 12.8 million) and "mass risks" (small business and private individuals). This distinction means that the ability to sell insurance to individual consumers on a Community-wide basis will be limited.

The EC has achieved greater progress in liberalizing *non-life* insurance than in liberalizing *life* insurance.

Non-Life Insurance[5]

The *First Non-Life Insurance Directive,* implemented in 1973, coordinated member states' laws governing the establishment of insurance business. This directive covers how insurance firms should be legally formed, what the supervision and cooperation among states should be, what the restrictions on providing insurance should be, what the rules on fiscal soundness should be, and what the procedures for setting up branches and subsidiaries throughout the EC should be.

The *Second Non-Life Insurance Directive,* which allows cross-border insurance services for all large commercial and industrial risks, became effective June 30, 1990. The directive covers all non-life direct risks, including accident, health, auto, fire, marine, aviation, and transport insurance.

The EC also began consideration of a so-called *Third Non-Life Insurance Directive* which would define the regulatory climate for non-life insurance (motor, home, theft).

Life Insurance[6]

As for *life* insurance, a directive allowing freedom of establishment was adopted in 1979, but the Commission is still struggling to reach final agreement on this directive, which would allow branches to be established freely under a single license. The *Third Directive on Life Insurance,* when adopted by the member states, will enable insurance companies to operate freely throughout the EC according to their home countries' rules, and will also allow them to invest their resources anywhere in the EC. This directive is also based on the principle of a single passport and mutual recognition. The directive will not restrict companies to particular investments and will not oblige them to invest primarily within a member state. However, it will determine types of assets which can be acquired and the proportion of the company's total assets which each type can represent.[7]

The Issue of Reciprocity[8]

Reciprocity is a concept that can take several different forms. It can be used by a country to restrict the access of foreign country firms to its market unless those countries provide a certain degree of access for its firms. There are several possible standards for this form of reciprocity, including (1) *national treatment* combined with (2) *effective market ac-*

cess, and (3) comparable (or identical) competitive opportunities *("mirror-image" reciprocity .)*

National Treatment

National treatment requires a country to treat foreign firms and products in a manner identical to the treatment accorded its own domestic firms and products in like circumstances.

Effective Market Access

Effective market access implies a substantial degree of access for foreign firms to the competitive opportunities potentially available in a market. When taken together, the EC, for example, could require its trading partners to provide EC firms the same treatment accorded to domestic firms, and to ensure that EC firms have substantial access to their markets.

"Mirror-Image" Reciprocity

"Mirror-image" reciprocity is a much more restrictive standard. As a condition of access, a country could insist that its firms have access to opportunities in markets abroad which are comparable (or identical) to those provided foreign firms in its own market. The EC, for example, could choose to limit access to firms of third countries that are unwilling to adopt laws and regulations equivalent to those prevailing in the internal market. Most countries are unlikely to be willing to alter their systems simply to conform with EC regulations. As a result, an insistence on "mirror-image" reciprocity could result in discrimination against countries with open, non-discriminatory regulatory systems such as the United States, which differ from those of the EC.

Reciprocity and "Fortress Europe"[9]

The concept has received the most attention in the area of financial services. The original proposal for the *Second Banking*

Directive contained a *reciprocity* provision that appeared potentially to apply a *"mirror-image"* standard. This led some American officials to raise the notion of a "Fortress Europe."

Significant modifications were later made in response to concerns expressed by some EC member states and by the Community's trading partners. The original text proposed a bureaucratic "vetting" system which would be triggered automatically whenever a bank from outside the EC sought an EC licence. The compromise is the result of the criticisms made by the UK, which disliked its protectionist overtones, and from banks abroad, particularly the United States, which feared they might be excluded from the EC because of restrictive American banking laws.[10]

The directive, as adopted, is based on *national treatment* with the provision for the Commission to negotiate *equal access.* In the *Second Banking Directive,* article 7, the Commission, in deciding whether to allow foreign banks access to the new EC single banking license, will conduct periodic studies of the treatment of EC banks in other markets around the world. Where it appears to the Commission that a foreign country does not grant "effective market access" comparable to that enjoyed by banks from that country in the Community, the Commission may propose to the council that negotiations be opened, aimed at achieving such comparable access.

If EC banks not only are denied effective *market access,* but also fail to receive *national treatment* offering the same competitive opportunities as are available to domestic credit institutions, the Commission may on its own initiative open negotiations to remedy the situation. In such cases, the Commission may go one step further and suspend new license applications from the country in question for a period of up to three months. This is the ultimate sanction against countries which do not give *national treatment* to EC banks. It may be extended beyond three months only by a decision of the EC Council, acting on a qualified majority vote.

The Second Banking Directive and Reciprocity

This compromise has defused a troublesome issue, and probably set a pattern for EC reciprocity policy in other areas of financial services, such as investment, and insurance. Still to be resolved, however, is the question of precisely who should be responsible for implementation of reciprocity policy, the Council or the Commission. The opponents of reciprocity want to ensure that it remains at the political level – in the Council – rather than with the bureaucrats.

This directive on banking continues to provide a basis for the Commission to seek a mandate to negotiate "competitive opportunities" for EC banks in foreign markets comparable to those which will prevail in the internal market. It does not provide, however, for the imposition of discriminatory measures in the event these negotiations are unsuccessful. In recent statements, EC officials have stressed that their intention is to open foreign markets to EC banks rather than close the internal market to foreign banks.

The proposed directive on *investment services* also contained a reciprocity provision approximating the *"mirror-image"* formulation originally proposed for the *Second Banking Directive.* It has since been revised to incorporate the reciprocal national treatment standard included in the *Second Banking Directive.* Although approval by the Council of the revised provision is anticipated, it is not a certainty.

The proposed *Second Life Insurance Directive* also contains the original *"mirror-image"* reciprocity formulation. In December 1989, the EC Council reached an informal agreement to incorporate the formulation contained in the Second Banking Directive in this directive as well. The EC Commission has revised its original proposal to reflect this agreement.

Overview of the American Financial Market

More than any EC regulation, it is U.S. laws which place American banks at a competitive disadvantage in relation to EC banks. Among them, the combination of the *Glass-Steagall Act,* the *Regulation K,* the *McFadden Act,* and the *Douglas Amendment* has the most detrimental effects.

The Glass-Steagall Act and the Regulation K[11]

The *Glass-Steagall Act* separates commercial and investment banking in the United States and does not permit nonbank activities. The *Glass-Steagall Act* applies only to American domestic banking activities.

International operations permissible for U.S. banking institutions overseas are set forth in *Regulation K.* This regulation allows American banking organizations to be more competitive in foreign markets by permitting them to do a broader range of securities activities overseas than is permitted in the U.S. market. However, *Regulation K* limits the absolute and relative size of such activities, unlike the EC's regulatory framework, which is increasingly shifting toward universal banking.

The *Glass-Steagall Act* indirectly affects American overseas banking operations since the volume restrictions provided for in *Regulation K* depend, in part, on the restrictions on domestic equity underwriting imposed by the *Glass-Steagall Act.* American banks have also insisted that their inability to offer the same range of services in both domestic and international markets has hindered their efforts to compete with foreign banks.[12]

American banks are unable to compete with large EC universal banks for new corporate customers, or even retain their present customer base, without the ability to lead or participate substantially in equity underwriting and distribution.

Regulation K forces more costly organizational structure. It prohibits American member banks from conducting any non-bank activities in overseas branches. This result is in conflict with the philosophy of the EC's Second Banking Directive, which endorses a universal banking model, under which banks are free to conduct a wide range of activities within the parent bank or its branches.

The McFadden Act and the Douglas Amendment[13]

American interstate branching restrictions under the *McFadden Act* and the *Douglas Amendment* to the *Bank Holding Company Act* have resulted in a U.S. banking industry that is more fragmented than Europe's. The banking sector Europe is more concentrated than in the United States. The EC's 1992 program will likely increase banking concentration in the Community, as EC banks expand their presence from a national to a European scale. Thus, American banks will encounter even larger and more powerful EC competitors while facing handicaps from restrictions on their ability to grow domestically.

American Discrimination Against Foreign Institutions[14]

There are a few American laws, both federal and state, that exclude or discriminate against international banks either directly or indirectly. There are only limited instances of unequal treatment but their cumulative effect can be substantial.

At the federal level, there are also a number of regulations which *de facto* do not favor European institutions. For example, U.S. laws dealing with thrift institutions generally do not authorize them to purchase deposits of U.S. branches of international banks. This limitation excludes international banks from an important source of funding that is available to the American counterparts.

At the state level, a major issue relates to interstate expansion. Many states have established regional interstate compacts which permit banks based in the region to expand into other states in the region. But some states have enacted laws that expressly exclude international banks whose home states are in the region from participating in otherwise permissible interstate expansion. Even officials from the Department of Treasury criticize American discriminations against foreign financial institutions: "It is true that a few individual U.S. States have practices which discriminate against foreign financial institutions."[15]

***

There is little reason to believe that American financial firms will face overt discrimination in EC markets after the implementation of the internal market program. There will be expanded opportunities in specific market sectors, such as retail and private banking or insurance and investment products. American financial firms are well positioned to benefit from these opportunities because of their international networks and their experience in operating across borders.

Equal access and expanded opportunities alone, however, may not be enough to ensure that U.S. financial institutions will prosper in a post-1992 Community. EC banks are organized under a regulatory structure that allows them to compete better and to profit more easily from broader powers under the internal market program. U.S. banks, by contrast, remain governed by a regulatory philosophy that prohibits universal banking. As a result, American banks are likely to face larger, better capitalized, and more diverse EC universal banks armed with broader powers and capabilities under the internal market program.

Finally, this loss of prominence internationally with a worsening crisis for U.S. banks at home led the U.S. Treasury in February 1991 to propose radical changes in the banking system.[16] The proposals include: the repeal of the *Glass-Steagall Act* barriers between commercial banks and investment houses; the end of the *McFadden Act* restrictions on interstate branch banking; the modification of the *Banking Holding Company Act* restrictions on the ownership of banks by non-bank institutions; and a reform of the deposit insurance system.

The EC rules have had an indirect impact on the adaptation of the U.S. financial system. It might be the beginning of a process whereby EC rules will gain influence elsewhere. The EC might give the world its bureaucratic leadership.

Notes

1. Paul Quantock (ed.), *Opportunities in European Financial Services. 1992 and Beyond* (New York: John Wiley & Sons 1990), pp. 153-158.
   Michael Calingaert, *The 1992 Challenge From Europe* (Washington, D.C.: National Planning Association, 1988), pp. 51-53.
2. Quantock, pp. 67-98.
3. "Regulation on Investment Firms" in U.S. Department of Commerce, *EC 1992: A Commerce Department Analysis of European Community Directives* (Washington, D.C.: U.S. Government Printing Office, 1989/90), Volume 3, pp. 150-152.
4. U.S. General Accounting Office, *U.S. Financial Services' Competitiveness Under the Single Market Program* (Washington, D.C.: Publications of the General Accounting Office, May 1990), pp. 18-19.
5. U.S. Chamber of Commerce, *Europe 1992. A Practical Guide for American Business #2* (Washington, D.C.: Publications of the U.S. Chamber of Commerce, 1990), p. 41.
6. U.S. Department of Commerce, *EC 1992,* volume 3, pp. 153-155.
7. "Way Paved to Single Life Insurance Market," *Financial Times,* 21 February 1991.
8. Glennon J. Harrison, *The European Community: 1992 and Reciprocity* (Washington, D.C.: Congressional Research Service Report, 11 April 1989); 8 p.
9. Glennon J. Harrison, "Fortress Europe and Reciprocity: the Controversy over the Second Banking Directive" in Glennon J. Harrison, (ed.). *European Community: Issues Raised by 1992 Integration* (Washington, D.C.: Congressional Research Service Report, 1989), pp. 30-31.
10. U.S. International Trade Commission, *The Effects of Greater Economic Integration Within the European Community on the United States. Report to the Committee on Ways and Means of the United States House of Representatives and the Committee on Finance of the Senate* (Washington, D.C.: USITC Publication, July 1989), pp. 5-10 to 5-12.
11. James V. Houpt and the Board of Governors of the Federal Reserve System, "International Trends for U.S. Banks and Banking Markets" in U.S. Congress. Committee on Banking, Finance and Urban Affairs, *Oversight Hearings on European Community's 1992 Program.* Hearing. 101 Cong. 1 sess. (Washington, D.C.: Government Printing Office, 26-28 September 1989), pp. 405-406.
12. U.S. General Accounting Office, *U.S. Financial Services' Competitiveness* , pp. 42-44.
13. Carter H. Golembe and David S. Holland, "Banking and

Securities" in Gary C. Hufbauer (ed.), *Europe 1992. An American Perspective.* (Washington, D.C.: The Brookings Institution, 1990), pp. 91-94.

14. Commission of the European Communities, *Report on United States. Trade Barriers and Unfair Trade Practices* (Brussels: Service of the Commission of the European Communities, 1990), pp. 54-57.

Commission of the European Communities, *Report on United States. Trade Barriers and Unfair Trade Practices* (Brussels: Services of the Commission of the European Communities, 1991), pp. 66-71.

15. David C. Mulford, "Statement" in U.S. Congress. Committee on Banking, Finance and Urban Affairs, *Oversight Hearings on European Community's 1992 Program,* p. 77. David C. Mulford is Under-Secretary for International Affairs at the Department of Treasury.

16. Peter Riddell, "A System in Urgent Need of Overhaul," *Financial Times,* 21 January 1991.

Peter Riddell, "U.S. Plans Overhaul Banking Regulations," *Financial Times,* 6 February 1991.

CHAPTER 9

THE URUGUAY ROUND

The aim of this chapter is to analyze the impact of EC-1992 on the evolution of GATT and *vice versa*. At the end of the 1980s, it was common wisdom in the United States that the success of EC-1992 would lead to a radicalization of the Community's position in the GATT negotiations.

Numerous experts saw in EC-1992 the danger of an economic bloc that contradicts the universalist philosophy of GATT. Many Cassandras predicted that any failure of the Uruguay Round would split the world into a triad of rival, closed trading blocs in America, Europe and the Asian/Pacific region – or into dollar, D-Mark/ECU and yen zones.[1]

In order to assess this assumption we first sum up the origin and the main objectives of the Uruguay Round. In a second part, we analyze the positions of the Community and the United States in the main sectors treated in GATT. As a leading thread, we will try to see in what ways the progress accomplished by the EC on its way toward 1992 has contributed to promote, or to hinder, the Uruguay Round negotiations.

Background

GATT has played a role by contributing to keep trade growing faster than world output through the 1950s and 1960s. Its main instrument is the principle of the most-favoured nation (MFN) status, under which a trade advantage granted to one country must be unconditionally extended to other GATT members.[2]

But in the 1970s countries found ways to circumvent GATT rules. The most famous are the bilateral voluntary export restraint agreements (VERs), shielding domestic industries from competition. In all, around 250 protective arrangements were put in place. These were, for example, negotiated for consumer electronics, for Japanese cars and consumer electronics, for European speciality steels.

Moreover governments subsidized domestic industries under formulae which, they claimed, did not infringe on GATT's subsidies code. In the 1980s the U.S. and the EC increasingly imposed anti-dumping charges on imports of Japanese electronic products and on each other's manufactures, allegedly for being sold at prices lower than those charged in home markets.

After industrial nations had lowered tariffs on imports to an average of less than 5 percent in the industrial nations, GATT's limitations became more evident. It did not cover farm produce - grains, meat, and dairy products – nor the services that, by the 1980s, accounted for more than half of the GDP of the economically advanced nations. Exemptions to its rules had been allowed for textiles and clothing, where trade is controlled by a Multi-Fibre Arrangement based on import quotas. GATT's procedure for settling disputes was too slow and did not sufficiently penalize offenders. By the early 1980s it was apparent that a revision of the whole system was needed.

On September 20, 1986, a meeting of GATT trade ministers held in Punta del Este launched the Uruguay Round of multilateral Trade Negotiations. Member states committed themselves to two objectives: (1) a "standstill" on new trade measures inconsistent with their GATT obligations; and (2) a "rollback" program aimed at phasing out existing inconsistent measures.[3] In the four-year time frame of the Uruguay Round, negotiations were undertaken in fifteen sectors. In Montreal (December 1988), for the mid-term review meeting of the Trade Negotiations Committee, agreements were reached in eleven of the fifteen negotiating sectors.[4] At the same time, there was agreement on some measures such as: strengthening the disputes settlement system, regular assessment of the trade policies of each GATT contracting country, and on concessions concerning tropical products covering trade worth around $20 billion.

In order to introduce the issues, we will sum up briefly the main topics of discussion as well as the state of play in the negotiations in 1991:[5]

The Uruguay Round - State of Play in 1991

Opening Markets

Tariffs: the objective was to get further liberalization, especially on high tariffs and tariff *escalation.* In 1991 offers were still short of 33 percent overall reduction in customs but the target was reachable.

Non-tariff measures: the aim was to reduce significantly or even phase out such measures, including quantitative restrictions. Real bargaining over reductions never started. There were difficulties on rules of origin and pre-shipment inspection of goods.

Tropical products:[6] negotiations should have ensured the fullest liberalization of trade in this sector (both tariff and non-tariff measures). Developed countries promised full liberalization but the whole issue was linked to progress in agriculture talks.

Natural-resource based products: liberalization efforts aimed, in particular, at trade in minerals, nonferrous metals, forestry, and fishery. Success in this area depends upon results from other areas.

Textiles and clothing:[7] the objective was eventual elimination of the multifiber arrangement. There has been serious discussion on liberalization. Defeat of the U.S. textile industry lobby is vital to success.

Agriculture: the goal was the establishment of effective GATT
rules, better market access, reduced subsidies, and elimination
of the adverse trade effects of sanitary and phytosanitary
regulations. The keys to the whole round in this area are the
enormous gap between the U.S. and EC positions and the concomitant need for top-level governmental decisions to be made.

Improving GATT

Amending GATT Articles:[8] a review of existing GATT provisions
was done, especially where not covered by other negotiating
areas. An impasse came rapidly with developing countries
demanding the right to protect markets when facing balance-of-
payments difficulties.

GATT codes: aims were improvement, clarification or expansion,
as appropriate, of Negotiating Trade Measures (NTM) agreements
and arrangements. Japan and other Asian exporters confronted
the U.S. and the EC over anti-dumping measures; new rules for
government procurement were likely.

Safeguard measures against unexpected surges in imports:[9]
the negotiation aimed for a comprehensive agreement that would
have included consideration of bilateral export restraints. The
EC battled to keep the right to take selective action against
offenders.

Subsidies and countervailing measures: the objective was improvement to the disciplines contained in Articles VI and XVI
of the General Agreement and in the Tokyo Round subsidies
agreement. The U.S. and the EC have hardened positions but a
deal limiting industrial subsidies was reachable.

Dispute settlement:[10] the discussions aimed at improving the system to ensure prompt and effective resolution of disputes and compliance with adopted recommendations. There was unanimity of most negotiators on this question. An agreement on a faster mechanism with a new appeals body was close.

Functioning of the GATT system: possible institutional changes to the GATT included enhanced surveillance of trade policies, improved decision-making, and an increased contribution by GATT to achieving greater coherence in global economic policy-making. Agreement came on ways to improve GATT surveillance of trade policies, but despite many projects, trade ministers clashed over an expansion of their role and over the creation of a new world trade organization.

Expanding GATT

Trade-related aspects of intellectual property protection, including trade in counterfeit goods: the main issue concerns the clarification of existing GATT rules that bear upon intellectual property protection, as well as the elaboration of new disciplines in counterfeit goods. In this area, the main conflict is between industrial nations and developing countries.[11]

Trade-related investment measures:[12] these concern the trade restricting or distorting effects of national investment measures and the possible elaboration of new provisions in GATT to avoid these adverse effects. Agreement to remove some restrictions on foreign investment was seen as possible.

Trade in services:[13] the Declaration of Punta Del Este envisaged the establishment of a multilateral framework of rules for trade in services, including the elaboration of possible disciplines for individual service sectors. Originally, the U.S.

called for a General Agreement on Trade in Services (GATS) embracing all services. But the question of "coverage" slowly emerged. The whole negotiation has been blocked over the scope of a new general agreement: for which sectors would exemptions or special reservations be allowed? Concrete difficulties arose when the American shipping and civil aviation industries, which can call on considerable support in Congress, wanted their sectors excluded from an international agreement.[14] The EC shipping industries, for different reasons, also wanted to exempt this sector. They were not alone. For instance, airlines and civil aviation authorities, whose interests are protected by a multiplicity of bilateral agreements on landing rights, also resisted the inclusion of their sectors. In September 1990, the EC demanded that the most-favoured nation or non-discrimination principle should not apply to traffic on inland waterways and to cross-border road transport.[15] The U.S., whose domestic legislation links inland waterways with "cabotage" or coastal shipping, insisted that waterways be handled in the shipping sector and not as part of land transport. Moreover, AT&T and other privately-owned U.S. basic telephone networks, concerned about competition from subsidized foreign suppliers of public networks, pressed for exemption for telecommunications.[16]

The solution adopted by negotiators for GATT was that "awkward" sectors should be dealt with in annexes to GATS, accommodating the scope and pace of the application of GATS's general principles to their special circumstances.[17] The problem was that no country was ready to commit itself to liberalizing any of its services as long as it feared that sectors in which it has particular export interests might be subject to exemptions. Therefore, a paradoxical situation arose: some developing countries – which first opposed the U.S. position in order to retain protection for their infant services – accepted the idea for reaching agreement on the U.S. basis at the same time the U.S. retreated from its original objectives.

Commentary

The difficulties of the negotiations in 1991 were due to numerous factors. It is impossible to mention all the elements. To be comprehensive, one should consider all historical, political, economic, and cultural particularities of more than 100 countries. For instance, Japan has refused to cut its subsidies on rice for "cultural reasons." This example suggests how difficult is an explanation of the deadlock of the Uruguay Round.[18] Nevertheless, it is possible to recall what the main difficulties of the negotiation were.

First, the whole Uruguay Round package had to be weighed in order to offer a balance of trade benefits over concessions to most countries. So one reason why the talks were blocked was that governments were holding back from making important concessions until the final pattern of "trade-offs" became clearer.

For instance, developing countries were not ready to subscribe to an agreement that would have forced open their markets to multinational service companies or to adopt stricter rules on intellectual property as long as they were not sure that the industrial nations would open their doors wider to imports of textiles, clothing, tropical goods, and farm produce.[19] Another example: Japan was not inclined to raise its level of food imports or to change its rules for public procurement before the EC and the U.S. had accepted tighter discipline on their antidumping actions.

For its part, the EC linked the dismantling of its restrictions on textile imports to securing an accord that would let it apply safeguard measures to protect industries against disruptive import surges and selectively against offending products or countries. The U.S. made everything conditional on its receiving satisfaction over farm reform. Most nations wanted any agreement to insure that curbs were put on U.S. laws under which it was allowed to take unilateral punitive trade action against other countries.

Parallels Between the Uruguay Round and EC-1992

The policy agenda of the EC-1992 has a lot of common features with the Uruguay Round objective.[20] Both address tariff and nontariff barriers and look for expanding rules to cover issues beyond trade in goods. The Community is pursuing its path of harmonizing trade regulations and reducing nontariff barriers and other commercial restrictions just as GATT countries are addressing many of the same issues on a world level.

Let's take the important sector of services. The EC-1992 program covers a wider scope than the Uruguay Round agreement could consider.[21] As a matter of fact, the internal market not only embraces free movement of services, but also includes cross-border trade in services and free establishment of persons. Moreover, with regard to the free movement of persons, the EC opposes coverage by the GATT of labor movement other than that of "skilled and key personnel and for a limited duration."

The GATT's exercise contains numerous sectors of overlap with developments in the EC program. Each initiative has affected the substance, timing, and process of the other. For such overlapping topics, the concern was whether inconsistencies would arise between decisions made in Brussels and the agreements sought in Geneva. Therefore, the question is to know to what extent the two processes conflicted with or strengthened one another.

Differences Between the Uruguay Round and EC-1992

Although some issues under negotiation in the Uruguay Round were addressed in EC-1992 (expanded government public procurement, intellectual property rights, investment, and services), others were not.

More fundamentally, the final objectives and methods of EC-1992 are broadly different. As already said, the internal market follows a double strategy of harmonization and mutual recognition of regulations coupled with the removal of internal barriers among the Twelve. This scheme is supported by a coherent and comprehensive legal order and thirty-year-old rules of competition. Furthermore, in order to keep solidarity and stability within the Community, there is an important set of horizontal and accompanying policies, such as Research and Development programs, and funding of social and regional policies.

The GATT, however, works with around 100 states divided by their political, economic, and cultural disparities. It also lacks a superior existential commitment to achieve an aim transcendent to liberalization of trade, i.e., a genuine political and economic union. Political and economic union pursued by the Community is not only a general commitment, it is also a terrific tool for giving direction to the whole process and promoting convergence of policies. This does not exist at the GATT level. Furthermore, contrary to the Community, there is no automatic primacy of GATT over national legislation and no legal and institutional mechanisms to ensure full compliance with the law. Finally, the GATT lacks minimum harmonization of rules, particularly in the fundamental sector of services.

Despite the differences, the EC-1992 program has had a lot of varying effects on the Uruguay Round process. It is not yet clear whether it will strengthen or conflict with the Uruguay Round negotiating objectives. An initial assessment is nevertheless already feasible.

Negative Impact of EC-1992 on the Uruguay Round

The fact that EC-1992 and the Uruguay Round occurred at the same time raised problems.[22] As for the Community, the issues of the integration program were more immediate; thus EC countries devoted their first priority to efforts on this program rather than to their interests in the Uruguay Round.[23] As a matter of fact, the timing of the 1992 process created a lot of *faits accomplis* when related issues arose in the Uruguay round, leaving the Community little room for negotiating flexibility.[24]

A previous example of *fait accompli* occurred in the Kennedy Round. The United States tried to negotiate with the EC on its

Common Agriculture Policy (CAP). After several delays and many proposals and counterproposals, the parties were de facto forced to negotiate on the basis of the CAP.

Also, on standards negotiations, the Community did its best to complete its internal process before becoming fully engaged in the Uruguay Round. Such an approach slowed the multilateral negotiations.

One of the principal U.S. concerns was that the EC would seek compensation in the Uruguay Round for any liberalizing effects of market integration. Many Americans especially feared that the EC might resort to reciprocity, a position that could have seriously frustrated aims sought in the Uruguay Round.

As a matter of fact, while the EC agreed at the mid-term review in Montreal in 1988 on the need to apply national treatment to trade in services, its policy statements on EC integration did not unequivocally support this stance. For instance, one statement claimed that the EC was perfectly willing to open up its services sector "provided its major trading partners are prepared to do likewise." It also cautioned that "the EC cannot deprive itself of negotiating leverage by making unilateral concessions in this sphere." Insistence on reciprocity could reduce competition. Although reciprocity is a useful negotiating lever for opening up foreign markets, it may not represent the optimum in economic efficiency.

One feature of the Community's position is its overall approach of including a sectoral agreement on financial services in the final agreement on services. In contrast, the United States has indicated its preference for a separate deal on financial services independent of the general negotiations on services – a move that would limit the scope for political bargaining in the Round. This is due to the limitations of the U.S. system on universal banking and interstate business.

There have also been concerns in the United States that the adjustment pressures caused by the elimination of internal barriers to trade and investment could make the Community less willing to liberalize external barriers. These fears were based on alleged uncertainties regarding the impact of EC-1992, difficulties in reconciling the conflicting interests of the member states and industry, and finally, EC problems in reconciling social, economic and strategic objectives with its trade interests.

For the sectors in which member states are preoccupied with adjusting to completion of the internal market, they may have perceived external liberalization to be an additional burden to be undertaken only at a later stage, if at all. This can explain prior reticence about the straightening of GATT rules on safeguards and dispute settlement.

Moreover, the EC employs a variety of mechanisms to develop its industrial base and strengthen its internal cohesion. The Community is forced to protect some sectors by redistribution policies for the affected regions. This is the case in sensitive areas of industry such as textiles where the costs of pursuing free trade may be concentrated in particular regions.

The questionable way in which EC rules of origin on semiconductors and photocopiers were modified exemplifies this. And, despite the "standstill" commitment under the Punta del Este declaration, the EC has concluded VERs on steel.

On the downside, one should also underline the important question of the EC's decision-making. The decision-making procedures themselves influence the balancing of economic interests and how they are reconciled with political and other goals. EC policy-making might permit protectionism, i.e., the possible abuse of anti-dumping regulations, rules of origin, and VERs. For instance, the delay in decision-making on the long-term strategy for the textile and automobile industries has been consciously played by the EC's protectionist sectors. It has also been said in the U.S. that an expanded central EC authority could have drawbacks for negotiations. For example, bilateral channels with individual EC states (the UK, Germany) could have become less effective as a means for U.S. negotiators to win support for American positions on certain topics.

Positive Impact of EC-1992 on the Uruguay Round

First, one should remember that the aim of the internal market is to promote economic efficiency and international competitiveness. This liberal philosophy corresponds to the general objective of GATT, i.e., to contribute to economic growth and development and to the welfare of the world's peoples by liberalizing world trade and placing it on a secure basis. For instance, the internal market structure, with its tough rules on competition, state aid, standards, and non-discrimination within the EC is, in general, a considerable guard against protectionism.[25]

Without any doubt, the successful process of completing the internal market of the Community gave expanded authority to the EC Commission. Many EC directives have reinforced the Commission's authority in its negotiations with its partners in the Uruguay Round. EC-1992 offers a lot of advantages to EC trade negotiators seeking to achieve consensus at international level. If the Commission can more easily arrive at a consensus on a united policy in the GATT process, the whole Round benefits. On the other hand, non-EC negotiators are still able to deal with one unique EC authority on many more issues, whereas previously they had to deal with each EC member state on an individual basis.

Much legislation of the internal market contains provisions that would subject EC rules to future GATT obligations.[26] The best example concerns government procurement. Negotiations to expand the GATT code were in a deadlock for many years as the EC had no competence over the public procurements of the Twelve in the "excluded sectors" and in purchases of services by public entities. But progress in the internal market's objective gave the Commission the authority to negotiate at an international level.[27]

Another example concerns the Community's approach to intellectual property and counterfeit goods. Previously, the Community was reluctant to deal at an international level on the trade-related aspects of intellectual property protection and trade in counterfeit goods. For a long time, there was an "agreement to disagree" among the GATT partners on the appropriate forum for dealing with this issue and the wisdom of tackling this question at the GATT level. This EC caution had to do with the lack of common Community rules on intellectual property and counterfeit goods. But the Green Paper on intellectual property gave the Commission a framework for its policy at the GATT level. Thereafter, the EC was capable of dealing with GATT articles affecting intellectual property, issues of guaranteeing a fair return on investments, and the like.

One should also mention the positive contribution of EC internal liberalization of agriculture. The relatively disproportional weight of agriculture in overall EC policy has declined through the development of numerous other EC programs. If, during the early 1980s, agriculture represented 80 percent of the EC's budget, its part (although as high in absolute figures) is proportionally smaller due to the development of the technological programs, and structural funds.

Furthermore, one can observe that many European lobbies of sectors that have been strengthened by the EC-1992 process want to extend liberalization at a world level. They are therefore more inclined than ever to push the Community to make concessions on agriculture in order to solve problems in other areas. Finally, reform in agriculture is also underway at the EC level. Although this process is largely insufficient for the Community and especially for the United States, it is nevertheless a good omen for an international agreement on agriculture.

In other words, thanks to the Uruguay Round process, GATT disciplines, and American pressures, EC liberals found leverage to counteract protectionist pressure within the EC. This is especially the case the new areas of investment, intellectual property, and services.

The EC policy toward Third World countries has also played a positive role in the evolution of the GATT Round. To be sure, the success of the EC internal market roused a lot of concern in the developing countries. But these fears forced the EC to strengthen the Lomé process[28] and to soften its attitude in the Uruguay Round.

For instance, the EC has shown flexibility on the sensible question of the removing of import restrictions on tropical products, textiles, and clothing. This openness has helped to avoid alienating developing countries from the negotiations. Contrary to America, which has demonstrated little willingness to ease trade restrictions in these areas, the EC has allowed seeking a compromise on behalf of all, the United States included.

***

There has been a kind of race between the EC-1992 process and the Uruguay Round. The scope and the extent of both exercises have a lot in common, although the level of integration pursued by the Community is much wider and deeper. To be sure, the Community has won the competition by being quicker than GATT. Although the Uruguay Round was scheduled to be completed in December 1990 – earlier than the EC domestic market (1992) –the EC has been able to adopt most of its program by 1991.

The GATT philosophy has been positive on the evolution of the EC's internal process toward liberalization, although it is difficult to mention any specific EC directive that has been directly influenced by the pressures of the EC's partners in the GATT negotiations. But it is also true that the construction of the Community's internal market contributes to world trade liberalization. EC-1992 gives more authority to the Commission for promoting negotiation on long-term deadlocked sectors, for reassuring developing countries, and for contributing to fighting protectionist tendencies in the United States.

The U.S. government is not well advised to criticize EC policy in those sectors because its own record is not shining. Therefore, it is wrong to argue, as many did in the U.S., that EC-1992 might have negatively influenced the Community in international trade negotiation. It is also extreme to accuse the Community of having been diverted by its own integration, and of lacking negotiating flexibility. Although the Uruguay Round is in a serious deadlock, one should nevertheless stress that the whole exercise is not useless. New opportunities have indeed been created by the Uruguay Round, that is something of a success. Take, for example, the institutional reforms that were implemented after the mid-term review in 1988. The GATT has switched to new and more efficient dispute settlement procedures. And progress is looming in the direction of insuring more effective implementation of panel findings. Another example is the new Trade Policy Review Mechanism. This has brought national trade policies under GATT surveillance in a concerted and comprehensive manner.

Of more significance has been the extent to which the Uruguay Round has allowed holding the line on new protectionist measures by governments. Participants have generally lived up to their undertaking to insure a standstill on new measures of protection and have largely avoided intensifying existing ones, with some exceptions. Turning to the services sector, privatization of services in many countries and deregulation of financial services are trends that have been affected by concepts relating to liberalization of trade in services and greater competition developed in the Uruguay Round services negotiations.

But on the whole, despite some success, the whole Round has not been a success. One does not know if in a few years success failure can be avoided but a positive outcome in the short term can be excluded. Agriculture is the key that could have unlocked the whole Round. It provided the most deep-rooted confrontation between Washington and Brussels. As the issue of agriculture is so complicated and so specific, the following chapter will be entirely devoted to it.

Finally, in the last chapter of this economic part, we will see if the failure of the Uruguay Round – due mainly to disagreements between the U.S. and the EC – might not lead paradoxically to an integration of both markets, through the creation of a "U.S./EC Economic Area."

Notes

1. Andrew Stoeckel, David Pearce and Gary Banks, *Western Trade Blocs,* (Canberra: Centre for International Economics, 1990); 119 p.
2. Daniel Jouanneau, *Le GATT* (Paris: Presses universitaires de France, 1987); 128 p.
3. General Agreement on Tariffs and Trade, *GATT, What it is, What it Does?* (Geneva: GATT Information and Media Relations Division, 1989), pp. 10-12.
4. Ibid., p. 12.
5. This synthesis has been made by compiling the annual review *GATT Activities,* the monthly newsletter *GATT Focus* and the regular bulletins, *News of the Uruguay Round.* The excellent regular articles by William Dullforce in the *Financial Times* have also been useful. We would also like to thank the very helpful people of the GATT Secretariat in Geneva who have given us so much valuable information.
6. Chakravarthi Raghavan, *Recolonization. GATT, the Uruguay Round & the Third World* (Penang: Third World Network, 1990), pp. 183-188. This book gives a critical "third-worldist" view on the Uruguay Round talks.
7. William R. Cline, "Textiles" in Jeffrey J. Schott (ed.), *Completing the Uruguay Round. A Results-Oriented Approach to the GATT Trade Negotiations* (Washington, D.C.: Institute for International Economics, 1990), pp. 63-79.
8. The U.S. position is well summed up in U.S. Information Agency, *Global Trade Issues. U.S. Policies and Proposals* (Washington D.C.: Publication of the U.S. Information Agency, June 1990); 54 p.
On the EC position, see Willy De Clercq and Leo Verhoef, *Europe Back to the Top* (Brussels: Roularta Books, 1990), pp. 51-53.
9. Colleen Hamilton and John Whalley, "Safeguards" in Schott (ed.), *Completing the Uruguay Round ,* pp. 79-91.
10. Robert E. Hudec, "Dispute Settlement" in Schott (ed.), *Completing the Uruguay Round,* pp. 180-204.
11. Robert Rice, "Patent Differences Holding Up Deal to Protect Ideas," *Financial Times,* 13 November 1990.
Sophie Gherardi, "La défense de la propriété intellectuelle," *Le Monde,* 21 November 1990.
12. Edward M. Graham and Paul R. Krugman, "Trade-Related Investment Measures" in Schott (ed.), *Completing the Uruguay Round,* pp. 147-163.
13. The best introduction to the issue of services – although outdated – within the GATT negotiation is the book edited by Patrick Messerlin and Karl Sauvant, *The Uruguay Round. Services in the World Economy* (Washington, D.C.: World Bank/UN Centre

on Transnational Corporations, 1990), 220 p. (Annexes with the Punta del Este Declaration and the Montreal Ministerial Declaration).

More recent, Brian Hindley, "Services" in Schott (ed.), *Completing the Uruguay Round,* pp. 135-143.

Stephen Woolcock, *The Uruguay Round: Issues for the European Community and the United States* (London: Royal Institute of International Affairs, 1990), pp. 22-23.

14. William Dullforce, "Transport Services Split Could Imperil GATS Pact," *Financial Times,* 4 October 1990.

15. Philippe Lemaître, "Services compris ou non. La CEE reproche aux Etats-Unis de préférer des arrangements bilatéraux à un accord global," *Le Monde,* 13 November 1990.

16. William Dullforce, "US Blocks GATT Telecoms Deal at Last Minute," *Financial Times,* 19 October 1990.

17. William Dullforce, "EC Commits Itself to Liberalising Trade in Services," *Financial Times,* 5 December 1990.

18. One needs more reflection on the deep causes of the Uruguay Round's setback. According to some American analysts, the GATT is condemned to fail because the United States is not strong enough to absorb the cost of world economic leadership. "Such principles as national treatment" and *most-favoured nations* are inherently disadvantageous to the most liberal and open societies. When America's power was truly exceptional, this all could be masked. But with America in relative decline the real penalties resulting from liberalism and openness have been exposed - with them, the weakness of GATT's original structure." Clyde V. Prestowitz, Alan Tonelson and Robert W. Jerome. "The Last Gasp of GATTism," *Harvard Business Review.* March-April 1991, pp. 130-131.

19. Raghavan, *Recolonization,* pp. 178-192.

20. United States International Trade Commission, *The Effects of Greater Economic Integration Within the European Community on the United States. Report to the Committee on Ways and Means of the United States House of Representatives and the Committee on Finance of the Senate* (Washington, D.C.: USITC Publication, July 1989), pp. 15-5 to 15-13.

21. Patrick Messerlin, "The European Community," in Messerlin and Sauvant (ed.), *The Uruguay Round,* pp. 141-146.

22. Michael Calingaert, *The 1992 Challenge From Europe* (Washington, D.C.: National Planning Association, 1988), pp. 123-125.

23. Lenore Sek, "1992, the GATT, and the Uruguay Round," in Glennon J. Harrison (ed.), *European Community: Issues Raised by 1992 Integration* (Washington, D.C.: Congressional Research Service, 1989), pp. 89-92.

24. Joseph Greenwald, "Negotiating Strategy," in Gary C.

Hufbauer (ed.), *Europe 1992. An American Perspective* (Washington, D.C.: The Brookings Institution, 1990), pp. 346-347.

25. Anna Murphy, *The European Community and the International Trading System. Volume II. The European Community and the Uruguay Round* (Brussels: Centre for European Policy Studies, 1990), pp. 69-74.

26. Woolcock, *The Uruguay Round: Issues for the European Community and the United States* , p. 7.

27. See supra chapter 6 on public procurements.

28. The core of the EC policy toward developing countries is based on the so-called Lomé conventions (from the name of the capital of Togo where they were signed).

CHAPTER 10

AGRICULTURE

The conflict between the United States and the European Community dates back to the creation of the European Community.[1] The debate has evolved and become more complicated but its deep cause is the same as it was three decades ago. This time, nevertheless, the acuity of the controversies reached such a level that it led to a deadlock never before seen in the history of GATT.

In this chapter we will introduce the whole problem in a synthetic manner by summing up the numerous arguments put forward on both sides. It is indeed very difficult to get access to a pedagogical, objective, and conceptual presentation of what is at stake in agriculture.[2] With this objective in mind, we will recall in a first step what the basic elements of the Common Agriculture Policy (CAP) are. Later, we will try to understand why the Community has had so much difficulty in making a genuine reform of the CAP. Finally, we will give a summary of the main arguments put forward by the U.S. and the EC for justifying their mutual intransigeance.

Basic Elements of the Common Agriculture Policy (CAP)

The CAP is one of the central pillars in the Community's system. The CAP has played a pioneering role in the unification of Europe.[3] Agriculture accounts for the largest proportion of Community legislation and more than two thirds of expenditures under the Community budget. There are at least three reasons why agriculture is such a special case in Europe.[4]

First, agricultural policy fulfills at the same time the roles of employment policy, incomes policy, regional policy, and population policy.

Second, agriculture is dependent on soil and climate, which often cause major fluctuations in harvests. Incomes must be enough to prevent too sharp a fluctuation.

Third, insuring the security of food supplies is one of the main areas of European policy. One way to do this is to attain more or less complete self-sufficiency, which means there is a tendency to overproduce so as to guarantee supplies when harvests are poor.

The main lines of the Common Agricultural Policy were laid down immediately following the entry into force of the EEC Treaty at a conference held at Stresa in July 1958. It had to incorporate the different national systems in one single system.

Objectives of the CAP

The main *objectives* of the CAP are:

(1) to increase agricultural productivity;
(2) to assure a security of supply;
(3) to maintain a fair standard of living for the farmers;
(4) to stabilize markets;
(5) to ensure that supplies are available to consumers at reasonable prices;
(6) to maintain the environment.

The basic *principles* of the CAP are: *unity of the market; community preference;* and a *common pricing system:*

Unity of the Market

Unity of the market means the free movement of agricultural goods throughout the whole EC territory. This implies: (1) common rules on competition; (2) common prices; (3) stable exchange rates in the agricultural sector; and (4) the approximation of administrative and public health regulations.

Community Preference

Community preference means the principle whereby priority must be given to the sale of Community produce. The main dilemma of CAP is the following: since costs of production are in general higher in the EC than in the other main producing countries, the CAP is supposed to protect the internal market against cheap imports and excessive fluctuations on the world market. Therefore, according to EC reasoning, EC prices must be above the world market level in order to guarantee Community production. In cases where no protection is possible, subsidies are paid to make the prices of Community products competitive with those of imported goods.[5]

Common Pricing System

Precisely, a common pricing system was introduced to guarantee uniform price levels. This involves three types of prices:

(1) the *target price,* which is the price that EC farmers are ideally supposed to receive. This price is fixed every year by the Council.

(2) the *intervention price,* when the EC intervenes to stabilize the situation, for example, if the actual market price drops below the target price. At the intervention price, the member states have to buy up the product concerned in unlimited quantities.

(3) the *threshold price* is the minimum price for agricultural imports into the Community. To prevent the Community market from being flooded with cheap imports from non-member countries, a levy is imposed to bring import prices up to the threshold level.

The levies are part of the Community's own resources. Conversely the Community pays agricultural exporters a refund, i.e., an export subsidy to offset the difference between the world price and the Community price. This enables Community farmers to sell their products on the world market despite the fact that their prices are generally higher.

This is the basic theory underlying the Common Agricultural Policy. In practice, it poses a number of problems. Setting prices that were out of line with market conditions led to surpluses. This in turn led to the accumulation of large stocks (butter, fruit and vegetable mountains) and to unfair competition at the world level.

Why Is the EC Not Capable of Reforming the CAP?[6]

Farming lies at the heart of European history, geography, culture, and environment. It plays a more important role in the European economy and society than is indicated by the figure (3.1 percent of the EC's GDP). Real reform of Europe's agricultural economy would cost millions of European farmers their jobs.

Ten million farmers and their families depend on agriculture; 2.5 million workers are employed in the food processing industries. *Nolens, volens,* the EC has made a political and cultural choice to maintain a living countryside and to sustain rural communities. How can it be otherwise, when, for example, the average size of a European farm is 13 hectares and an American farm is 186 hectares?

As Ray Mac Sharry, the EC Agriculture Commissioner said: "There can be no question of setting aside these achievements or to put them at risk in the pursuit of dubious text book economic theories of comparative advantage and international specialization."[7]

Direct Payments

Some economists argue that the only long-term solution is to make direct payments to producers that do not act as an incentive for inefficient producers to increase their output and that do not therefore lead to the use of trade-distorting export subsidies. According to this theory, farmers should be paid for their role as guardians of the countryside. Farmers are suspicious of this approach for at least two reasons. One is that they instinctively shy away from the image of "park-keepers" or social security recipients. The other is that reshaping the CAP from a system based on price supports to one which makes payments directly to the producer is a deceptively symmetrical idea.

The U.S. Position

For a long time the United States adopted an extreme position in GATT, demanding complete elimination of all aids that had any impact on trade in agricultural produce. For example, in Montreal in 1988, the U.S. called for the total abolition of all export subsidies by the end of the 1990s. It has denounced the CAP as an expensive policy, out of control and harmful to the interests of developing countries.

In May 1990, the U.S. attacked again at the OECD ministerial meeting. This was resisted, but resurfaced in July in Houston, Texas. American proposals had strong support in the talks from the Cairns Group of agricultural free traders, an alliance of thirteen rich and poor agricultural exporters.

The U.S. proposal seeks to reform trade in agriculture in four key areas, which are the following:

Market Access

Countries would convert all of their nontariff barriers to agricultural trade to equivalent tariffs through a process known as "tariffication." If implemented, all agricultural trade restraints – such as U.S. quotas on cotton, sugar, and dairy products; the European Community's variable levies; voluntary import restraint agreements; and restrictive licensing practices would be converted to bound tariffs. Until the year 2000, new and previously existing tariffs on agriculture would be reduced substantially through multilateral negotiations.

To facilitate the transition process, countries would be able to use tariff-rate quotas (a two-tiered tariff system with low tariffs on a certain quota level of imports and higher tariffs applying to all imports beyond the quota level) and a temporary safeguard measure (a tariff "snapback" when imports go above certain quantitative limits). After the transition period, "bound" tariffs – tariff levels that cannot subsequently be raised – would be the only form of import protection remaining.

Export Competition: Countries would phase out agricultural export subsidies and differential export taxes over a five-year period. Only *bona fide* food aid would be exempted.

Internal Support Measures: States would phase out the most trade-distorting forms of government support for agriculture. Support measures that interfere less with trade would be subject to discipline, and those having a relatively minor effect on trade would be permitted as long as they met specific criteria.

Sanitary and Phytosanitary Measures: Government regulation and barriers relating to animal, plant, and human health would come under an international process for dispute settlement and harmonization.

Some Government Support Could Remain

Permitted policies would include income support policies not linked to production or marketing, environmental and conservation programs, bona fide disaster assistance and domestic food aid, certain marketing programs such as information and inspection services, general services such as education and research, programs to remove land or other production factors from agriculture, and programs to stockpile food reserves.

Later, in the second half of the 1980s, the U.S. softened its negotiating position. It revised its plan for world farm reform and called for cuts of 90 percent in export subsidies and 75 percent in internal supports and tariff barriers.

The U.S. has modified its original proposal in at least three ways. First, instead of calling for the total elimination of export subsidies in five years, it sought reductions of 90 percent over ten years. Second, Washington dropped its demand that some domestic subsidies be phased out completely during the transition period. (This would have included America's own deficiency payments to farmers which, together with other internal supports, averaged $23 billion a year in 1988). Third, under border protection cuts, the Americans have accepted the EC's demand for introduction of a "corrective factor" that would shield farmers against abrupt swings in prices or exchange rates.

The original U.S. proposal allowed governments to levy a tariff surcharge if the volume of imports of a product exceeded 120 percent of the imports of that product during the previous year. The revised draft provides for a second emergency relief mechanism based on price. Governments would be able to impose a surcharge if the import price of a product fell below 75 percent of the average import price for the product over the three preceding years.

However, the trigger mechanism applies to import, not export, prices. Moreover, nothing in the U.S. plan offered provisions for countering exchange rate fluctuations. There was also no concession to the EC's "rebalancing" requirement, which would enable it to raise tariffs on products such as oilseeds, provided cuts in other areas met the overall reduction target.

The U.S. proposed an average of 1968 to 1988 levels for internal supports and border protection and an average of 1987 to 1989 for export subsidies. The U.S. wanted to limit the use of an Aggregate Measure of Support (AMS) to monitoring reduction targets for internal supports. The EC wanted to use an AMS covering all farm supports as the main instrument determining reductions in general.

The EC Position[8]

The Community considered U.S. proposals as an unbalanced attack on the basic essence of the CAP. The EC was not ready to accept that its system of protection could be jeopardized, especially by the border measures such as import levies and export subsidies. The general EC position is based on the following arguments:

First, since 1988 with the operation of stabilizers, important efforts have been made to keep the CAP below the guideline set for agriculture expenditure.[9] This occurred despite the world market deterioration. This has been the case especially in dairy products, where the EC's trading partners refused to comply with GATT minimum prices, in beef where there is a decline in consumption, and in cereals where there is an increase in world production.

Second, the Community points out that its market is not so protected when anti-trade combination, as in 1988, the EC had an agricultural trade deficit of $27.5 billion while the U.S. enjoyed a trade surplus of $18 billion in agriculture.[10] The U.S. also has special tricks to support farm exports. These are frequently much more difficult to identify than the Community's export refunds. The U.S. spent $11,250 per farmer on farm aid in 1987 – almost five times what the Common Agricultural Policy cost per farmer.[11]

Third, the EC refuses to admit that its agricultural policy is unfair toward less-developed countries. On the contrary, the EC argues that it does much more for those countries than the U.S. because it has created a special system under the Lomé Convention.[12] Thanks to this Convention, nearly 130 Third World countries from Africa, the Caribbean, and the Pacific (the ACP countries) are allowed to export almost all their products to the EC free of duty. Moreover, the EC has created the Stabex system. This mechanism guarantees ACP countries minimum returns on the export of certain raw materials to the Community. The system covers many agricultural commodities such as coffee, cocoa, and tea. This means that some exports by ACP country are protected from the speculative fluctuations of world markets. The Community recalls also that it runs large agricultural trade deficits with the ACP countries partners. Under the Fourth Lomé Convention, ACP countries continue to benefit from preferential access for their agricultural products. The EC has also given improved access, even for sensitive products, to the emerging democracies of Eastern and Central Europe.

Fourth, the EC contests that the CAP disrupts world markets. Its share of total world agricultural exports has only moved from 11.8 percent in 1980 to 12.8 percent during the eighties. Within this overall trend there are variations. In cereals its share of world trade has risen (from 9.4 percent in 1980 to 14.6 percent in 1989). But its share of world trade in dairy products has fallen from 59.9 percent from 1984 to 50.9 percent in 1989.[13]

Fifth, the reforms undertaken have already led since 1986 to a 10 percent reduction in support for arable crops and a 15 percent reduction in support for livestock. In cereals, for example, prices have been reduced cumulatively by 3 percent in each of three consecutive years.

Sixth, if reforms proposed by the U.S. and the Cairns Group were adopted, the risks would be the same ones that the Reagan and Bush administration have imposed on rural America: depopulation, economic concentration, erosion and groundwater pollution.

Seventh, most farmers in the U.S. oppose the Bush proposal on agriculture. The Administration is isolated in its own country. It is therefore groundless to jeopardize the whole GATT negotiation over reforms on agriculture that would likely be refused by the U.S. Congress. As a matter of fact, Congress is not ready to sacrifice farmers to "larger" continental business interests.[14]

EC Counter-Proposals

The EC reacted to U.S. proposals.[15] Its counter offer was broadly to propose a system based on an aggregate measure of support (AMS). The idea is to capture all the different forms of protection in a single measure and agree upon targets for how this single measure should be reduced, thereby leaving it to governments to decide which measures to cut.

The problem is that the EC did not want to convert its various trade barriers to tariffs because it would have needed to "rebalance" the present pattern of support, i.e., increase some existing tariffs.

The EC also proposed a two-tier tariff, part fixed (and subject to negotiated reductions) and part variable to compensate for big shifts in prices or currencies. One of the main difficulties to resolve was the conflict over the EC's controversial demand for "rebalancing" – the freedom to raise tariffs on foodstuffs (such as oilseeds) now imported duty-free to compensate for overall tariff cuts.

On export subsidies there was also an impasse. The EC argued that cuts in domestic price-supports would automatically lead to lower export subsidies because one is a mirror-image of the other. Moreover, it argued that its dual-pricing system, which fixes domestic prices higher than world prices, is sacrosanct. The EC, which has imposed budget curbs on farm payments since 1986, wanted to use 1986 as the base year for calculating reductions.

Motives of U.S. Refusal of EC Counter-Proposals[16]

First, the 30 percent that has been proposed by the European Commission is not the same as the 75 percent that has been offered by the U.S. Washington questioned EC proposals because the Community called for a 30 percent cut which actually incorporates a 15 percent cut that had already taken place since 1986. The Community proposal is to cut 30 percent from the level that existed in 1986, and 15 percent of that already took place prior to this year.

Second, the EC's proposal covers different time periods. The Community offer goes back five years and forward five years. The U.S. goes forward ten years from 1990, although both proposals use similar base periods. The Community's is 1986, which is the highest level of support; the U.S.'s is 1986-1988.

Finally, the issue was not as clear-cut as this presentation would suggest. At the beginning of 1991, the U.S. Congress was writing a new farm bill. Its terms were conditioned by the outcome of tense budget negotiations that imposed limits on deficiency payments to farmers.

Moreover, farm costs rose due to the higher fuel and fertilizer prices resulting from the embargo on Iraq. The embargo also closed one of the largest markets for U.S. wheat at the same time that world market prices for cereal crops were falling. The American administration could not apply to its own farmers the heavy cuts in farm supports it was proposing in the Uruguay

Round. With this downgrading of expectations, the GATT trade talks also became one of the victims of the political rebellion in Congress unveiled by the budget crisis.

***

The disadvantages of CAP are both domestic and external. First, CAP consumes about two-thirds of the EC budget and has created large surpluses of many agricultural products. Second, EC export subsidies contribute to creating a distorted market in agricultural commodities.

Some EC member states bear an enormous responsibility for the failure of the Uruguay Round. In January 1991, the EC Commission gave them the possibility of reforming the Common Agriculture Policy by calling for severe cuts in Community subsidies to farmers.[17] Those cuts would have virtually eliminated the exports subsidies. But the so-called "liberal camp" composed of the UK,[18] France,[19] the Netherlands, and Denmark opposed what they see as discriminatory measures which will penalize their large producers. Facts are nevertheless facts and the failure of the CAP is a reality. EC farm spending rose in 1990 by about ECUS 7 billion, or 25 percent, to over ECUS 32 billion.[20] In 1992 it would rise further by 12.5 percent. Some 80 percent of the farm budget goes to 20 percent of EC farmers, concentrated in the northern triangle running from East Anglia up to Denmark and down to the Paris Basin.

A reform of the CAP is a necessity not only for the sake of the Uruguay Round and good relations with America. It is also inevitable because the prospect of a Community enlargement to embrace some EFTA and eventually Central and Eastern European countries with such different levels of agriculture (from the most subsidized to the poorest) demands such an adaptation.

Notes

1. For a good historical summary: Romain Yaremtchouk, "L'Europe face aux Etats-Unis," *Studia Diplomatica,* 29/1986, No 4-5, pp. 468-481.

2. See, nevertheless, Catherine Pivot, "Logiques comparées des politiques agricoles américaines et européennes," in Jacques Bourrinet (ed.), *Les relations Communauté européenne-Etats-Unis* (Paris: Economica, 1987), pp. 193-206.

Also interesting: Denis Bergmann, "Problèmes de fond dans le conflit entre la CEE et les Etats-Unis en matière agricole," Ibid., pp. 207-222.

3. Commission of the European Community, *A Common Agricultural Policy for the 1990s* (Brussels/Luxembourg, Office for Official Publication of the European Communities, 1989), p. 5.

4. Bibliography in Commission of the European Community, *A Common Agricultural Policy for the 1990s,* pp. 87-90.
See also, Dimitrios Demekas, Kasper Bartholdy and al. "The Effects of the Common Agricultural Policy of the European Community: A Survey of the Literature," *Journal of Common Market Studies,* 1988, 27/02, pp. 113-145.

5. Alan L. Winters, "The Economic Consequences of Agricultural Support: A Survey," *OECD Economic Studies,* 9, 1987, pp. 7-22.

6. Richard Howarth, *Farming for Farmers? A Critique of Agricultural Support Policy"* (London: Institute of Economic Affairs, 1985), 143 p.

7. Ray Mac Sharry, "Commemoration 30 Years of the Common Agricultural Policy Speech at the Dublin Horse Show," *European Community News* (Washington, D.C.: EC Embassy, 19 July 1990), p. 2.

8. Commission of the European Communities, "Outline of the Current Proposals," *GATT, Global Negotiation Proposal on Agriculture* (EC Mission in Geneva, 1990), 4 p. (not published).

9. "Rocking a Lifeboat is Dangerous," *The Economist,* 8 December 1990.

10. Ray Mac Sharry, "Commemorating 30 Years of the Common Agricultural Policy," p. 2.

11. Commission of the European Communities, *Report on United States. Trade Barriers and Unfair Trade Practices* (Brussels: Service of the Commission of the European Communities, 1990), p. 10.

12. Commission of the European Communities, *A Common Agriculture Policy for the 1990s,* pp. 42-43.

13. Commission of the European Communities, "The Background in Graphs and Charts," *GATT, Global Negotiation Proposal on Agriculture,* pp. 2-7.

14. Philippe Lemaître, "Etats-Unis: la CEE un concurrent déloyal," *Le Monde,* 4 December 1990.

15. Philippe Lemaître, "La CEE propose de réduire de 30% les soutiens aux exploitants agricoles," *Le Monde,* 8 November 1990.

16. U.S. Information Agency, *Global Trade Issues,* pp. 4-7. See also Philippe Lemaître, "Etats-Unis : la CEE un concurrent déloyal," *Le Monde,* 4 December 1990.

17. David Gardner, "Brussels Examines Deeper Cuts in EC Farm Support," *Financial Times,* 17 January 1991.

18. Sir Simon Gourlay, President of the National Farmers Union, said the plans were "the biggest threat to British agriculture since the Second World War. See also David Blackwell, "EC Plan 'Biggest Threat to UK Agriculture Since the War'," *Financial Times,* 25 January 1991.

19. Louis Mermaz, the French Agriculture Minister, judged the proposals of the Commission as inacceptable. Philippe Lemaître, "M. Mermaz juge 'inacceptables' les projets de la Commission de Bruxelles," *Le Monde,* 26 January 1991.

20. "EC Farm Reform: That's the Way the Money Goes," *The Economist,* 26 January 1991.

David Gardner, "A Slimmer Sacred Cow," *Financial Times,* 24 January 1991.

David Gardner, "No End in Sight to EC Farm Quagmire," *Financial Times,* 12 April 1991.

CHAPTER 11

TOWARD A "U.S.-EC ECONOMIC AREA"?

This chapter is more of an exercise, a general analytical reflection on the future of U.S.-EC relations, than a study based on empirical evidence. We will try to imagine the main difficulties of negotiating a "U.S.-EC Economic Area." If the U.S. and the EC want to integrate their markets, they will have to find common rules in order to erase most non-tariff barriers between their two blocs.

To be sure, reflection on this concept has not started yet. Digestion of the deadlock of the Uruguay Round negotiations will take time. Acrimonious accusations over "who is responsible for the set-back?" will never cease. A period of increased tension cannot be excluded. And the "sea-snake" issue of the Common Agriculture Policy is far from being solved. Moreover, the EC is much too preoccupied with its own integration, without mentioning its relations with EFTA and former Communist countries, to even accept the idea that such a "U.S.-EC Economic Area" could be an issue in the future.

Prospects for a "U.S.-EC Economic Area"

The assumption of an integration of U.S. and EC markets nevertheless has some basis. First, one should note that, in June 1990, the Italian Presidency of the Community Council developed its own view of the concept of integration around concentric circles. According to this interpretation, the United States –

and Canada are countries belonging to the fourth circle of the
European architecture:

> On the level of foreign relations, the presidency's action
> will be based on the concept of concentric circles, the first
> of which will be made of EFTA countries. As far as East
> European countries are concerned, the presidency should
> conclude negotiations on the association agreements. The
> fourth circle of this European architecture, built around the
> Community's core, will be formed on one side by the United
> States and Canada and on the other by the Soviet Union.[1]

Second, one can also find the same idea of integrating U.S. and
EC markets in a brochure published by the most important American
business organization. According to the U.S. Chamber of Commerce:

> A failure of the Uruguay Round would mean that ultimate
> access to the single market would not be governed by multi-
> lateral rules but by bilateral agreements based upon recip-
> rocal market access and treatment.[2]

A quite similar assumption has been made by Professor Lester
Thurow, Dean of the Sloan School of Management at the Massachusetts Institute of Technology. According to his prediction, the
rules the EC is writing for its states will gain acceptance
elsewhere:

> Not only will Europe's economic growth lead the world, but
> also Brussels will be writing the rules. . . . It will be the
> Europeans who give the world its economic sizzle and its
> bureaucratic leadership.[3]

Finally, one should remember that the common Declaration on
U.S.-EC Relations adopted on 23 November 1990 pleads that both
blocs do the following:

> Will further develop their dialogue, which is already under-
> way, on other matters such as technical and non-tariff
> barriers to industrial and agricultural trade, services,
> competition policy, transportation policy, standards, tele-
> communications, high technology and other relevant areas.
> . . . In education, scientific and cultural cooperation, the

partnership between the European Community and its member States on the one hand, and the United States on the other, will be based on continuous efforts to strengthen mutual cooperation in various other fields which directly affect the present and future well-being of their citizens, such as exchanges and joint projects in science and technology, including, inter alia, research in medicine, environment protection, pollution prevention, energy, space, high-energy physics, and the safety of nuclear and other installations, as well as in education and culture, including academic and youth exchanges.[4]

Scope of a "U.S.-EC Economic Area"

To create such a "U.S.-EC Economic Area" it is indispensable to determine what could be the basic legislation. Our assumption is that the Community legislation *(acquis communautaire)* relevant to the so-called four freedoms of movement necessary to complete the 1992 Single Market could be the basis of the negotiation. To this will be added horizontal and flanking measures, as well as legal and institutional questions.

Free Movement of Goods

This includes problems already raised in the Uruguay Round negotiations such as: competition policy, government aid, public procurement, intellectual and industrial property rights, trade in counterfeit goods, rules of origin, technical regulations and standards, trade facilitation, and textiles. To those areas, one can add technical barriers to trade in a variety of fields ranging from the chemical industry to foodstuff legislation and toys, border controls and formalities, indirect taxation, phyto-sanitary controls, product liability, transport of dangerous and toxic materials, and veterinary controls.

One can easily imagine that Washington would question some essential requirements contained in some "new approach" directives. For instance, if the U.S. considered that its level of protection of health, safety, and environment is sometimes better than the average EC legislation, there would be discussions on how to ban European products.

There could also be controversies about the question of temporary derogations, as well as of permanent exemptions. Will it be possible to get periods of transition? Another issue could be the question of safeguard clauses and rebalancing measures (taken to compensate for the effects of a safeguard clause). Should a safeguard clause be general in nature? Or is it possible to imagine that the safeguard clauses and rebalancing measures might be specific and take the risk that they serve as *de facto* permanent exemptions?

Free Movement of Capital and Services

This negotiation could deal with the following issues: capital movements, economic and monetary cooperation, financial services (banks, insurance, securities), information services, audiovisual services, telecommunication services, and transport.

According to the principle of free circulation of capital, EC capital could be freely invested in American land and real estate, and reciprocally. But Americans as well as Europeans could fear that foreigners might control their economies. There is numerous legislation banning sale of land, houses, and apartments to foreigners. There are, both in the U.S. and in the EC, also limitations on the free flow of capital and on bank acquisition. These kinds of problems could lead to acute clashes because they touch very sensitive points of sovereignty.

On banking, the negotiation might be now easier than in the past, as the U.S. seems to be on its way to abolishing the *McFadden* and the *Glass-Steagall Acts*. But there could be clashes on the issue of administrative assistance that other countries' authorities should give such as the right to look into sensitive taxation relations.

Free Movement of Persons

These kinds of problems include: free movement of employees and self-employed persons, mutual recognition of diplomas, the right of establishment and freedom to provide services by self-employed professionals.

Practically, the free circulation of persons means that any EC citizen could settle, get a job, and buy a house in any part of the U.S. and reciprocally. The U.S. has a xenophobic tradition and a system of quotas. In a first step, the discussion could turn only on the questions of the free circulation of key personnel.

Flanking and Horizontal Policies

Through this expression, one understands: civil protection, company law, consumer protection, economic and social cohesion, education, the environment, research and development, social policy, small and medium-size enterprises, statistical cooperation, tourism, and nuclear safety.

Another issue concerns the question of a common regime toward third countries. Is it possible to imagine the EC and the U.S. speaking with one voice in most international forums?

Legal and Institutional Questions

These types of problems include the legal character of the treaty; ways of integrating the relevant "U.S.-EC Economic Area's" legislation into the treaty; the structure of common decision-making, surveillance, and enforcement mechanisms; a joint judicial body; the uniform interpretation of treaty provisions; and other matters related to legal aspects of the negotiating groups.

For instance, the U.S. and the EC would have to examine the issue of the *direct applicability* and *direct effect* of "U.S.-EC Area's" rules. The question is the following: how will it be possible to invoke the "U.S.-EC Area's" rules before the national and regional courts and authorities in New York or Paris? Will they have the competence to recognize and enforce the "U.S.-EC Area"?

Another example, would the United States accept the principle that it would have to make the "U.S.-EC Area" part of its national legal system, so that national courts and authorities could directly apply them.

There could also be difficulties about the question of a *surveillance mechanism*, i.e., a body which should be competent to act on its own initiative when there are alleged violations of "U.S.-EC Area's" rules. The EC Commission exercises those powers in certain sectors, such as competition, state aid, and public procurement. Will the exercise of corresponding competences in the "U.S.-EC Area" be the same? Or will it be preferable for certain aspects to use existing national surveillance mechanisms?

Another question that could be further looked into is how to arrange this surveillance practically. Is it better to establish one joint U.S.-EC body, or to add a U.S. participation to the Commission machinery, and/or to set up a U.S. surveillance mechanism as a bridge between such a U.S. mechanism and the EC Commission?

With regard to the *mechanisms for securing a uniform interpretation* of "U.S.-EC Area"'s rules between the contracting parties, what could be the best solution? To create a "U.S.-EC Area's" Court consisting of judges from the EC Court of Justice and from the U.S.? Or to settle a court of justice based on the EC Court and to add, when necessary, judges from the U.S., and reciprocally?

As for a *common decision-making mechanism*, difficulties are numerous because it has to do with the sovereignty of each bloc. First, the U.S. should demand a role in the *shaping* of the Community decisions that influence the further development of the "U.S.-EC Area." Evidently, for the U.S., in a balanced relationship it should also have the right to launch initiatives. Therefore, there should be time frames which allow American propositions to be delivered at different stages of the EC decision-making process.

Moreover, a common body for U.S. parliamentarians and representatives of the European Parliament should also be foreseen. Finally, regarding the crucial stage of the adoption of final decisions, there should be a U.S.-EC *Council* which acts as a decision-making body, where the U.S. and the EC would be represented on an equal footing and where decisions would be taken by consensus.

***

A "U.S.-EC Area" is a very difficult matter. It would necessitate a complicated negotiations on the nature, scope, conditions, exceptions, legal dimension, and decision-making of this Area. For the U.S. the main problem will be how to avoid satellization, i.e., to accept EC legislations without having sufficient influence on it.

To be sure, future U.S.-EC relations won't be asymmetrical. America will never accept passive adaptation and will resist it. U.S. power will remain important. Nevertheless, some political, legal, and technical problems should already be raised. It will take years to imagine a genuine U.S.-EC integration.

Many Third World countries, especially from Asia and Africa, could be the main victims of this U.S.-EC bilateralism. As a matter of fact, according to the assumption of success of these U.S.-EC negotiations (even if there is a triad with Japan), these countries would lag even more behind the developed countries. This could lead to widening the gap between rich and poor countries. This type of bilateral agreement could also lead to even more disinterest in the terrible difficulties of the developing countries.

Notes

1. Italian Presidency of Community Council, second half of 1990: *Objectives in Europe,* 26 June 1990, Document No. 1629, p. 2.

2. U.S. Chamber of Commerce, *Europe 1992. A Practical Guide for American Business #2* (Washington, D.C.: Publications of the U.S. Chamber of Commerce, 1990), p. 51.

3. Tim Carrington, "Will the European Era Follow the Shooting?" *Wall Street Journal,* 4 February 1991.

See also, Kalypso Nicolaidis, "Mutual Recognition: The New Frontier of Multilateralism?" *Project Promethee Perspectives* (No. 10, June 1989), pp. 21-34.

4. "Declaration on U.S.-EC Relations," *Daily Bulletin,* (Geneva, U.S. Mission, 23 November 1990), EUR503, p. 5. See also **Document 4** in appendix.

PART THREE

POLITICAL AND STRATEGIC
ASPECTS OF U.S.-EC RELATIONS

CHAPTER 12

THE AMERICAN POSITION
TOWARD THE COMMUNITY

To analyze contemporary U.S.-EC relations, we made a distinction between economic and politico-strategic aspects. This dichotomy is of course theoretical because one can never isolate the two dimensions. This is even more true in the case study of the U.S.-EC because there is everywhere a dialectical interlinking of economic and political aspects.

In order to blaze the trail of the politico-strategic dimension, we will introduce the theoretical positions of both the U.S. and the EC toward their respective future relations. This an *intentionalist* analysis and is of course not sufficient because history is shaped not merely by the intentions of the actors. Many other – still unknown – factors will occur. Unfortunately, the complexity of the future international order cannot be integrated into one – or even a few – theories.

The American position on U.S.-EC relations is much more articulated and comprehensive than the EC one. The U.S. has only one center of decision in foreign and military affairs (despite conflicts within the administration and with Congress). Furthermore, America is still – and will remain – a political and military Gulliver. Therefore, it is less difficult to analyze American intentions toward the EC than the reverse.

The first months of the Bush administration coincided with the first hints of a crumbling of communism in Europe. This conjuncture led the American government to reaffirm the political values of a stronger European Community. The sympathy of the U.S. administration has something to do with an important factor: the personality of George Bush, a friend of Europe, a man who is less nationalistic than Ronald Reagan, and who has a serious international background. Therefore, a few weeks after the inauguration of the new president, directives were given to avoid clashes with the Community on petty matters.[1] Thus, since spring 1989, American policy has been to create more international cooperation, to limit East-West tensions, and to strengthen links with its Western allies. Almost instantly, one could observe some improvements in U.S.-EC relations and abandonment of polemical themes such as "Fortress Europe."

The positive attitude of the Bush administration vis-à-vis the EC coincided with the process of disintegration in Central and Eastern Europe. Interestingly enough, many bureaucrats of the Bush administration understood faster than most Europeans the necessity of preparing the transition to the post-Cold War era.[2]

American Objectives in Europe

Since spring 1989, the Bush administration has seen in the EC a body which could fulfill at least four functions: (1) anchoring Central and Eastern Europe to the Western world; (2) easing German reunification; (3) sharing more of the burden of the Atlantic Alliance; and (4) maintaining the Atlantic Alliance partnership.

Attracting Eastern Europe

For the Bush administration, the EC has a "natural vocation"[3] for promoting economic and political reforms in former Communist Europe. As early as May 1989, President Bush said that: "a resurgent Western Europe is an economic magnet, drawing Eastern Europe closer, towards the commonwealth of free nations."[4]

Washington has considered that the EC as such should play a leading role in bridging the divide between the two parts of Europe. Therefore, it was on American initiative that, in July 1989, the European Commission was nominated to coordinate twenty-four rich countries' aid to Poland and Hungary.

But, according to some sources, the motive for the American initiatives is not entirely flattering to the EC. The idea of giving the Commission a role in Eastern Europe was to "counteract the Community's natural tendency to be insular." Moreover, a policy review in July 1989 concluded that Europe would continue to become more integrated and that any American opposition would be counter-productive.[5] Thus, in July 1989 in Paris, the Americans pressed hard upon a somewhat reluctant and badly prepared Community to coordinate help to Poland and Hungary, to lead the G24 (Group of Twenty-Four OECD countries),[6] and to create a European Bank for Reconstruction and Development (EBRD)[7] with a majority of capital belonging to the EC countries (contrary to the World Bank and IMF).

There are also a few Americans who fear that the Community could set an independent course toward Eastern Europe that would limit U.S. economic opportunities.[8] This conception does not seem to be based on any empirical evidence as yet.

Anchoring German Reunification

Since the early fifties, European integration has been viewed as a way to insure that the links between Germany and its Western European partners are so important that they cannot be severed. A strong EC political identity helps to insure that German reunification happens under conditions in which the old instabilities do not arise again.

Use of European integration to anchor German reunification in the Western Alliance has always been one of the most fundamental aims of American policy toward Europe. Let us remember the enthusiasm (after some hesitation) of the Eisenhower administration for the European Defence Community (EDC) and later the support of John Foster Dulles for EURATOM and the European Economic Community. In 1989-1990, the American motives were in many aspects the same as in the fifties: first, to strengthen the European pillar of the Atlantic Alliance against the USSR thanks to German power; second, to fight German neutralist tendencies, which could have led to exchanging of the Atlantic Alliance for reunification; and, third, to reassure former victims of Germany, particularly France.

It is mainly for those political motives that the United States supported most moves toward European integration, although since the fifties the Americans have been fully aware that a genuine common market contained the risk of discrimination for the U.S. The Americans nevertheless always supported EC integration and went as far as opposing anti-EC trends in the United Kingdom, their best ally. For the same reason America rejected any British attempt to torpedo the EC *(Maudling Plan* and EFTA),[9] arguing exaggeratedly that their economic power of discrimination would be as important as that one provoked by the EC, without granting to the U.S. enough political advantage.

In the years 1989-1990, one finds less public American senti-ment expressing as clearly as in the fifties that the EC should play an important role in integrating German unification within a European framework. Every official person was careful to avoid injuring German pride.[10] Therefore, there has been a debate only among intellectuals devoted to the rather artificial question: "European Germany or German Europe?" According to Stanley Hoffmann, stronger economic and political links within the Community have been considered as ways to divert Germany from nuclear ambitions.[11] But is Washington aware that a stronger EC could provide Germany with more influence than it would have if fully sovereign?

There are also serious hints that Americans fear that German reunification alters the Atlantic Alliance, especially because in coping with Soviet demands, Bonn has accepted significantly reducing its army and sought to remove most U.S. nuclear weapons from its territory.[12] To be sure, in return the Soviets have agreed removing gradually their troops from eastern Germany.

This deal leads Americans to rethink their role in Europe. Would removal of U.S. nuclear weapons from Germany signal the end of extended deterrence? Would other European states, such as France and Britain, agree to supply a nuclear deterrent for Europe? Is such a force necessary in light of political reforms in Eastern Europe and the Soviet Union? What tactics and strategy, with the end of extended deterrence and flexible response, would be utilized by U.S. conventional forces in Europe?

Sharing the Burden

The notion of "burden-sharing" is almost as old as the American presence in Europe. This concept – repeated continuously in any period of Euro-American tension – means simply that Europeans should contribute more to their defense and relieve the Americans of a part of their economic, political, and military contribution.[13]

In the context of the years 1989-1990, the sea-serpent of "burden-sharing" reappeared due to the conjunction of three factors: first, the triple American deficit, external, budgetary and structural; second, the economic dynamism brought by EC1992; and, third, withdrawal of most American and Soviet troops from Europe.[14] These three factors naturally led the Americans to ask the Europeans to share the burden of the Atlantic Alliance in Europe. They saw in a strengthened Community the best means of achieving this objective.[15]

Therefore, America asked the EC to help the former communist countries economically and to offer them some kinds of association. Moreover, the Bush administration supported trends toward more EC political unification in order to balance, through a homogeneous and coherent structure, the political and strategic instability induced by the crumbling of communism, departure of the Soviets, withdrawal of the Americans, and emergence of the "German colossus."[16]

In this perspective, the EC-1992 program is seen by the U.S. as a good means to strengthen the European economy. A more efficient use of economic resources will promote economies of scale; then the reduction of costs of producing weapons systems may prove to be an important factor in leading EC states to cooperate more closely. Moreover, EC habits taken in the civilian arena could promote more cooperation in the Western European Union (WEU) and the Independent European Programme Group (IEPG).[17]

Thanks to free flow of capital and labor across borders and promotion of economies of scale, it will be less expensive to produce costly weapon systems. Thanks also to habits developed in the civilian economic arena, it will be easier to share military planning.

As the EC grows more confident in its military technology and as public procurement in the defense sector liberalizes, European defense cooperation in WEU and IEPG is likely to increase. The Europeans will also have more capacity to provide a larger share of their own defense needs, at a time when the U.S. is preoccupied with its own structural problems. EC-1992 could relieve the United States of some of its current burden in Europe.

One finds here again, when dealing with the burden-sharing issue, two dilemmas often underlined: on the one hand, the Americans want to keep their world leadership while spending less money. On the other hand, Europeans demand less American leadership without accepting to pay more and without agreeing to lose the American military guarantee.

Maintaining the Atlantic Alliance Partnership

The Bush administration's overall sympathy for the EC cannot be solely explained by the rather rational arguments mentioned above. The pro-EC attitude of the Bush administration should also be analyzed as a consequence of a fear of a collapse of the Atlantic Alliance. The U.S. commitment to European security is questioned more and more as the Soviet military threat becomes less dangerous. The disappearance of the common enemy could lead to Euro-American conflict and finally to the end of the American leadership in the world.

Moreover, EC-1992 means a less malleable partner. A more unified internal market will likely raise EC self-confidence in dealing with political issues. The Twelve also seem more assertive of their military technology and defense capacities than at any time since the Second World war. A stronger Western European identity leads to an erosion of NATO as the single viable institution where European security could be debated and implemented.

Furthermore, if the Twelve use the EC as a means to work out their differences before confronting the U.S., it will reduce the flexibility of the Alliance and alter the way it operates. In the past, America used to achieve more by dealing with 14 small NATO allies separately than with one large one. Divide and rule policy will be more difficult. And possibilities of "special relations" (like with the UK and the FRG) will disappear.

Therefore, since May 1989, George Bush reaffirms that: "The Alliance with Western Europe is utterly unlike the cynical power alliances of the past."[18] Furthermore, the President insists that the Alliance "is based on far more than the perception of a common enemy."[19] And he repeats that there is a tie of culture, kinship and shared values, a "moral and spiritual community between Western Europe and the U.S."[20]

Even, in the July 1990 NATO declaration, the European Community is mentioned as a positive factor, contributing to strengthen the Atlantic alliance:

> Part of the growing political and economic integration of the European Community will be an indispensable factor of stability, which is needed in the heart of Europe. The move within the European Community toward political union, including the development of a European identity in the domain of security, will also contribute to Atlantic solidarity and to the establishment of a just and lasting order of peace throughout the whole of Europe.[21]

Although there is a lot of American sympathy for the Community, one should nevertheless remain cautious and avoid exaggeration. For the American government, NATO is and should remain the vital foundation of stability in Europe. The Atlantic Alliance should continue to be the transatlantic forum in which mutual security issues are addressed. From a strategic point of view, America still keeps three priorities: to save NATO as much as possible; to maintain unified Germany in NATO; and to resuscitate WEU as a complement to NATO in preference to a European Defense Community which would be too dependent upon the EC. These American priorities can be easily explained: the EC is completely independent from the American leadership which is not the case of NATO and of WEU (although to a lesser extent).

In conclusion, the Bush administration wants to preserve NATO but nevertheless understands that NATO is: (1) not sufficient anymore to keep Europe under its influence; (2) its sphere of action is mainly limited to the European theater (and Asian Turkey); (3) its structure is too military-oriented; and (4) it could not fully integrate Central and Eastern European countries (as long as the Soviet Union exists as such).

The American Plan Toward the EC

Washington, especially the State Department, seeks to forge closer institutional links with the EC. This initiative aims at complementing traditional U.S. ties to Europe through the NATO alliance. According to this concept, the EC will form one institutional grouping, and the U.S., possibly joined by Asian countries, will form another. The approach appears to be mutually advantageous. For the U.S. this plan could have three advantages: first, to create an alliance of free democracies, second, to strengthen the European Community, and, third, to reorganize its foreign aid budget priorities. For the Europeans, the new role would enable them to argue that the Community has not become preoccupied with its own continental drama of the Single Market, German reunification and the European monetary union.

Concretely, the American plan toward the EC contains the five following objectives: (1) Institutionalization of U.S.-EC relations; (2) strengthening the WEU; (3) stabilization of Turkey; and (4) co-administration of the world.

Institutionalization of U.S.-EC Relations

This idea is contained in the November 1990 "Declaration on U.S.-EC Relations."[22] The concept of institutionalization was already mentioned by President Bush's call in May 1989 for "new mechanisms for consultation and cooperation on political and global issues"[23] and by Secretary Baker's proposal to achieve "a significantly strengthened set of institutional and consultative links" in his December 1989 Berlin speech.[24] The agreement already establishes regular consultation procedures at various levels to avoid presenting either side with non-negotiable positions and to enhance the practice of joint action.

Originally, the Americans also wanted to develop a regime that could integrate all levels of issues in order to protect fully their interests. The U.S. did not suggest, however, a supranational organ of control. The American model is close to the inter-governmental practiced by the EC states in the EPC or in the *Schengen agreement.*[25] The creation of a small secretariat may be envisaged. As a consequence, this might prod the Commission and the Council to reconcile their respective roles on matters of so-called mixed competency.

Strengthening the WEU

During the Reagan administration, the Americans were reluctant to support any European initiative toward a more integrated regional dimension. They feared a further fragmentation of the European foreign policy decision-making setup. They considered the NATO bodies to be the genuine institutionalized framework for the transatlantic defense dialogue.

But the Bush administration was aware early of the potentiality of WEU and the EC.[26] Washington of course prefers NATO as the vehicle for its security presence in Europe and would like to extend NATO competences to civil issues. The U.S. also wants to extend the sphere of intervention of NATO outside Europe and the Atlantic to the Third World, especially to the Middle East. But most Americans know that the alliance will have tremendous difficulties in playing an "out of area" role.[27]

Washington seems yet to understand why Europe wants to develop the WEU as its own forum for talking about security. After all, for forty years America has wanted Europe to develop a more coherent security identity. In the nineties, from a U.S. perspective, the WEU is the best vehicle for further European cooperation. WEU is closely linked with NATO, and its limited membership means that certain disparate views which surface in NATO could be excluded.

The Bush administration seems also ready to accept the development of a mechanism for tackling regional security problems along the lines of the one used in the Persian Gulf in 1987 and employed especially against Iraq in 1990-1991. This could lead finally to a kind of co-administration of WEU by both NATO and the EC. One might envisage, for example, the creation of a European crisis planning mechanism in order to coordinate the management of European national forces.[28]

Finally, one can already imagine the difficulties which might emerge: on the one hand, if the system is too favorable to the Europeans, Washington would not welcome a caucus of nine that would bring *faits accomplis* to NATO. But, on the other hand, if the decision-making reserves too many rights for the U.S., Washington might have a kind of veto over WEU, i.e., its rights will be as important as the ones of a dozen European countries. One can already forecast multiple clashes between the U.S. and the EC over WEU. For sure, it would be the first time in history that a military organization would be administered by two major blocs.

Stabilization of Turkey

Washington is more aware of the difficulties in Turkey than the Europeans. The Bush administration emphasizes the need to take into account Turkey's place and prospects in the post-Cold War era. Dismantling of NATO could provoke an isolation of Turkey.[29]

America suggests that the EC be more receptive to the membership application of this country. A rejection of Turkey by Western Europe could lead to the following problems: destabilization by fundamentalist Moslems; lack of solidarity against Iraq; irredentism on the Cyprus question; and expansionist tendencies toward the Turkish cultural territories in the crumbling Soviet Union.

A future point of discord between the U.S. and the EC concerns the proposal to establish a free trade zone between Turkey and America. Trade preferences offered to the U.S. would technically be incompatible with any customs union between the EC and Turkey.[30]

Co-management of the World

The U.S. position toward the EC can only be understood in the perspective of maintaining American domination in the world by using the EC. The Bush administration aims at creating between the EC and America an alliance able to confront the challenges of the new international order.

This implies first that the EC welcomes Japan as a partner.[31] In the Bush administration's concept of a new world order, U.S.-EC links are good and U.S.-Japan links are satisfactory, but the Japan-EC links are weak. Japan's motivation for an agreement with the EC is chiefly political but the EC's objective is mainly economic. It is objectively difficult to broaden relations with the EC beyond the economic sphere because the Commission deals almost exclusively with economic questions. Improved access to markets is the EC's objective. Financial services, investments, telecommunications, technology and computers are especially singled out as areas for liberalization.[32]

One can imagine that an EC-Japan declaration will be issued - modelled on the "transatlantic agreement" between the EC and the U.S. – and that an institutional framework for annual meetings will be established between the Japanese prime minister, the president of the Commission, and the EC presidency, as well as regular meetings between Japanese ministers and EC commissioners.

This scenario can occur only if the Europeans become less suspicious vis-à-vis Japan. It is difficult to evaluate how far the Americans will try to force the Europeans to set up this special relationship with Japan. Underlying prejudices from many Europeans against the Japanese will make difficult a durable U.S.-EC-Japanese alliance (Trilateral concept). Even Jacques Delors, the president of the Commission, recognizes that "in the Japan-United States-EC triangle, the EC-Japan side is by far the weakest side."[33]

The United States also aims at working together with the EC on regional conflict and proliferation. Washington wants the European Political Cooperation (EPC) to play a greater international role.[34] The model is the one used in the beginning of the Kuwait Crisis to avoid dislocation of the embargo against Iraq.[35] The

Bush administration desires more unity of action and greater common leadership within the CSCE. More original, since 1989, Washington also suggests associating the EC with a "Program for Democracy and Development in Central America."[36]

***

The American scheme for a new transatlantic partnership might sound like a repetition of similar calls launched by previous American administrations (Kennedy and the "Atlantic partnership," Kissinger and the "Year of Europe"). This time, however, there is at least one important difference: the U.S. can no longer impose a non-egalitarian partnership on Western Europe. The American leadership is aware of its structural economic weakness and of the post-Cold War isolationist mood of the American population.

The new international structure envisioned by the U.S. is based on two main powers: America and the EC, with potential support by Japan. Washington would be ready to associate with Japan but knows that the Europeans are broadly reluctant toward Japan and that Tokyo will have difficulties moving its public opinion to accept any serious global duty in such a context.

Implicitly, this American "Weltanschauung" excludes the Soviet Union, the Middle East, Latin America, Asia (except Japan) and Africa. This model of U.S.-EC relations leads clearly to domination by the Western world, a minority of the world population, who possess most of its wealth and weaponry.

Notes

1. The following sentence was pronounced by George Bush already in May 1989: "What a tragedy; what an absurdity it would be if future historians attribute the demise of the Western Alliance to disputes over beef hormones and wars over pasta."

George Bush, "Remarks at the Boston University Commencement Ceremony, 21 May 1989" in *Beyond Containment, Selected Speeches by the President George Bush* (Washington D.C., United States Information Agency, 1989), p. 13.

2. Stanley Hoffmann, "A New World and its Troubles," *Foreign Affairs* (Fall 1990), pp. 115-122.

3. James A. Baker, "A New Europe, A New Atlanticism: Architecture for a New Era," *Press Department of State*, Berlin, 12 December 1989, p. 6.

4. George Bush, "Remarks at the Boston University Commencement Ceremony," p. 13.

5. "Baker and the Dozen," *The Economist*, 9 June 1990.

6. Promises of financial aid to the countries of Eastern Europe total $23 bn in 1991. This includes $8 bn in the form of grants, $1.7 bn in structural loans from EC bodies such as the European Investment Bank, $11.4 bn pledged as capital for the European Bank for Reconstruction and Development and $2 bn in bilateral loans and credits.

7. The Bank is located in London and directed by Jacques Attali, a former senior advisor to French President Mitterrand. The EBRD's mission is to promote private and enterpreneurial initiatives in the Central and East European countries. European Community states and institutions have a 51 percent majority of votes; the rest is shared among the other West European countries, Eastern Europe, the Soviet Union and a few non-European countries including the U.S., which, with 10 percent, is the largest single contributor.

No more than 40 percent of the Bank's funds are awarded to the public sector, reserving the majority for private enterprises. The Bush administration prefers a relatively narrow focus for the bank in encouraging the private sector in Eastern Europe, as the Community supports the broader view of the bank as the first truly pan-European organization of the post-Cold War era.

Commission of the European Communities, *La Communauté et la Banque européenne pour la reconstruction et le développement* (Bruxelles/Luxembourg, Office of official publications of the European Community, 25 July 1990) COM(90) 190/2 final; 90 p.

8. Robert Hunter and John Yochelson, *Beyond 1992: U.S. Strategy Toward the European Community* (Washington, D.C.: The Center for Strategic and International Studies, September 1990), p. 28.

9. See Chapter One.

10. See nevertheless the semi-official view of the Congressional Research Service: "A European Community allows to capture reunited Germany and to limit any tendency of such a state to dominate Europe's economic and political future."
Paul E. Gallis and Steven J. Woehrel, "Germany's Future and U.S. Interests," *Congressional Research Service Issue Brief,* 23 February 1990, pp. 10-11.
See also, Paul E. Gallis and Steven J. Woehrel, "Germany's Future and U.S. Interests," *Congressional Research Service Issue Brief,* 2 October 1990, p. 11.
11. Stanley Hoffmann, "Today's NATO –and Tomorrow's," *The New York Times,* 27 May 1990.
12. Paul Gallis, "U.S.-West European Affairs: Responding to a Changing Relationship," *Congressional Research Service Issue Brief,* updated 9 November 1990, pp. 4-5.
13. David P. Calleo, *Beyond American Hegemony* (New York: Basic Books, 1987), pp. 109-126.
14. Stanley R. Sloan, "A New Europe and U.S. Interests," *Congressional Research Service Issue Brief,* updated 8 November 1990, pp. 8-9.
15. Stanley R. Sloan, "The United States and a New Europe: Strategy for the Future," *Congressional Research Service Issue Brief,* 14 May 1990, pp. 32-33.
16. Gallis, "U.S.-West European Affairs," updated 9 November 1990, p. 10.
17. Paul Gallis, "A New Global Role for the EC?" in Glennon Harrison (ed.), *European Community: Issues Raised by 1992 Integration,* 1989, p. 81.
See about the WEU and the IEPG, Chapter 13 of this book.
18. George Bush, "Remarks at the Boston University Commencement Ceremony," p. 13.
19. Ibid., p. 13.
20. Ibid., p. 13. The latest expression is by Raymond Aron.
21. "Text of the Declaration after the NATO Talks," *The New York Times,* point 3, 8 July 1990.
22. "Declaration on U.S.-EC Relations," *Daily Bulletin,* (Geneva, U.S. Mission, 23 November 1990), EUR503, pp. 2-6.
See the whole text in Document 4.
23. Bush, "Remarks at the Boston University Commencement Ceremony," p. 13.
24. Baker, "A New Europe," A new Atlanticism: Architecture for a New Era," *Press Department of State,* Berlin, 12 December 1989, p. 6.
25. In 1985, five EC countries (France, Germany, and Benelux) agreed to abolish their physical internal frontiers and to adopt common immigration and visa policies. This took place in Schengen, a village in Luxembourg. Later, Italy joined the *Schengen*

agreement. Formally, the *Schengen agreement* is not a part of the Community.

26. Robert Mauthner, "U.S. Backs Stronger European Security and Defence Role," *Financial Times,* 18 December 1990.

27. "What to do with WEU," *The Economist,* 2 February 1991.

28. Willem Van Eekelen, "The WEU: Europe's Best Defense," *European Affairs.* Vol. 4, 1990, pp. 10-11.

Willem Van Eekelen is Secretary General of the Western European Union.

29. Robert B. Zoellick, "Practical Lessons for the Post-Cold War Age," *European Affairs,* Volume 4, 1990, p. 84.

Robert Zoellick was in 1990 Counselor of the State Department.

30. John Murray Brown, "U.S. Deal Signals Turkey's Frustration with EC," *Financial Times,* 11 October 1990.

31. Dick K. Nanto, "Japan's Response to EC Integration," in Glennon J. Harrison (ed.), *European Community: Issues Raised by 1992 Integration* (Washington, D.C.: Congressional Research Service Report, 1989); pp. 61-70.

32. Andrew Hill and Stefan Wagstyl, "Community's Hand of Friendship Carries a Price for Japan," *Financial Times,* 12 April 1991.

33. Jacques Delors, "Europe's Ambitions," *Foreign Policy,* no. 80 (Fall 1990), p. 16.

34. Zoellick, "Practical Lessons for the Post-Cold War Age," pp. 84-85.

35. See Chapter 14 in this book.

36. Zoellick, "Practical Lessons for the Post-Cold War Age," p. 84.

CHAPTER 13

THE EC POSITION
TOWARD THE UNITED STATES

The Community is still a political dwarf despite recent progress, and Community foreign policy has a *papier maché* quality. European Political Cooperation (EPC) has had its successes, notably in the Conference on Security and Cooperation in Europe, but it is essentially a paper mill producing joint statements, often too late (because of the need for consensus) to get noticed.

But a lot has changed in Europe. In the beginning of the 1990s, the Community has achieved an impressive degree of economic and political integration and is aiming for still more. The USSR domination in Europe has dissolved and the military threat much diminished, while the U.S.'s own financial capacities to play a lone leadership role have been vividly exposed (Kuwait crisis).

EC Progress Toward Integration

It is more difficult to analyze the Community's position toward the U.S. than the contrary. This is due mainly to the backwardness and the fragility of its political integration, itself linked to the diverging interests of its member states. There is therefore an epistemological problem: how to study the EC as a comprehensive whole though its appearance of coherence often disguises disagreements among the Twelve and is the result of a common position based on the smallest common denominator.

There is nevertheless more and more convergence among France, Germany, Italy, and Benelux on a future political union. Even

Britain has shifted its attitude, after the resignation of Margaret Thatcher from fierce opposition to non-opposition. And in the UK, the Labor party and the majority of the business community support a more pro-European stand in the direction of more political integration.

Therefore, a new political and security dimension is emerging. Although the decisions taken during the intergovernmental conference on political union in December 1990 did not propel the Community to the stage of being a genuine political union, that stage might nevertheless arrive before long because of the inexorable pressure of events both inside and outside Europe which demand continuing momentum toward an ever fuller European union.

Take just three of these trends. First, inside Europe the potential queue of new EC member states waiting to join the Community gets longer with almost every passing month. Therefore, the Community will have to shift towards a more federal constitution to permit essential day-to-day decisions to be taken. Second, the involvement of the United States in the security of Western Europe will run down even more rapidly in the future. The EC will have to deal with a range of highly political questions involving the very heart of foreign and defense policy in the last years of this decade. Third, NATO is in decline. Although part of its functions could be passed over to the CSCE, Western Europe will need its own peace-keeping role in the near future, given the dangers of instability in parts of Central and Eastern Europe. Therefore, the Community objectives in the beginning of the 1990s turn around the following points:

Completion of the Internal Market[1]

The objective of completing the internal market is achievable although difficulties remain in sectors such as the removal of the fiscal and the physical barriers. Reform of the decision-making mechanism through the intergovernmental conference on political union should permit voting with a qualified majority system (instead of unanimity) on some important sectors such as social rights, environment, and technological cooperation.[2]

This will accelerate the process of completion of the internal market until it is finished by the end of this century.

The Monetary Union[3]

There has also been some progress on the way to a monetary union thanks to another intergovernmental conference that started in December 1990 and should finish its work in June 1991. Its plan includes three stages:[4]

Stage 1 is broadly completed. Its major objective was to strengthen monetary and economic policy coordination and to include all EC currencies in the Exchange Rate Mechanism (ERM) of the European Monetary System (EMS). In 1990-1991, important progress was made toward this goal, thanks to (1) the total free circulation of capital in France, Belgium, Italy, and Spain[5] and (2) Britain's accession to the ERM.

Stage 2 should begin as early as January 1, 1994, and its main characteristic is the establishment of a bank called European Monetary Institute (EMI). The EMI will simply co-ordinate 12 monetary policies, still run by national central banks. It will however not control national monetary policies. Before the end of 1996 the institute and the European Commission will report on the Community's readiness for phase three, taking note of how much progress has been made towards economic convergence.

Stage 3 should lead to a single Community currency.[6] The most optimistic experts do not expect that it will start before 1997. Its main steps would be: (1) making rules decided at the Community level in the macroeconomic and budgetary fields binding; (2) locking exchange rates; (3) assuming by the European System of Central Bank (ESCB) full responsibility for the formulation and implementation of monetary policy on exchange rates; (4) pooling official reserves under the management of the ESCB; and (5) changing to a single currency.

One main issue must nevertheless be resolved: the coordination of the member states' fiscal policies. Given that fiscal policies are closely interlinked with the conduct of monetary policy, states will eventually have to relinquish sovereignty. This will be a difficult area on which to reach agreement.

A More Efficient EPC[7]

Since the beginning of the 1980s many voices have been raised in the Community to develop further unification in the foreign policy area. The Stuttgart Declaration of 1983 (following the Genscher/Colombo initiative) even originally intended to include defense matters in European Political Cooperation.[8]

This was refused by the Greek, Danish, and Irish reservations. Consequently, in the Stuttgart Declaration, the security policy cooperation was limited to "political and economic" aspects, thus enlarging the formula of "political" aspects only, first agreed upon in the London Report in 1981. The combined formula was taken up in the Single European Act.[9]

Until 1990, a consensus vote's rule applied in the EPC for all areas of the Community's political cooperation. But the aim is to change the decision-making process from unanimity voting to majority voting.[10] But not all areas can be transferred to a majority vote rule. Member states have special relations with certain parts of the world and geopolitical positions which are firmly anchored in their history. More importantly, the Twelve do not always share the same assessment of their responsibilities or of their general and specific commitments in various parts of the world. Therefore, only a few areas can be transferred to a "common policy."

In other words, efficiency of decision-making depends greatly upon the method used. And the method depends on the scope of foreign policy.[11] The more the areas transferred from the scope of political cooperation to that of a "common policy," the more efficient the EPC will be. Unfortunately it is impossible to know yet what areas will be considered of vital interest and excluded from a "common policy." It is very difficult to compile a list of vital common interest because there are insurmountable difficulties of interpretation.

Assuming nevertheless that at least some areas of common interest can be defined, the Foreign Ministers could take decisions by a qualified majority. This would however be an augmented qualified majority requiring the votes of eight member states.[12] Concretely, EC states would continue to set broad lines of foreign policy (such as aid to frontline Gulf states) by unanimity, but most implementing decisions (such as who pays) would be taken by majority vote.

"Communitization" of the EPC

This means that the Commission would like to get a greater right of initiatives on foreign policy matters.[13] The Commission does not demand any monopoly of right of initiative as in the EEC and ECSC, fully aware of the specificity of foreign policy and the susceptibility of the member states.

It nevertheless wishes to share the right of initiative between the Council presidency, the member states and the Commission. Then the body responsible for preparing decisions could include the present political secretariat (although strengthened) and representatives of the Commission. Furthermore, the Committee of Permanent Representatives (COREPER) would be reorganized so that it could be apprised of foreign policy matters before the Council makes a decision.[14]

As regards implementation of the most important decisions, the essential requirement is that once a common position has been decided on, the Community must speak with one voice.

Inclusion of a Security Dimension in the EC

By April 20, 1990, France and West Germany launched a joint initiative to achieve a European political union.[15] This declaration called for preparatory work on an intergovernmental conference with the aim of defining and putting into effect a common foreign and security policy.[16]

On the French side, the joint initiative came from the conviction that the best response to German unification and the upheavals in Eastern Europe was to press ahead with the development of the European Community.[17] The fundamental French interest was the desire to tie down Germany. French President Mitterrand

was especially annoyed by German Chancellor Kohl's lack of consultation with France both on his ten-point plan for German unity
in November 1989 and by proposals for German monetary union.
Clear indications of Mitterrand's misgivings came in his visit to
Kiev in December 1989 to see Gorbachev, and his earlier trip to
East Berlin and Leipzig. Mitterrand's tactics misfired. Both
visits failed to have any effect on the breakneck pace of German
unity.

Bonn was also at the origin of the initiative in order to head
off Community worries about the effects of German unity. Many
Germans also realized that it would not have been so easy to move
toward unification in the absence of a strong EC to reassure
those who worried about the prospect of unification. Helmut Kohl
was also concerned with proving that German unity was not slowing
down European integration as many had claimed it would. Mr. Kohl
is moreover inspired by the memory of his political mentor Konrad
Adenauer. Chancellor Kohl grants importance to his future role in
the annals of history.

In a security-oriented Community, member states would continue
to keep their autonomy over defense matters and the organization
would maintain some existing structures, such as the Independent
European Programming Group, NATO's Eurogroup, and the Western
European Union (WEU). But a common military strategy and a comprehensive arms procurement policy might be developed in this
body. It could also organize joint training and joint maneuvers.
In the future it could have its own research and development
budget. It might possibly "manage" a European nuclear deterrent.
This would exist as an equal partner with the American one. It
could also develop more military integration "both in terms of
joint forces and specialization of roles."

EC Technological Cooperation

A European Community stronger in technology could lead to less
American political influence. According to the Single European
Act, "The Community's aim shall be to strengthen the scientific
and technological basis of European industry and to ensure it to

become more competitive at international level."[18] As a consequence, there could be less importing of American weaponry and
technology, and therefore less U.S. political influence, if the
Europeans coordinate their programs of high technology, make more
arms together, and protect their own industries through "privileged treatment."[19]

There is a so-called "dual-use" in technology because this
sector has broken down the barriers between defense and commercial policy. For example, it is often difficult to determine
whether a computer chip has a defense or a commercial status.
Attainment of prominence in technology is seen as the chief
ingredient for reaching EC foreign policy goals. The EC Commission has been introduced in sectors that were previously national. Therefore, the United States may lose its influence in
security matters by losing contracts.[20]

The Americans do not like centralized planning in technology.
Many argue that this tradition is reflected in the 1992 program.
In February 1990, the French firm Thomson-CSF and British Aerospace created a joint venture company for research and development of guided weapon systems. This new company will enable them
to pool R&D funds and relevant personnel in an effort to attract
defense contracts. But the SEA does not envisage an "industry
policy." Officially, this policy implies a support to precompeti-
tive research only, which is not always the case of policies
implemented by some of the member states.

The Community rejects the accusation that it is making a
state-directed industrial and trade policy with distorting effects. The EC fund participation in the programs is at a maximum
of 50 percent as a rule. Theoretically, the conditions for participating in EC research programs are clear and non-discriminatory
with respect to Community-based firms with foreign parentage. If
their work is done in the Community, by two or more firms which
are not established in the same member state, and is to be mar-
keted in Europe, they should be treated exactly the same as EC
companies.

Participation by American EC-based firms in EC programs with
U.S. ownership or control is only 1.5 percent. But only 0.18

percent of U.S. publicly funded R&D goes to U.S.-based, but non-U.S. owned or controlled, organizations.[21]

In spring 1990, Science and Technology Commissioner Filippo Pandolfi suggested that the U.S. and the EC cooperate on technology projects in the areas of biotechnology, energy, environmental protection, microelectronics, and information technology, including space stations and ocean exploration.[22]

Certainly, under pressure from Japanese competition, the EC shows more interest in collaboration with the U.S. than the reverse. The U.S. nevertheless accepts EC overtures but seems to be reluctant to put emphasis on the most important sectors. It is interesting to note that the U.S.-EC joint declaration is rather ambiguous in its formulation of the objectives of future cooperation. It says that both partners "should strengthen mutual cooperation in research in medicine, environment protection, pollution prevention, energy, space, high-energy physics, and the safety of nuclear and other installations."[23]

Arms Procurement

In arms procurement, countries might be forced to drop their national preferences, abiding by the same procurement rules that apply to other sectors. The Treaty of Rome excludes public procurements of weapons from the Community's competence (art. 223). The Commission however wishes that defense equipment production and trade will be fully under the discipline of the common market. This quite old claim[24] has been refused by a coalition of "national champions," ministries of defense, NATO, WEU, and IEPG. To be sure, such an evolution of the EC may incite a rivalry in the division of labor between a changing NATO, the WEU, and the EC.

At the EC level, the Commission is pushing a number of directives on public procurement which, if adopted, will encourage less national favoritism in awarding defense contracts.[25] While Article 223 of the Treaty of Rome might render military procurement exempt from such initiatives, the Commission appears to be striving for a narrower interpretation of this provision.[26] Another issue involves EC tariffs on military equipment imported from the U.S., a move that the Commission is considering. In fact there is an EC Commission proposal to limit member states' ability to waive customs duties on defense imports.[27] The proposal asserts a need for tariffs to foster European defense industries that are not yet able to compete on even terms with those of the United States. Duty suspensions are limited to a list of items which, even if expanded, would inevitably omit much.

Mutual duty waivers on defense imports are prescribed under the bilateral, reciprocal procurement Memoranda of Understanding (MOU) that the U.S. has with its allies in the EC. In conformity with these agreements, the Department of Defense (DoD) waives duties on virtually everything it imports from MOU partners, and it expects them to reciprocate. According to the Pentagon, this proposal would have adverse effects on burden-sharing, on procurement cooperation, and on the purchasing power of EC members' defense budgets.

At the Independent European Program Group (IEPG) level, the Group 5 had repeatedly demonstrated a strong preference for a security policy future denominated in Community terms.[28] It was with some dismay, then, that the U.S. greeted the series of IEPG defense technology initiatives that appeared at the end of 1988. Washington fears that the interlinking between EC-1992 and the Independent European Group (IEPG) could strengthen European cooperation in armaments to the detriment of American interests.

It should be remembered that the IEPG, of which thirteen of the fourteen European NATO states and eleven of the twelve EC states are members (except Ireland), has taken some steps to move into this gap that the European Community has not yet filled.[29]

The IEPG aims at building a common market for arms production. Its objective is to improve the competitiveness of European defense industry. The IEPG's objectives are:[30] (1) to build a European armaments market; (2) to remove obstacles restricting border-crossing competition; (3) to place contracts more readily with suppliers in other countries; and (4) to have research activities provide for the fullest possible exploitation of European resources in talents and funds.

Because of very important national interests, IEPG countries will only be prepared to admit border crossing competition if they are sure of getting an equitable and fair return in a suitable time, corresponding to their vital interests and their possibilities. Therefore some kind of "juste retour" has to be arranged.

But IEPG does not work too well because there is nothing compulsory. Decisions taken – although by unanimity –are not compelling because they cannot be put in force. Moreover, the IEPG has never been able to deal with major armament contracts and has therefore never touched fundamental national interests.

U.S. officials criticize the practice of IEPG representatives who attend Conference of National Armaments Directors (CNAD) meetings to determine defense needs and budgetary priorities of member countries, and then utilize that information for the benefit of IEPG efforts at winning contracts. But the United States is not a member of the IEPG, and many Americans believe that it is attempting to take over functions already assigned to a NATO body, the Conference of National Armaments Directors (CNAD).[31] CNAD was formed to pool the resources of all Alliance countries to develop selected joint defense projects.

A Defense Dimension

Most EC governments would prefer to introduce defense into the Community through WEU, a non-EC institution –just as the European Monetary System (EMS), conceived outside the Community womb, has introduced money into the EC. The issues mentioned under the previous point demonstrate the problems of overlapping between a more defense-oriented Community on the one hand, and WEU and NATO on the other hand. In the mind of most EC states, there is a dialectic relationship between the Community and the WEU. For example, the Single European Act, an amendment to the Treaty of Rome, the EC Constitution, reserves a special role to the WEU. The SEA states explicitly that:

> Nothing should . . . impede closer cooperation in the field of security between certain of the High Contracting Parties within the framework of the Western European Union or the Atlantic Alliance.[32]

Moreover, one of the most important WEU documents, the Platform on European Security Interests, adopted by the Council of Ministers in the Hague on October 27, 1987, emphasizes the links between WEU and the EC:

We recall our commitment to build a European Union in accordance with the Single European Act which we all signed as members of the European Community. We are convinced that the construction of an integrated Europe will remain incomplete as long it does not include security and defence. . . . We intend therefore to develop a more cohesive European defence identity which will translate more effectively into practice the obligations of solidarity to which we are all committed through the modified Brussels and North Atlantic Treaties.[33]

In 1987, the WEU declaration was intended to say that under the then – presumed Soviet military superiority, a substantial presence of American nuclear and conventional forces was an irreplaceable part of the defense of Europe. But at the same time the Western European states wanted to recall that a strengthened "European pillar" would make a valuable contribution to the Alliance as a whole.

But the WEU suffers from many handicaps. First, an expanded WEU caucus could jeopardize NATO cohesion by creating three factions: WEU members, the U.S., and those states in NATO Europe but not in the WEU. Second, the WEU lacks inclusiveness. It groups only nine European countries out of more than thirty.

In September 1990, Gianni De Michelis, the Italian foreign minister, made the suggestion that the Community take over the WEU when the latter's Brussels treaty comes up for possible revision in 1998.[34] Since then, there have been numerous plans to merge in way or another the WEU with the EC.

For instance, the Commission recommends "that the Treaty on Political Union incorporate the undertaking contained in Article 5 of the 1948 Brussels Treaty of the WEU which specifies that, in the event of an armed attack against one of the contracting parties, the others are obliged to provide aid and assistance."[35] And the EC inter-governmental conference on political union is supposed to address "the proposals put forward by some Member States on the future of Western European Union."[36]

There are, however, disagreements about how the WEU should fit in with NATO. Broadly speaking, the French, Italians, and, to a lesser extent, the Germans, see it having a transitional role on the way to a genuine European security and defense policy. The United Kingdom, on the other hand, wishes to see the union as a strengthened defense arm of NATO.

For France, the issue is the following: it does not take part in NATO's integrated command, the WEU is interesting because it provides a way to be involved in a post-Cold War European defense structure, still linked to the U.S. but under a European commander.

Therefore, Paris aims at the following mechanism: the European Council (as summits of EC leaders are known) will have the capacity to decide what should be fed into a common EC security policy, but defense ministers and chiefs of staff should continue to meet in the WEU, which itself would draw progressively closer to the Community. The WEU would work on common security policies under the guidance of the European Council.

While Germany has never been keen on the WEU because of its origins (it was set up to control German rearmament), it seems to follow France in its proposals and accept the Paris' plan. Spain, Italy, Belgium, Portugal, Greece, and Luxembourg express broad support for the Franco-German plan. They also go along with French and German ideas on the way the Community should conduct foreign policy. The European Council would decide by unanimity which subjects are ripe for a common foreign policy. The foreign ministers would then decide policy in these areas, voting by majority if the European Council decided they should.

Fearful of weakening NATO, the UK (and Holland)[37] oppose the idea of EC-WEU fusion; a Community that sets up its own defense policy could spell the end of NATO. As analyzed in the next chapter, the Kuwait Crisis has done nothing to diminish Britain's support for NATO and skepticism towards a European defense identity independent of the United States.

But, contrary to a widespread misinterpretation, Britain accepts the idea of "bridges" between the two organizations and the idea of a revitalized WEU.[38] Since the Americans are taking part of their army out of Europe, London is prepared to pay a price and accept some links between the Community and the WEU if France could be brought into European defense and enticed back into full NATO membership. The main condition for the UK is that the WEU should also be a "bridge" to NATO, and that it should not be seen as automatically submissive to the European Council:

> We agree that the construction of an integrated Europe must include security and *defence*. But European defence without the United States does not make sense. . . . A mechanism to ensure co-ordination between common foreign and security policy and NATO will be crucial. The Western European Union is in our view the answer most likely for European co-ordination within the alliance and as the *defence arm of the union*.[39]

But more serious problems exist for the three EC states that do not belong to the WEU: Ireland, Denmark, and Greece. Ireland is deeply wary of any EC defense involvement, as is Denmark where pacific sentiment is strong. They share the UK's concern that foreign policy should remain subject to national veto and they do not want to be members of the WEU. Ireland says that any Community links with the WEU would compromise its neutrality. Denmark fears that any EC defense policy would make it harder for its neutral friends like Sweden to join the Community. Greece's case is different. The conservative government wants to join the WEU but the present members fear that, if Greece got into a scrap with Turkey, they might have to fight.

Other European nations also fear that they will lose out. For instance, Turkey and Norway, both NATO members with borders with the Soviet Union (but not in the EC or in the WEU), have voiced concerns that their interests could be neglected in any new defense arrangements.

Support may rally around the compromise that the Twelve should just write the WEU's mutual defense clause into the EC treaties, and take over the rest of the WEU when that organization's treaty expires in 1998. The Rome Treaty could incorporate the undertaking contained in Article 5 of the 1948 Brussels Treaty on the WEU which specifies that, in the event of an armed attack against one of the contracting parties, the others are obliged to provide aid and assistance. More than that, the new EC Constitution could, in general terms, point the way towards a common security policy, including defense. Security is more than just a matter of military defense, it covers all means of guaranteeing cohesion at the national and Community level and protection of citizens against terrorism and serious crime.

The best strategy would not be to start a rapid build-up of a European army but rather a step-by-step "bottom-up" approach consisting of shaping multinational units that are militarily significant and could be political symbols. Moreover, an operational role for the WEU would preferably grow from some practical activities such as verification and on-the-spot coordination.[40]

But will Ireland and future EC members from EFTA and Eastern Europe accept a security-oriented Community? It might not be a bad idea if the memberships in the EC and WEU remain different. Such a "variable geometry" might be a way of easing neutral countries' entry into the Community: the WEU would be an optional extra to standard membership.

EC Attitude Toward a Partnership with the U.S.

Until 1990, the EC was not ready to go very far in the process of improving its relations with America.[41]

Therefore, on November 23, 1990, when the U.S. pressed the EC to conclude an agreement on U.S.-EC relations, the Community was not yet ready to go further in the direction of the partnership proposed by the U.S. If one looks at the main American proposals, one notices that the EC was obliged to limit U.S. ambitions and to sign only a declaration with a much narrower perspective.

Institutionalization of U.S.-EC Relations

At that stage, the Community could only promise to be resolved to develop and deepen the existing U.S.-EC procedures for consultation so as to reflect its own evolution, namely:[42] bi-annual consultation between the president of the United States and the

president of the European Council and the president of the EC
Commission; bi-annual consultations between the U.S. secretary of
state and the EC foreign ministers, with the Commission; ad hoc
consultations between the U.S. secretary of state and the presidency foreign minister of the Troika; bi-annual consultations
between the U.S. government and the Commission at cabinet level;
briefing by the presidency to U.S. representatives on EPC meetings at the ministerial level.

Common Administration of Regional Conflicts

The Community did not like the American idea of common management of regional conflicts. There is, for instance, no mention of
Latin Americain the November 1990 declaration. Certainly, the
Community has enough problems to solve in Europe without dealing
with Latin America.[43] The EC is nevertheless ready to provide
adequate support, in cooperation with other states and organizations, to the nations of Eastern and Central Europe that are
undertaking economic and political reforms.

Co-Management of the World

The EC agreed to fulfill its responsibility to address transnational challenges. In particular, it will act in the following
fields: combatting and preventing terrorism; putting an end to
the illegal production, trafficking, and consumption of narcotics
and related criminal activities, such as the laundering of money;
and fighting international terrorism.[44] On the question of
terrorism, one should remember that the EC has begun special
cooperation within the 1986 Trevi Group. EC nations have agreed
to cooperate on the identity, movement, and funding of suspected
terrorists. The Trevi Group is generally seen as an important
step forward into the direction of genuine political cooperation.
As a principle of U.S.-EC partnership, the EC and its member
states and the U.S. will bring their positions as close as
possible. In appropriate international bodies, they will seek to
reach closer cooperation, and to strengthen security and economic
cooperation in the framework of the CSCE, and in other fora.

More interestingly, the EC agreed to join its effort with the
U.S. for "preventing the proliferation of nuclear armaments,
chemical and biological weapons, and missile technology."[45]
This is clearly a clue to a possible evolution of the Community
in the direction of more involvement in the political aspects of
security.

***

The U.S.-EC political future will be dictated by strategic
considerations dependent on the constitution (or not) of a
genuine European identity in foreign, security, and defense
policy.

One finds here a paradoxical dilemma.[46] On the one hand, the
United States will certainly continue its withdrawal from Europe
(although maintaining nuclear missiles based on submarines and
some installations in the UK and in Italy). The time should be
ripe for the EC to develop a much more active foreign policy and
expand its security and defense identity because only the Community's member states are now capable of filling the political and
military vacuums in Europe. But, on the other hand, as the
decline of the Soviet threat makes a strong European defense
identity less pressing (although it pushes the debate more toward
the softer areas of security policy), the EPC's credibility is
very much questioned and no consensus is looming on future
relations between the EC, the WEU and NATO.

Without a true challenge, Western European countries will
accommodate to the current situation, i.e., a Community slightly
more integrated politically, but dependent fundamentally on the
U.S. and NATO for its protection. The real test of European
identity in security matters will come with conflicts in Europe
or at its door. Potential sources of conflict are indeed many in
central and eastern Europe. And the Mediterranean basin is far
from being stabilized. If one assumes that important tensions
will erupt there, then the Community will have incentives to
intervene through diplomatic mediation or by sending troops. The

Community might act independently or in collaboration with the United States but it is doubtful that the Americans will be the main intercessor if a conflict erupts in Europe or nearby.

Nobody knows yet if the Community will be capable of speaking and acting with one voice. For instance, will the Germans have the same position as the French in the conflict in Croatia? On the one hand, the Community could profit from a crisis at its border, to realize rapidly its foreign, security, and military integration. But, on the other hand, it might have a reverse effect if a conflict erupts again, for example, in Macedonia, and Greece takes radical measures refused by other EC member states. So much uncertainty makes any forecast impossible, as has been demonstrated by the Kuwait crisis.

Notes

1. For more details on the EC-1992, the internal market, see Chapter 3.

2. European Council, *Conference on Political Union: European Council, Presidency Conclusions,* Rome, 14-15 December 1990 (part 1), SN 424/1/90, pp. 8-9.

3. See Chapter 3.

4. Commission of the European Communities, *Union économique et monétaire* (Brussels-Luxembourg: Office of Official Publications of the European Community, 21 August 1990), SEC(90) 1659 final, pp. 25-32.

5. Ireland has until 1992 to remove its exchange rate controls and Portugal until 1994.

6. In summer 1990, John Major, then the UK Chancellor of the Exchequer, submitted an alternative approach to the Delors plan. He proposed creating a hard ECU, a thirteenth currency, which would compete with other currencies. None of the member states indicated support for Major's proposal. Finally, Britain changed its proposal and John Major, not yet Prime Minister, did not try anymore to torpedo the objective of a single currency. "Softer Stance on Hard Ecu," *Financial Times,* 9 January 1991.

7. David Allen, Reinhardt Rummel and Wolfgang Wessels (eds.), *European Political Cooperation. Towards a Foreign Policy for Western Europe* (London: Butterworth, 1982); 184 p.

De Schoutheete, Philippe. *La coopération politique européenne.* (Brussels/Luxembourg: Labor/Office des publications officielles des Communautés européennes, 1990); 260 p.

Roy H. Ginsberg, *Foreign Policy Actions of the European Community: The Politics of Scale* (Boulder: Lynne Riener, 1989); XIII-203 p.

8. Jean De Ruyt, *L'Acte unique européen* (Brussels: Université de Bruxelles, 1987), pp. 47-65.

9. Commission of the European Communities, "Single European Act," *Bulletin of the European Communities,* Supplement 2/86, article 30 (6a), p. 18.

10. European Council, *Conference on Political Union,* p. 6.

11. "La lettre commune de MM. Kohl et Mitterrand," *Le Monde,* 9-10 December 1990.

12. Commission of the European Communities, *Commission Opinion of 21 October 1990 on the Proposal for Amendment of the Treaty Establishing the European Economic Community with a View to Political Union* (Luxembourg: Documents, COM(90) 600 final), p. 6.

13. Ibid., p. 5.

14. European Council, *Conference on Political Union,* p. 6.

15. "Time for a New Constitution," *The Economist,* 7 July 1990.

16. "Gymnich-Type Parknasilla Meeting/Political Union/EMU: the Foreign Minister Start this Weekend in Ireland the Reflection Requested by the European Council," *Europe,* 19 May 1990.

17. Stanley Hoffmann, "La France dans le nouvel ordre européen," *Politique étrangère* (Fall 1990), pp. 507-508.

18. Commission of the European Communities, *Single European Act,* title VI, article 130 F, p. 14.

19. Glenn J. McLoughlin, "EC 1992: Science and Technology Cooperation," in Glennon J. Harrison (ed.), *European Community: Issues Raised by 1992 Integration* (Washington, D.C.: Congressional Research Service Report, 1989), p. 96.

20. Joseph C. Rallo, "Alliance Security Policy After 1992," *Hearing on Europe 1992 and its Effects on U.S. Science, Technology and Competitiveness* (Washington, D.C.: House of Representatives, Committee on Science, Space, and Technology, 16 May 1989), pp. 70-71.

21. Filippo Maria Pandolfi, *Science and Technology and European Market Integration* (Washington, D.C.: U.S. National Academy of Sciences Forum), 5 March 1990, p. 12.

22. Ibid, pp. 13-20.

23. "Declaration on U.S.-EC Relations," *Daily Bulletin,* (Geneva: U.S. Mission, 23 November 1990), EUR503, p. 5. See the whole text in the appendix, Document 4.

24. Commission of the European Communities, *Proposal for a Council Regulation Temporarily Suspending Import Duties on Certain Weapons and Military Equipment* (Brussels: 15 September 1988, COM (88) 502 final); 16 p.

25. Commission of the European Communities, "Commission Opinion of 21 October 1990 on the Political Union," p. 5.

26. Ibid., p. 5.

27. Simon Webb, *NATO and 1992: Defence Acquisition and Free Markets* (Santa Monica: Rand Corp., July 1989), p. 87.

28. Joseph Rallo, "Alliance Security Policy After 1992," p. 16.

29. M. Wilkinson, *Rapport sur le Groupe européen indépendant de programmes (GEIP) et l'Union de l'Europe occidentale* (Paris: Assemblée de l'Union de l'Europe occidentale), 25 May 1990; 21 p.

30. Independent European Programme Group, *European Armaments Market Action Plan,* 13 July 1988, IEPG/III-D/36; 6 p. (not published).

31. Paul E. Gallis, "U.S.-West European Affairs: Responding to a Changing Relationship," *Congressional Research Service Issue Brief,* Updated 9 November 1990, p. 9.

32. Article 60, paragraph 6 c). of the SEA.

33. Western European Union, *Platform on European Security Interests,* The Hague, 27 October 1987.

34. David Buchan, "Italian Foreign Minister Proposes Military

Dimension for EC," *Financial Times,* 19 September 1990.

35. Commission of the European Communities, *Commission Opinion of 21 October 1990 on the Proposal for Amendment of the Treaty Establishing the European Economic Community with a View to Political Union* (Luxembourg: Documents, COM(90) 600 final), pp. 4-5.

36. European Council, *Conference on Political Union: European Council, Presidency Conclusions,* (part 1), SN 424/1/90; p. 6. See the whole text in the appendix, Document 5.

37. The Dutch, however, favour majority voting in the EC decision-making process in foreign affairs.

38. Douglas Hurd, "No European Defence Identity Without Nato," *Financial Times,* 15 April 1991.

39. Ibid. (My emphasis).

40. See the proposals by the Secretary General of the Western European Union, Willem Van Eekelen, "The WEU: Europe's Best Defense," *European Affairs,* Vol. 4, 1990, pp. 8-11.

41. Robert J. Guttman, "E.C. Outlook: E.C. Commissioner Frans Andriessen," *Europe,* April 1990.

42. "Declaration on U.S.-EC Relations," p. 6. See also appendix Document 4.

43. Lionel Barber, "Washington sees dual role for EC in Latin America," *Financial Times,* 25 April 1990.

44. "Declaration on U.S.-EC Relations," pp. 5-6. See also Document 4.

45. Ibid., p. 6.

46. Helen Wallace, "Political Reform in the European Community," *The World Today* (January 1991), p. 2.

CHAPTER 14

THE KUWAIT CRISIS

Through the Kuwait crisis the EC member States have had to face a severe test of their political cohesion and will to continue with the process of unification. Ironically, the reactions of the West European countries during the first months of the crisis were generally considered to be an historical success: the actions of both the Community and the West European Union (WEU) were rather impressive in regard to their previous achievements and augured further progress.

Preparation of the War and European Integration

There was a great deal of unity in the Community's initial political response to the crisis. It had a relatively coherent attitude in the weeks following Iraq's invasion of Kuwait. The Community fully backed the UN Security Council's resolutions calling upon Iraq to withdraw its troops from Kuwait, with most West European countries involved in the embargo effort in some way or other.

As early as August 2, 1990, the Community and its member states condemned the Iraqi invasion of Kuwait.[1] On August 4, 1990, the EPC adopted a resolution calling for an immediate and unconditional withdrawal of Iraqi forces from Kuwait and decided to introduce an embargo against Baghdad.[2] On August 6, the Council of the European Communities adopted other measures in order to put a total embargo against Iraq and occupied Kuwait. Never in the past had the EC reacted so promptly and cohesively.[3] On August 21, the Community developed a policy of solidarity vis-à-vis its citizens held as hostages by Baghdad. The EC adopted a symbolic declaration:

> Any attempt to injure or threaten the security of any citizen of the European Community will be considered as an offensive act against the Community and all its member States and will provoke a unanimous response from the whole Community.[4]

One can find in this sentence the first draft of the text adopted by the European Community intergovernmental conference on December 15, 1990, which for the first time put forth formally the idea of "a commitment by Member States to provide *mutual assistance* ."[5]

Moreover, on August 21, at a WEU meeting, West European governments gave the go-ahead signal to one of the most important operations ever launched by a common European body. Their ministers clearly intended that the principle of European coordination should go much further than mine-sweeping in the Gulf under a loose WEU umbrella as was done in 1987-88.[6] It was agreed that cooperation would cover overall operational concepts and specific guidelines for coordination among forces in the region, including areas of operation, sharing of tasks, logistical support, and exchange of intelligence.[7] Belgium and Italy sent warships to the Gulf to enforce the embargo. Spain and Greece (a non-member) contributed for the first time to European efforts by dispatching a naval force. Moreover, Denmark and Turkey also took part in the WEU meeting as observers and agreed to its conclusions.

More important, this relaunching of the WEU was made in close collaboration with the European Community. It was the French government's idea to underline the close links between the organization's security interests and the broader process of European integration by inviting all twelve members of the European Community to attend the WEU's meeting, even though only nine are members of the WEU. Immediately following the WEU meeting, the twelve foreign ministers of the EC held a separate meeting to discuss and coordinate the European response to Iraq's restraints on Westerners in Iraq and Kuwait. This EC session was held in order to stress symbolically the continuity of the Community's integration process.

The two meetings, in promoting a kind of osmosis between the EC and WEU, were seen at that time not only by many Europeans –but also by American observers – as a turning-point in the history of European integration toward the establishment of a defense and security role for the Community.[8]

Gianni de Michelis, at that time President of the European Council of Ministers, did his best to present the experience of the Kuwait crisis as a harbinger of a common security and defense policy among EC governments. A merger of Community political cooperation and the WEU seemed to be attainable on the condition of including special provisions to enable a neutral country such as Ireland to "opt out" of the military aspects of EC policy-making. This fall 1990 the preparation of the war seemed indeed to give an important extra push to the process of European integration. European political unification was, of course, accelerated by German unification, but the Kuwait crisis acted "as if a turbo-charger had been switched on."[9] The period of crisis, without military involvement of the Coalition, contributed a lot to the proposals of the December 1990 Rome inter-governmental conference.[10]

The crisis of Kuwait seemed to have provided a possible scheme for the political integration of Europe, around concentric circles. In the first circle, WEU members would stress military aspects. In the second circle, EC States who are not members of the WEU would be consulted in a very narrow way. In the third circle are countries like Turkey, Norway, or Austria, which would be added according to circumstances. Finally, other EFTA neutral countries, as well as Hungary, Poland, and the Federal Republic of the Czechs and the Slovaks, would be regularly informed.

Negative Impacts of the Kuwait Crisis

The twelve members of the European Community, it is true, all subscribed to the resolutions calling upon Iraq to withdraw from Kuwait and to impose a trade embargo on Iraq. Yet there has been a considerable disparity in the extent to which individual European countries have committed themselves to the different problems of the crisis. They went their separate ways, not only as far as the size and nature of the contributions they have made to the anti-Iraq coalition's military effort but also in their political commitment to the use of their forces to dislodge Saddam Hussein from Kuwait. For instance, until January 1991, the French, positioned on Kuwait's western flank, were solely under national command, although the British, in contrast, were directly integrated with the U.S. First Marine Expeditionary Force on the Gulf coast.

Things started to come apart at a meeting of foreign ministers in Luxembourg on January 4, 1991, when it seemed that U.S. Secretary of State James Baker and Iraqi Foreign Minister Tariq Aziz would never meet. France wanted EC foreign ministers to talk to Mr. Aziz anyway. It also wished to offer Iraq "linkage" between withdrawal from Kuwait and a general Middle East peace conference, meaning an international attempt to settle the Israeli-Palestinian issue.

Britain and Holland vetoed both ideas. At one point the Dutch minister, Hans Van den Broek, argued so vigorously against acting independently of the Americans that Roland Dumas, the French minister, said: "If the EC had majority voting on foreign policy you would be outvetoed."[11] Douglas Hurd, Britain's foreign secretary, replied coldly: "That is exactly why Britain wants to maintain unanimity."[12] In other words, for the UK, the EC should not try to mask disagreements by changing procedure.

On January 14, when the EC foreign ministers decided (minus French Foreign Minister Roland Dumas, who did not turn up) that further EC steps would be pointless, France made its final offer in the Security Council. Several EC countries backed the plan, but Iraq showed no interest in it, and Britain and America opposed linkage between the withdrawal from Kuwait and the Palestinian problem, so it died just before the deadline. Yet President Mitterrand's maneuvering upset London. The new British prime minister, John Major, lunched with President Mitterrand a few hours before the French plan was unveiled, but heard nothing of it.

British Prime Minister John Major made clear on January 22 that the European Community's response to the Kuwait crisis cast doubts on its goal of political union. He told the House of Commons:

> Political union and a common foreign and security policy in Europe would have to go beyond statements and extend to action. Clearly, Europe is not ready for that and we should not be too ambitious when it comes to the inter-governmental conference on political union.[13]

Assessment

Two different sets of conclusions have been drawn. The first is that the crisis has underlined the urgency for moving toward the realization of European political union. It illustrated not the impossibility, but the need to develop an agreed-upon defense and foreign policy. Many believed that if the EC had been fully responsible for its own security policy, it would have been more effective in pursuing a strategy for avoiding war.

The alternative view prevailed, however, as most observers admitted that Europe, in general, and the Community, in particular, cut a sorry and ineffectual figure during the crisis in several ways. The rift between Britain and France especially was seen as further evidence that twelve countries with different historical backgrounds and interests can never agree on a common foreign policy. Attitudes to the Gulf crisis seemed to prove that no member countries would be prepared to abandon decision-making by consensus in the foreign policy field. This analysis has been expressed particularly in Britain, but was heard elsewhere, notably from people who argued that when push comes to shove the only superpower that matters is America. They argued that the EC should – more than ever – give priority to preserving the Atlantic Alliance under American leadership.

Impact on the American View of a United Europe

The Kuwait crisis also had an impact on the American view of a politically united Europe. First, this war changed Americans' self-perception of their position in the world. To be sure, even if the United States had not been contested in its number one leadership position, it would have opposed Saddam Hussein's policy militarily. Although Washington did not organize the war against Iraq in order to reestablish its hegemony – as if George Bush dispatched troops in the Gulf in order to prove that Joseph Nye[14] was right in his argument against Paul Kennedy[15] – it is true that the "declinist" mood which prevailed in the United States in the first half of 1990 constituted a fertile field for an operation that could demonstrate that America was still number one.

For the United States, moreover, the Europeans bore a large responsibility for selling so many sophisticated and non-conventional weapons to Saddam Hussein. The Europeans behaved like novices in Iraq and they have to learn that they cannot act without America. Their defense has a price and they have to pay for their past mistakes by financing the American intervention. One should not, however, overstress the impact of the Kuwait crisis. It has been more a mirror of underlying forces than the cause of them. Britain has always been reluctant to join any true political union. France has followed its own way since de Gaulle. America has criticized the Common Agriculture Policy since the late 1950s. The Gulf crisis added nothing new. The Community was neither more nor less politically united after than before the Iraqi invasion. This crisis did not stop the inter-governmental conference on political union from discussing the future shape of western Europe's alliances and defense mechanisms, and did not hinder seeking maximum political understanding of approaching foreign policy questions as they arise.

The Kuwait crisis had another impact on U.S.-West European relations: accelerating the American withdrawal from Western Europe. As a matter of fact, the U.S. removed an enormous military capability from Europe – and, hence, out of NATO –for use in the war against Iraq. In 1991, many NATO and EC governments believed that these forces either would be kept in the Gulf as part of an attempt to create a local security structure or would be returned directly to America. This put the long-term future of NATO even more into question and obliged European members of

NATO – through the WEU – to provide the main prop for the remainder of the Atlantic Alliance. This vacuum pushed the European Community to provide for a stronger long-term security structure and to assume a greater share of its own defense burden.

***

Paradoxically, experts on the Community – generally "Euro-optimists" – drew pessimistic conclusions from the Kuwait crisis. But specialists of NATO – usually "Euro-sceptics" – discerned the necessity of strengthening the European pillar of NATO. As a matter of fact, for the former, the Kuwait crisis led them to the conclusion that there won't be any rush toward the development of a genuine European identity in political, security, and defense matters.

In contrast, for the experts on NATO, ironically, this crisis has been seen as another demonstration of the Atlantic Alliance's weakness, and the need for creating a true European defense capable of sharing burden and responsibilities with America.

Notes

1. "Déclaration des Douze sur l'invasion du Koweit par l'Irak, Brussels, 2 August, 1990," in Assemblée de l'union de l'Europe occidentale, "La sécurité de l'Europe et les événements survenus au Proche et au Moyen-Orient: la crise du Koweit," *Report by Mr Pieralli*, Paris, 36th session (2nd part), document 1242, 20 September 1990, annex III, p. 26. (Translated from French.)

2. "Déclaration des Douze sur l'invasion du Koweit par l'Irak, Brussels, 4 August, 1990," Ibid., annex III, p. 26. (Translated from French.)

3. Claude Berger, "Crise du Golfe, embargo et après-crise," *Revue du Marché Commun*, no 341 (November 1990), pp. 615-620.

4. "Déclaration des Douze sur la situation des ressortissants étrangers en Irak et au Koweit. (Réunion ministérielle extraordinaire de la CPE), Paris, 21st August, 1990," in Assemblée de l'union de l'Europe occidentale, "La sécurité de l'Europe et les événements survenus au Proche et au Moyen-Orient: la crise du Koweit," *Report by Mr Pieralli*, Paris, 36th session, (2nd part), document 1242, 20 September 1990, p. 28. (Translated from French.)

5. European Council, Rome, 14 and 15 December 1990, *Presidency Conclusions*, SN 424/1/90. See also in appendix, Document 5. (My emphasis).

6. Assemblée de l'Union de l'Europe occidentale, "La sécurité de l'Europe et la crise du Golfe," *Report by Mr De Decker*, Paris, 36th session (2nd part), document 1244, 14 November 1990, pp. 9-10.

7. Assemblée de l'Union de l'Europe occidentale, "Les conséquences de l'invasion du Koweit: les opérations dans le Golfe," *Report by Mr De Hoop Scheffer*, Paris, 36th session (2nd part), document 1243, 20 September 1990, pp. 7-12.

8. For instance, Ian Mather wrote in the *European:* "Last week may be seen by historians as the moment the EC first moved towards acquiring a common defence policy." Ian Mather, "Let's not Kill off Nato Just Yet," *The European*, 19-21 October 1990.

In the same vein, Ian Davidson added in the *Financial Times:* "For the moment we only know that a war in the Gulf would be deeply damaging for the Atlantic Alliance." Ian Davidson, "High Risks for the Western Alliance in a Gulf Conflict," *Financial Times*, 13 September 1990.

On the *French side*, see Marie-Pierre Subtil, "L'UEO et les Douze réunis à Paris. Les pays européens commencent à faire bloc," *Le Monde*, 24 August 1990.

On the *American side*, see the State Department Deputy Spokesman Richard Boucher, *U.S. News* (American Mission to Geneva)

"Declaration on U.S.-EC Relations Agreed Upon," EUR503, 23 November 1990, p. 3.

And the American Ambassador to the EC, Thomas Niles, "A Word from Ambassador Niles," *Letter from Brussels,* Volume 3, No. 4, (25 October 1990), p. 1.

9. Ian Davidson, "The Gulf Prods EC Unity," *Financial Times,* 15-17 October 1990.

10. European Council, Rome, 14 and 15 December 1990, *Presidency Conclusions,* SN 424/1/90. See also appendix, Document 5.

11. "A Light is Dimmed," *The Economist,* 19 January 1990, p. 38.

12. Ibid., p. 18.

13. Ivo Dawnay, "Major Skeptical of United EC Goal," *Financial Times,* 23 January 1991.

14. Joseph Nye, *Bound to Lead: the Changing Nature of American Power* (New York: Basic Books, 1990); XII-307 p.

15. Paul Kennedy, *The Rise and Fall of the Great Powers: Economic Change and Military Conflict from 1500 to 2000* (New York, Random House, 1987, XXV-667 p.

16. David Buchan, "Common EC Defence Policy Vital, Says NATO Chief," *Financial Times,* 25 January 1991.

See also *Transcript of the Secretary General's Address to the Centre for European Policy Studies,* Brussels, 24 January 1991, pp. 3-4. (Not published.)

CONCLUSION

This study questions some myths associated with the economic as well as the political aspects of U.S.-EC relations. At the *economic level,* the two main issues are EC-1992 and the Uruguay Round negotiations. First, EC-1992 is no longer equated by the Americans with a "Fortress Europe." On the contrary, the American business community, as well as the Bush administration, supports EC-1992 because it offers the following advantages: (1) a contribution to free-trade, (2) expanded market opportunity, (3) increased economic growth, (4) added economic and monetary stability in the world, (5) a magnet for developing and stabilizing Eastern Europe, (6) and a partner to maintain order in the world.

There are, nevertheless, some grievances against the EC, but they concern relatively minor issues. On the issue of standards, the problem is the following: European committees for standardization could adopt standards which are not used in the U.S. or at an international level. This could put some American firms outside the European market. On tests and certifications, there is American anxiety over the future of existing bilateral agreements; tests required in the EC but not in the U.S.; extension of the principle of mutual recognition to American products; and conformity of American laboratories to proceed to certification.

In the public procurement area, the Community's directive on the so-called excluded sectors has also raised U.S. concerns. It contains a "Buy European" clause authorizing the EC to reject proposals which contain less than 50 percent Community content and which proposes preference of price of 3 percent for all Community companies. As to the rules of origin requirements, local content rules, and quantitative restrictions, the U.S.

209

dislikes the fact that the Community sometimes uses anti-dumping measures to tax or ban foreign products. According to Washington, the EC exercises too much pressure on some foreign countries to limit their exports (VERs), especially on semiconductors and automobiles.

The impasse of Uruguay Round talks represents a major blow for U.S.-EC relations. We do not share, nevertheless, a widespread American interpretation that the internal market process has necessitated numerous internal compromises, leaving little room for agreements with America. The EC-1992 program does not hinder the GATT negotiations for the following reasons: (1) the philosophy of the European Community is liberal in nature. For example, the internal market with strong rules of competition constitutes a serious barrier against protectionism. (2) Success of the Commission in its action gives it more authority to negotiate at an international level. Numerous directives have been adopted in sectors where the Commission could not act previously due to a lack of domestic consensus (intellectual property, public procurements, services). (3) Pro free-trade European lobbies have been strengthened by the success of EC-1992. They want to achieve at an international level the same objectives that they got at the level of the Community. (4) The whole logic of the Community's integration beyond 1992 (projects of monetary, economic, and political union) pushes the Twelve to make more concessions to their foreign partners.

The relatively positive impact of EC-1992 on the Uruguay Round negotiations should not of course lead to any underestimation of the seriousness of the deadlock. It is very difficult to imagine any positive outcome of the Uruguay Round negotiations in the near future. Even if a general agreement emerges, it will have to receive the blessing of more than a hundred parliaments. In the EC as well as in the U.S., such ratifications are far from being sure. There is a convergence of parliamentary opposition in America as well as in the Community that is strongly motivated to block any substantial agreement within the GATT framework.

Ironically, however, setbacks in the Uruguay Round negotiations could strengthen – after a period of serious U.S.-EC tension – the commercial and economic relations between the U.S. and the

EC. Convergence of economic, political, and bureaucratic developments of both blocs makes it possible for the creation of a "U.S.-EC Economic Area." This necessitates of course further reflection on which issues could be included in such an "area." Is it possible to establish a common decision-making mechanism? What kind of jurisdictional body will be set up?

The Community could be, indeed, the locomotive for the market integration of industrialized countries. The Community's bureaucracy, as it dictates the trading rules for the Twelve, EFTA, and other European countries, could prescribe the rules of the new world trading game. The EC is characterized by an efficient bureaucratic leadership, something less developed in America. Not only might Western Europe's economic growth replace American economic leadership, it could also be writing the rules of the new international economic order, as it is already doing in financial services. Whatever rules the EC puts forward, the U.S. and other trading partners will have to be able to cope with them.

At a *political-strategic* level, contrary to a common misinterpretation in Europe, the Bush administration, like its predecessors, manifests a lot of sympathy for the European integration idea. It wants a strong relation with the EC which would compel the Community to collaborate with the U.S. in almost all areas. The EC member states agree with this overall objective. To play again a role at a world level is not without its own attraction for mostly former colonialist countries. They also know that if the most wealthy countries do not exercise their political and military responsibilities, instability provoked by poverty will touch them.

Official American support for the Community has to do with the following reasons. First, the Americans like the idea of an institution whose final objective is to create the "United States of Europe." Second, no U.S. government can be indifferent to the strategic interest of European integration. The EC contributed greatly to eliminating tension between France and Germany and is still useful in anchoring Germany to the West. It has also strengthened the European pillar of NATO against the Soviet Union, and promoted free trade and international prosperity.

Despite its pro-European rhetoric, however, the Bush administration contributes in practice to the difficulties of European construction. This seems a repetition of the past. The strategic concept of the Atlantic Alliance – as defined by the U.S. – still causes setbacks to European integration. This already occurred in the early sixties when the American doctrine of centralized nuclear deterrence contributed to General de Gaulle's refusal of the UK membership in the EC. Other examples have been mentioned dealing with the 1973 Israel-Arab conflict, the Siberian pipeline issue, and more recently, the Kuwait crisis. Interestingly, one can observe at the beginning of each decade the same kind of contradiction between European aspirations toward integration and the setbacks caused by American leadership in defense matters.

In the Kuwait crisis, it is once again American logic which created crisis within the Community. EC member states defended very different positions, from the most pro-American posture (UK) to a very neutral one (Ireland). As a result, the EC has been judged by the American government as too inefficient to be respected, while the Community was rejected by the Iraqi government for being too much aligned with America.

This observation does not mean that any prospect of European integration in foreign, security, and defense policies is definitely out. Progress in the negotiations within the inter-governmental conference on political union is auspicious. There is a fair amount of probability that a progressive European integration might occur in areas such as the opening of public armaments procurements and security cooperation.

In foreign affairs, progress in the direction of a decision-making mechanism by consensus (instead of unanimity) seems to be a realistic option. Moreover, internal EC reforms will certainly occur on the following issues: democratic deficit, notion of *subsidiarity,* more efficiency of the executive, and "communitization" of the *Schengen agreement* .

Finally, the EC internal market will be completed by the *horizon 1992* despite some difficulties in matters such as indirect fiscal policy and abolition of physical barriers. The monetary union's project is also well managed although a single currency (not only common) won't be introduced before the end of this century.

There is indeed no sign that the Community might fail and be dismembered. Never in the past did the EC member states (UK included) go so far in the direction of an economic, political, and security dimension for the Community. Compared to the declarations of 1973, one can easily measure the distance covered within the last twenty years. Although there is no setback in the European integration process, it is true that the UK and almost all EC states are still convinced that American support is necessary for their defense.

Predictable regional insecurity at the doors of Western Europe might be the decisive test for judging the real capacity of the European Community to be more than an economic giant. To be sure, such a challenge might also lead to the Community's paralysis if the member states have too divergent interests. If the Community, however, demonstrates a capacity to intervene in coordination with the WEU and NATO, then a U.S.-EC partnership could take shape.

APPENDIXES

DOCUMENTS ON U.S.-EC RELATIONS

SECRETARY OF STATE JOHN FOSTER DULLES
AND THE EUROPEAN COMMUNITY

In January 1956, John Foster Dulles summed up in a secret document what are the European Community's main advantages for the U.S.:

"a. Problem of tying Germany organically into Western Community so as to diminish danger that over time a resurgent German nationalism might trade neutrality for reunification with view seizing controlling position between East and West.

   b. The weakness of France and need to provide positive alternative to neutralism and "defeatism" in that country.

   c. The solidifying of new relationship between France and Germany which has been developing since 1950 through integration movement.

Six-country supranational Euratom would be a powerful means of binding Germany to West and may be most feasible means for achieving effective control over weapons-quality material. If genuinely supranational, Euratom program would be compatible with national cooperation in OEEC.

United States does *not attach to common market proposals same immediate security and political significance* as we do to Euratom. However we believe that a common market which results in a general reduction of international trade barriers could contribute constructively to European integration."

Source: "Telegram from the Secretary of State to the Embassy in
           Belgium", *Foreign Relations of the United States 1955-
           1957,* Volume IV, January 1956, pp. 399-400.
           (Emphasis, R.S.)

JOHN F. KENNEDY:
DECLARATION OF INTERDEPENDENCE
ON AN ATLANTIC PARTNERSHIP

"The nations of Western Europe, long divided by feuds far more bitter than any which existed among the 13 colonies, are today joining together, seeking, as our forefathers sought, to find freedom in diversity and in unity, strength.

The United States looks on this vast new enterprise with hope and admiration. *We do not regard a strong and united Europe as a rival but as a partner.* To aid its progress has been the basic object of our foreign policy for 17 years. We believe that a united Europe will be capable of playing a greater role in the common defense, of responding more generously to the needs of poorer nations, of joining with the United States and others in lowering trade barriers, resolving problems of commerce, commodities, and currency, and developing coordinated policies in all economic, political, and diplomatic areas. We see in such a Europe a partner with whom we can deal on a basis of full equality in all the great and burdensome tasks of building and defending a community of free nations. . . .

Building the *Atlantic partnership* now will not be easily or cheaply finished. But I will say here and now, on this Day of Independence, that the United States will be ready for a *Declaration of Interdependence,* that we will be prepared to discuss with a united Europe the ways and means of forming a *concrete Atlantic partnership,* a mutually beneficial partnership between the new union now emerging in Europe and the old American Union founded here 175 years ago. . . .

Acting on our own, by ourselves, we cannot establish justice throughout the world; we cannot insure its domestic tranquility, or provide for its common defense, or promote its general welfare, or secure the blessings of liberty to ourselves and our posterity. But joined with other free nations, we can do all this and more. We can assist the developing nations to throw off the yoke of poverty. We can balance our worldwide trade and payments at the highest possible level of growth. We can mount a deterrent powerful enough to deter any aggression. And ultimately we can help to achieve a world of law and free choice, banishing the world of war and coercion."

Source: "Address at Independence Hall, Philadelphia, July 4, 1962", *Public Papers of the Presidents of the United States, John Kennedy.* Washington, D.C., U.S. Government Printing Office, PUB 18, 1962; [278], pp. 538-539.

(Emphasis, R.S.)

RICHARD NIXON AND HENRY KISSINGER
ON PARTNERSHIP WITH WESTERN EUROPE

"Now, America and Europe are challenged to forge a more mature and viable partnership in which we cooperate:
- in developing a new and more equitable international economic system that enables the Europeans to reinforce their unity, yet provides equitable terms for the United States to compete in world markets;
- in providing a strong defense with the forces necessary to carry out a realistic strategy in light of the nuclear balance of the 1970's while meeting our mutual defense commitments with an equitable sharing of the burdens;
- in building a common framework for diplomacy to deal with fundamental security issues – such as mutual and balanced force reductions – in the new international environment, reconciling the requirements of unity with those of national interest....

Atlantic Partnership and European Unity

Throughout the postwar period, the United States has supported the concept of a unified Western Europe. We recognized that such a Europe might be more difficult to deal with, but we foresaw manifold advantages. Unity would replace the devastating nationalist rivalries of the past. It would strengthen Europe's economic recovery and expand Europe's potential contributions to the free world. We believed that ultimately a *highly cohesive Western Europe would relieve the United States of many burdens.* We expected that unity would not be limited to economic integration, but would include significant political dimension. We assumed, perhaps too uncritically, that our basic interests would be assured by our long history of cooperation, by our common cultures and our political similarities. . . .

The Europeans have thus been pursuing *economic regionalism;* but they want to preserve American protection in defense and an undiminished American political commitment. This raises a fundamental question: can the principle of Atlantic unity in defense and security be reconciled with the European Community's increasingly regional economic policies?"

Source: "Fourth Annual Report to the Congress on United States Foreign Policy, May 3, 1973", *Public Papers of the Presidents, Richard Nixon.* Washington, D.C., United States Government Printing Office, PUB 29, 1973, [141], pp. 402-405. (Emphasis, R.S.)

DECLARATION ON U.S.-EC RELATIONS,
23 NOVEMBER 1990

"The United States of America on one side, and, on the other, the European Community and its member States,

- mindful of their common heritage and of their close historical, political, economic and cultural ties,
- guided by their faith in the values of human dignity, intellectual freedom and civil liberties, and in the democratic institutions which have evolved on both sides of the Atlantic over the centuries,
- recognizing that the transatlantic solidarity has been essential for the preservation of peace and freedom and for the development of free and prosperous economies as well as for the recent developments which have restored unity in Europe,
- determined to help consolidate the new Europe, undivided and democratic,
- resolved to strengthen security, economic cooperation and human rights in Europe in the framework of the CSCE, and in other fora,
- noting the firm commitment of the United States and the EC member States concerned to the North Atlantic Alliance and to its principles and purposes,
- acting on the basis of a pattern of cooperation proven over many decades, and convinced that by strengthening and expanding this partnership on an equal footing they will greatly contribute to continued stability, as well as to political and economic progress in Europe and in the world,
- aware of their shared responsibility, not only to further common interests but also to face transnational challenges affecting the well-being of all mankind,

- bearing in mind the accelerating process by which the European Community is acquiring its own identity in economic and monetary matters, in foreign policy and in the domain of security,
- determined to further strengthen transatlantic solidarity through the variety of their international relations,

have decided to endow their relationship with long-term perspectives.

Common goals

The United States of America and the European Community and its member States solemnly reaffirm their determination further to strengthen their partnership in order to:
- support democracy, the rule of law and respect of human rights and individual liberty, and promote prosperity and social progress world-wide;
- safeguard peace and promote international security, by cooperating with other nations against aggression and coercion, by contributing to the settlement of conflicts in the world and by by reinforcing the role of the United Nations and other international organizations;
- pursue policies aimed at achieving a sound world economy marked by sustained economic growth with low inflation, a high level of employment, equitable social conditions, in a framework of international stability:
- promote market principles, reject protectionism and expand, strengthen and further open the multilateral trading system;
- carry out their resolve to help developing countries by all appropriate means in their efforts towards political and economic reforms;
- provide adequate support, in cooperation with other states and organizations, to the nations of Eastern and Central Europe undertaking economic and political reforms and encourage their participation in the multilateral institutions of international trade and finance.

Principles of U.S.-EC partnership

To achieve their common goals, the European Community and its member States and the United States of America will inform and consult each other on important matters of common interest, both political and economic, with a view to bringing their positions as close as possible, without prejudice to their respective independence. In appropriate international bodies, in particular, they will seek close cooperation.

The U.S.-EC partnership will, moreover, greatly benefit from the mutual knowledge and understanding acquired through regular consultations as described in this declaration.

Economic cooperation

Both sides recognize the importance of strengthening the multilateral trading system. They will support further steps towards liberalization, transparency,and the implementation of GATT and OECD principles concerning both trade in goods and services and investment.

They will further develop their dialogue, which is already underway, on other matters such as technical and non-tariff barriers to industrial and agricultural trade, services, competition policy, transportation policy, standards, telecommunications, high technology and other relevant areas.

Education, scientific and cultural cooperation

The partnership between the European Community and its member States on the one hand, and the United States on the other, will be based on continuous efforts to strengthen mutual cooperation in various other fields which directly affect the present and future well-being of their citizens, such as exchanges and joint projects in science and technology, including, inter alia, research in medicine, environment protection, pollution prevention, energy, space, high-energy physics, and the safety of nuclear and other installations, as well as in education and culture, including academic and youth exchanges.

- bi-annual consultations between the European Community Foreign Ministers, with the Commission, and the U.S. Secretary of State, alternately on either side of the Atlantic:
- ad hoc consultations between the Presidency Foreign Minister or the Troika and the U.S. Secretary of State;
- bi-annual consultations between the Commission and the U.S. Government at Cabinet level;
- briefings, as currently exist, by the Presidency to U.S. Representatives on European Political Cooperation (EPC) meetings at the Ministerial level.

Both sides are resolved to develop and deepen these procedures for consultation so as to reflect the evolution of the European Community and of its relationship with the United States.

They welcome the actions taken by the European Parliament and the Congress of the United States in order to improve their dialogue and thereby bring closer together the peoples on both sides of the Atlantic.

Trans-national challenges

The United States of America and the European Community and its member States will fulfil their responsibility to address trans-national challenges, in the the interest of their own peoples and of the rest of the world. In particular, they will join their efforts in the following fields:
- combatting and preventing terrorism;
- putting and end to the illegal production, trafficking and consumption of narcotics and related criminal activities, such as the laundering of money;
- cooperating in the fight against international crime;
- protecting the environment, both internationally and domestically, by integrating environmental and economic goals;

- preventing the proliferation of nuclear armaments, chemical and biological weapons, and missile technology.

Institutional framework for consultation

Both sides agree that a framework is required for regular and intensive consultation. They will make full use of and further strengthen existing procedures, including those established by the President of the European Council and the President of the United States on 27th February 1990, namely:
- bi-annual consultations to be arranged in the United States and in Europe between, on the one side, the President of the European Council and the President of the Commission, and on the other side, the President of the United States;
- bi-annual consultations between the European Community Foreign Ministers, with the Commission, and the U.S. Secretary of State, alternately on either side of the Atlantic;
- ad hoc consultations between the Presidency Foreign Minister or the Troika and the U.S. Secretary of State;
- bi-annual consultations between the Commission and the U.S. Government at Cabinet level;
- briefings, as currently exist, by the Presidency to U.S. representatives on European Political Cooperation (EPC) meetings at the Ministerial level.

Both sides are resolved to develop and deepen these procedures for consultation so as to reflect the evolution of the European Community and of its relationship with the United States. They welcome the actions taken by the European Parliament and the Congress of the United States in order to improve their dialogue and thereby bring closer together the peoples on both sides of the Atlantic."

Source: "Declaration on U.S.-EC Relations," *Daily Bulletin,* (Geneva, U.S. Mission, 23 November 1990), pp. 2-6. (Emphasis, R.S.)

CONFERENCE ON POLITICAL UNION:
EUROPEAN COUNCIL,
ROME, 14 AND 15 DECEMBER 1990,
PRESIDENCY CONCLUSIONS

Common foreign and security policy

The common foreign and security policy should aim at maintaining peace and international stability, developing friendly relations with all countries, promoting democracy, the rule of law and respect for human rights, encouraging the economic development of all nations, and should also bear in mind the special relations of individual Member States.

To this end, the conference will in particular address the Union's objectives, the scope of its policies and the means of fostering and ensuring their effective implementation within an institutional framework.

Such an *institutional framework* would be based on the following elements:

- one decision-making centre, namely the council;
- harmonization and, where appropriate, unification of the preparatory work; a unified secretariat;
- a reinforced role for the Commission, through a non-exclusive right of initiative;
- adequate procedures for consulting and informing the European Parliament:
- detailed procedures ensuring that the Union can speak effecti-

vely with one voice on the international stage, in particular in international organizations and vis-a-vis third countries.

The following elements should be considered as a basis for the *decision-making process:*
- the rule of consensus in defining general guidelines: in this context, non-participation or abstention in the voting as a means of not preventing unanimity:
- the possibility of recourse to qualified-majority voting for the implementation of agreed policies.

As regards *common security,* the gradual extension of the Union's role in this area should be considered, in particular with reference, initially, to issues debated in international organizations: arms control, disarmament and related issues; CSCE matters; certain questions debated in the United Nations, including peace-keeping operations; economic and technological co-operation in the armaments field; co-ordination of armaments expert policy, and non-proliferation.

Furthermore, the European Council emphasizes that, with a view to the future, the prospect of a role for the Union in *defence matters* should be considered, without prejudice to Member States' existing obligations in this area, bearing in mind the importance of maintaining and strengthening the ties within the Atlantic alliance and without prejudice to the traditional positions of other member states.

The idea of a commitment by Member States to provide *mutual assistance,* as well as proposals put forward by some Member States on the future of *Western European Union,* should also be addressed."

Source: European Council, *Presidency Conclusions,* Rome, 14-15
            December 1990, (part 1), SN 424/1/90; pp. 1-10.
            (Emphasis, R.S.)

SELECTED BIBLIOGRAPHY

Official Publications and Memoirs

European Community

Cecchini, Paolo. *The European Challenge 1992: The Benefits of a Single Market.* Aldershot, Gower, 1988; XXI-127 p.

Commission of the European Communities. *Completing the Internal Market [the White Paper].* Luxembourg/Brussels, Office for official publications of the European Communities, 14 June 1985, COM(85)310.

Commission of the European Communities. "Single European Act," *Bulletin of the European Communities,* Supplement 2/86; 26 p.

Commission of the European Communities. "The Economics of 1992: An Assessment of the Potential Economic Effects of Completing the Internal Market of the European Community," *European Economy,* no 35, March 1988; 233 p.

Commission of the European Communities. *Proposal for a Council Regulation Temporarily Suspending Import Duties on Certain Weapons and Military Equipment.* Brussels, 15 September 1988, COM (88) 502 final; 16 p.

Commission of the European Communities. *L'Europe de 1992 sera une "Europe partenaire".* Information Memo. Brussels, 19 October 1988, P(88)117; 4 p.

Commission of the European Communities. "One Market, One Money," *Information of the Spokesman's Service.* Brussels, 19 October 1990, P(90) 78; 6 p.

Commission of the European Communities. *Europe partenaire. La dimension extérieure du marché unique.* Brussels, 24 October 1988, SEC(88) 1492/7; 12 p. (not published).

Commission of the European Communities. *Public Procurements and Construction – Towards an Integrated Market.* Brussels, 1988; 107p. (European Documentation).

Commission of the European Communities. *A Common Agricultural Policy for the 1990s.* Brussels, 1989; 90 p. (European Documentation).

Commission of the European Communities. *Commission Opinion of 21 October 1990 on the proposal for amendment of the Treaty Establishing the European Economic Community with a View to Political Union.* Brussels/Luxembourg, Documents, COM(90) 600 final; 16 p.

Commission of the European Communities. *La Communauté et la Banque européenne pour la reconstruction et le développement.* Bruxelles/Luxembourg, office of official publications of the European Community, 25 July 1990, COM(90) 190/2 final; 90 p.

Commission of the European Communities. *Report on United States. Trade Barriers and Unfair Trade Practices.* Brussels, Services of the Commission of the European Communities, 1990; 57 p.

Commission of the European Communities. *Report on United States. Trade Barriers and Unfair Trade Practices.* Brussels, Services of the Commission of the European Communities, 1991; 87 p.

Commission of the European Communities. *Union économique et monétaire,* Brussels/Luxembourg, office of official publications of the European Community, 21 August 1990), SEC(90) 1659 final; 37 p.

Commission of the European Communities. *Union européenne - La politique extérieure commune.* 27 February 1991; 27 p. (draft).

De Clercq, Willy and Leo Verhoef. *Europe Back to the Top.* Brussels, Roularta Books, 1990; 185 p.

Delors, Jacques. "Europe's Ambitions," *Foreign Policy,* No 80, Fall 1990; 27 p.

Delors, Jacques. "European Integration and Security," Survival, Vol. XXXIII, No 2, March/April 1991; pp. 99-109.

European Council. *Presidency Conclusions.* Rome, 14-15 December 1990, (part 1), SN 424/1/90; 10 p.

France, Boyd. *A Short Chronicle of United States - European Community Relations,* Washington, D.C., European Community Information Service, 1973; 32 p.

Krenzler, Horst G. "The Dialogue Between the European Community and the United States of America: Present Form and Future Prospects" in Jürgen Schwarze (ed.), *The External Relations of the European Community.* Baden-Baden, Nomos Verlag, 1989; pp. 91–103.

Luxembourg Presidency. "Union politique : pour une politique étrangère et de sécurité commune - un document soumis à la CIG par la présidence," *Agence Europe,* 16 April 1991; 5 p.

Mc Sharry, Ray. "Commemoration 30 Years of the Common Agricultural Policy Speech at the Dublin Horse Show", *European Community News.* Washington, EC Embassy, 19 July 1990; 3 p.

Monnet, Jean. *La Communauté européenne et l'unité de l'Occident.* Lausanne, Centre de recherches européennes, 1961; 10 p.

Monnet, Jean. *Europe-Amérique. Relations de partenaires nécessaires à la paix.* Lausanne, Centre de recherches européennes, 1963; 13 p.

Pandolfi, Filippo Maria. *Science and Technology and European Market Integration.* Washington, US National Academy of Sciences Forum, 5 March 1990; 22 p. (not published).

Spaak, Paul-Henri. *Combats inachevés.* Paris, Fayard, 1969; 2 volumes.

Western European Union and Independent European Programme Group

Assemblée de l'union de l'Europe occidentale. *La sécurité de l'Europe et les événements survenus au Proche et au Moyen-Orient: la crise du Koweit.* Report by Mr Pieralli, Paris, 36th session, (2nd part), document 1242, 20 September 1990; 36 p.

Assemblée de l'union de l'Europe occidentale. *Les conséquences de l'invasion du Koweit: les opérations dans le Golfe.* Report by Mr De Hoop Scheffer, Paris, 36th session, (2nd part), document 1243, 20 September 1990; 21 p.

Assemblée de l'union de l'Europe occidentale. *La sécurité de l'Europe et la crise du Golfe.* Report by Mr De Decker, Paris, 36th session, (2nd part), document 1244, 14 November 1990; 16 p. Assemblée de l'union de l'Europe occidentale. *Les conséquences de l'invasion du Koweit : la poursuite des opérations dans la région du Golfe.* Report by Mr De Hoop Scheffer,

Paris, 36th session, (2nd part), document 1248, 7 November
1990; 30 p.

Assemblée de l'union de l'Europe occidentale. *Rapport sur le
Groupe européen indépendant de programmes (GEIP) et l'Union
de l'Europe occcidentale.* Report by Mr M. Wilkinson, Paris,
35th session, document 1228, 25 May 1990; 21 p.

Independent European Programme Group. *European Armaments
Market Action Plan.* IEPG/II-D/36m 13 July 1988; 9 p.
(Not published).

Independent European Programme Group. *Luxemburg Communique.*
IEPG/MIN/D.11, 9 November 1988; 6 p.

Van Eekelen, Willem. "The WEU: Europe's Best Defense," *European
Affairs.* Vol. 4, 1990; pp. 8-11.

U.S. Government

Baker, James A. "A New Europe, A New Atlanticism: Architecture
for a New Era," *Press Department of State,* Berlin, 12 December 1989; 11 p. Pr No. 245.

Bush George. "Remarks at the Boston University Commencement
Ceremony", *Beyond Containment, Selected Speeches by President
George Bush on Europe and East-West Relations.* 21 May 1989;
pp. 12-15.

Carter, Jimmy. *Keeping Faith. Memoirs of a President.* London,
Collins, 1982; XVI-622 p.

Carter, Jimmy."Address by the President before the Commission of
the European Communities, 6 January 1978" in U.S. State
Department, *American Foreign Policy: Basic Documents, 1977-
1980.* Washington, D.C., United States Government Printing
Office, 1981, Document 209.

Department of Commerce. Miller, Debra L. (ed.). *EC 1992: A Commerce Department Analysis of European Community Directives.*
Washington D.C., U.S. government printing office, 1989/90;
3 volumes.

Department of Defense. *1992: The Single European Market and
Defense Cooperation.* Washington D.C., 1989; 3 p. (Not published).

Department of State. *Financial Services and the European Community's Single Market Program.* Washington D.C., January 1989; 26 p. (Not published).

Department of the Treasury. *EC Single Market: Banking and Securities.* Washington D.C., 27 December 1988; 6 p. (Not published).

De Vos, Peter Jon. "Statement by the Deputy Assistant Secretary for Science and Technology Affairs of the Department of State", *Hearing on Europe 1992 and its Effects on U.S. Science, Technology and Competitiveness.* Washington D.C., House of Representatives, Committee on Science, Space, and Technology, 16 May 1989; 5 p.

Eisenhower, Dwight D. *Waging Peace, 1956-1961.* London, Heinemann, 1966; XXIII-741 p.

Foreign Relations of the United States. *1955-57, Western European Security and Integration.* Washington D.C., 1986, volume IV.

Hills, Carla A. "European Economic Integration (1992)", *Testimony by the U.S. Trade Representative Before the Senate Finance Committee.* 10 May 1989; 16 p.

Kennedy, John, F. "Address at Independence Hall, Philadelphia, July 4, 1962", *Public Papers of the Presidents of the United States, John F. Kennedy, PUB 18.* Washington, D.C., United States Government Printing Office, 1962; [278], pp. 538-539.

Key, Sidney. "Financial Integration in the European Community", *International Finance Discussion Papers 349.* Washington D.C., Board of Governors of the Federal Reserve System, April 1989; 120 p. (Not published).

Kissinger, Henry. *Years of Upheaval.* Boston/Toronto, Little, Brown and Company, 1982; XXI-1283 p.

Mc Allister Eugene J. "Testimony of the Assistant Secretary of State for Economic and Business Affairs", *Subcommittee on Europe and the Middle East, Committee on Foreign Affairs U.S. House of Representatives.* 10 May 1989; 14 p.

Murphy, James M. "Testimony of the Assistant U.S. Trade Representative For Europe and the Mediterranean", *Ways and Means Trade Subcommittee Hearing on "Europe 1992".* 20 March 1989; 12 p.

Murphy, James M. "Testimony of the Assistant U.S. Trade Representative For Europe and the Mediterranean", *Subcommittee on Europe and the Middle East, Committee on Foreign Affairs U.S. House of Representatives.* 10 May 1989; 16 p.

Nixon, Richard and Henry Kissinger. "Fourth Annual Report to the Congress on United States Foreign Policy, May 3, 1973," *Public Papers of the Presidents, Richard Nixon, PUB 29.* Washington, D.C., United States Government Printing Office, 1973, [141], pp. 401-407.

Straetz, Robert. "U.S. Exporters Should Find That Benefits of "Europe 1992" Program Will Outweigh Problems", *Business America.* 22 May 1989; pp. 10-11.

U.S. General Accounting Office. *European Single Market. Issues of Concern to U.S. Exporters.* Washington, D.C., Publications of the General Accounting Office, February 1990; 46 p. GAON-SIAD90-60.

U.S. General Accounting Office. *U.S. Financial Services' Competitiveness Under the Single Market Program.* Washington, D.C., Publications of the General Accounting Office, May 1990; 72 p. GAO/NSIAD-90-99.

U.S. Government Task Force on the EC Internal Market. *An Assessment of Economic Policy Issues Raised by the European Community's Single Market Program.* Washington, D.C., U.S. Government Printing Office, 1990; 31 p.

U.S. International Trade Commission. *The Effects of Greater Economic Integration Within the European Community on the United States. Report to the Committee on Ways and Means of the United States House of Representatives and the Committee on Finance of the Senate.* Washington, D.C., USITC Publication, July 1989; 310 p.

U.S. Representative to the European Communities. *Letter From Brussels.* Volume 2, No.4, 15 August 1989; 6 p.

Zoellick, Robert B. "Practical Lessons for the Post-Cold War Age," *European Affairs.* Volume 4, 1990; pp. 79-84.

U.S. Congress

Eubanks, Walter W. "The European Central Banking System and the 1992 Monetary Union," *Congressional Research Service Report for Congress,* 10 January 1990; 17 p.

Gallis, Paul E. "A New Global Role for the EC?" in Glennon Harrison (ed.) *European Community: Isssues Raised by 1992 Integration. Congressional Research Service.* 1989; pp. 79-82.

Gallis, Paul E. "U.S.-West European Affairs: Responding to a Changing Relationship," *Congressional Research Service Issue Brief.* Updated 6 March 1990; 14 p.

Gallis, Paul E. Germany's Future and U.S. Interests: Summary of a CRS Seminar," *Congressional Research Service Issue Brief.* 23 October 1990; 19 p.

Gallis, Paul E. "U.S.-West European Affairs: Responding to a Changing Relationship," *Congressional Research Service Issue Brief.* Updated 9 November 1990; 14 p.

Gallis, Paul E. and Steven J. Woehrel. "Germany's Future and U.S. Interests," *Congressional Research Service Issue Brief.* Updated 23 February 1990; 15 p.

Gallis, Paul E. and Steven J. Woehrel. "Germany's Future and U.S. Interests", *Congressional Research Service Issue Brief.* Updated 2 October 1990; 15 p.

Guicherd, Catherine. *A European Defense Identity: Challenge and Opportunity for NATO,* Washington D.C., Congressional Research Service Report, 12 June 1991; 85 p.

Harrison, Glennon J. (ed.). *European Community: Issues Raised by 1992 Integration.* Washington D.C., Congressional Research Service Report, 1989; 102 p.

Harrison, Glennon J. *The European Community: 1992 and Reciprocity.* Washington, D.C.: Congressional Research Service Report, 11 April 1989; 8 p.

Jackson, James K. *American Direct Investment Abroad: Effects on Trade, Jobs and the Balance of Payments.* Washington D.C., Congressional Research Service Report, 1988; 26 p.

Jackson, James K. "U.S. Direct Investment in the EC", in Glennon J. Harrison (ed.), *European Community: Issues Raised by 1992 Integration.* Washington D.C., Congressional Research Service Report, May 1989; pp. 19-27.

Mc Loughlin, Glen J. (ed.). "The Europe 1992 Plan: Science and Technology Issues", *CRS Report for Congress.* 16 March 1989; 23 p.

Nanto, Dick. "Japan's Response to EC Integration" in Glennon J. Harrison, (ed.) *European Community: Issues Raised by 1992 Integration.* Washington D.C., Congressional Research Service Report, 1989; pp. 61-70.

Rallo, Joseph C. "Alliance Security Policy After 1992", *Hearing on Europe 1992 and its Effects on U.S. Science, Technology and Competitiveness.* Washington D.C., House of Representatives, Committee on Science, Space, and Technology, 16 May 1989; 34 p.

Sloan, Stanley R. "The United States and a New Europe: Strategy for the Future", *Congressional Research Service Issue Brief.* 14 May 1990; 60 p.

Sloan, Stanley R. "A New Europe and U.S. Interests," *Congressional Research Service Issue Brief.* Updated 8 November 1990; 12 p.

U.S. Congress. Joint Economic Committee. *Europe 1992.* Hearing. 100 Cong. 2nd sess. Washington, D.C., Government Printing Office, 18 November 1988; 56 p.

U.S. Congress. House Committee on Foreign Affairs. Subcommittee on Europe and the Middle East. *Europe 1992: Economic Integration Plan.* Hearing. 101 Cong. 1 sess. Washington, D.C., Government Printing Office, February-May 1989; 446 p.

U.S. Congress. Joint Economic Committee. *Europe 1992: Long-Term Implications for the U.S. Economy.* Hearing. 101 Cong. 1 sess. Washington, D.C., Government Printing Office, 26 April 1989; 254 p.

U.S. Congress. Committee on Science, Space, and Technology. *Europe 1992 and its Effects on U.S. Science, Technology and Competitiveness.* Hearing. 101 Cong. 1 sess. Washington, D.C., Government Printing Office, 16-17 May 1989; 815 p.

U.S. Congress. Committee on Foreign Affairs. *The European Community's Plan to Integrate Its Economy by 1992.* Hearing. 101 Cong. 1 sess. Washington, D.C., Government Printing Office, 31 May 1989; 69 p.

U.S. Congress. Committee on Banking, Finance and Urban Affairs. *Oversight Hearings on European Community's 1992 Program.* Hearing. 101 Cong. 1 sess. Washington, D.C., Government Printing Office, 26-28 September 1989; 426 p.

U.S. Congress. Subcommittee on Exports, Tax Policy, and Special Problems. *European Community Approach to Testing and Certification: Should the U.S. Government Play a Role?* Hearing, 101 Cong. 2nd sess. Washington, D.C., Government Printing Office, 30 April 1990; 133 p.

U.S. Professional Organizations

Bhatia, Joe and U.S. Chamber of Commerce. "Europe-1992: Product Standards and Testing." Statement before *the Subcommittee on International Economic Policy and Trade and Subcommittee on Europe and the Middle East of the House Committee on Foreign Affairs.* 13 April 1989; pp. 294-307.

Business Roundtable."the United States and the European Community's Single Market Initiative: An Analytical Framework" in U.S. Congress, *Europe 1992: Economic Integration Plan.* Hearing. 101 Cong. 1 sess., Washington, D.C.: Government Printing Office, February-May 1989; pp. 425-436.

Cooney, Stephen. *EC-92: New Issues and New Developments. NAM's Third Report on the European Community's Internal Market Program and the Effects on U.S. Manufacturers* (Washington, D.C.,: National Association of Manufacturers Publications, April 1991); 55 p.

Cooney, Stephen. *Update on EC-92. An NAM Report on Developments in the European Community's Internal Market Program and the Effects on U.S. Manufacturers* (Washington, D.C.,: National Association of Manufacturers Publications, April 1990); 48

Cooney, Stephen. *EC-92 and U.S. Industry.* Washington, D.C., National Association of Manufacturers, 10 January 1989; 32 p. (Draft).

Cooney, Stephen. "The Implications of the European Community 1992 Plan". *Testimony before the Joint Economic Committee, United States Congress.* 26 April 1989; 10 p.

Cooney, Stephen. "Europe 1992: The Opportunity and the Challenge for U.S. Economic Interests", *SAIS Review,* Vol. 10, Spring 1990; pp. 73-85.

Cooney, Stephen. "The Impact of the European Community 1992 Internal Market Program on U.S. Competitiveness in Science and Technology", *Testimony before the U.S. House of Representatives Committee on Science, Space and Technology.* 17 May 1989; 12 p.

Cooney, Stephen. "EC-92 and U.S. Industry," in Joint Economic Committee. *Europe 1992: Long-Term Implications for the U.S. Economy.* Hearing. 101 Cong. 1 sess. 26 April 1989; pp. 18-

Cooney. Stephen. *Update on EC-92. An NAM Report on Developments in the European Community's Internal Market Program and the*

Effects on U.S. Manufacturers. Washington, D.C., National Association of Manufacturers Publications, April 1990; 63 p.

Olmer, Lionel H. "EC 1992 and the Requirement for U.S. Industry and Government Partnership", *Statement for the U.S. Chamber of Commerce before the House Committee on Ways and Means, Subcommittee on Trade.* 20 March 1989; 10 p.

U.S. Chamber of Commerce. *Europe 1992. A Practical Guide for American Business.* Washington, D.C., Publications of the U.S. Chamber of Commerce, 1989; 143 p.

U.S. Chamber of Commerce. *Europe 1992. A Practical Guide for American Business #2.* Washington, D.C., Publications of the U.S. Chamber of Commerce, 1990; 56 p.

Books

Adenauer, Konrad. *Erinnerungen, 1955-1959.* Stuttgart, Deutsche Verlags-Anstalt, 1967; 551 p.

Allen, David, Reinhardt Rummel and Wolfgang Wessels (eds.) *European Political Cooperation. Towards a Foreign Policy for Western Europe.* London, Butterworthand, 1982; 184 p.

Alting Von Geusau, Frans Alphons Maria (ed.) *The External Relations of the European Community.* London, Saxon House, 1974; 132 p.

Bourrinet, Jacques (ed.) *Les relations Communauté européenne-Etats-Unis.* Paris, Economica, 1987; 617 p.

Bressand, Albert and Kalypso Nicolaïdis (eds.) *Strategic Trends in Services.* New York, Harper & Row, 1989; XIII-360 p.

Brzezinski, Zbigniew. *Power and Principle: Memoirs of the National Security Adviser, 1977-1981.* New York: Farrar, Straus, Giroux, 1983; XVII-587 p.

Brugmans Henri. *L'idée européenne 1918-1965.* Bruges, Tempelhof, 1965; 292 p.

Bureau of National Affairs. *1992 - The External Impact of European Unification.* Washington, D.C., Buraff publications, (Newsletter).

Burstein, Daniel. *Euroquake. Europe's Explosive Economic Challenge Will Change the World.* New York, Simon & Schuster, 1991; 384 p.

Calingaert, Michael. *The 1992 Challenge From Europe.* Washington D.C., National Planning Association, 1988; 148 p.

Calleo, David P. *The Imperious Economy.* Cambridge, Harvard University Press, 1982; 265 p.

Calleo, David P. *Beyond American Hegemony.* New York, Basic Books, 1987; 288 p.

Campbell, Dennis. *Europe and 1992: the Challenge for American Enterprise.* Boston, Kluwer Law and Tax Publishers, 1989; VII, 100 p.

Coffey, Peter. *The External Economic Relations of the EEC.* London, MacMillan, 1976; 118 p.

Cook Paul, Gilmour Andrew. *Toward a "European Pillar?" Enhanced European Security Cooperation and Implications for U.S. Policy.* Washington D.C., Center for Strategic and international Studies, November 1988; 44 p.

De Ruyt, Jean. *L'Acte unique européen*. Brussels, Université de Bruxelles, 1987; 355 p.

De Schoutheete, Philippe. *La coopération politique européenne*. Brussels/Luxembourg, Labor/Office des publications officielles des Communautés européennes, 1990; 260 p.

Deutsch, Karl. *Political Community in the North Atlantic Area: International Organization in the Light of Historical Experience*. Princeton University Press, 1957; 228 p.

Deutsch, Karl. *Political Community in the North Atlantic Area: International Organization in the Light of Historical Experience*, Princeton, Princeton University Press, 1957; 228 p.

Duroselle, Jean-Baptiste. *Deux types de grands hommes. Le général de Gaulle et Jean Monnet*. Geneva, Institut universitaire de Hautes Etudes Internationales, 1977; pp. 17-22.

Feld, Werner. *The European Community in World Affairs*, Port Washington, N.Y., Alfred, 1976; 352 p.

Fontaine, André. *Un seul lit pour deux rêves. Histoire de la "détente" 1962-1981*. Paris, Fayard, 1981; 538 p.

Freedman, Lawrence. *Evolution of Nuclear Strategy*. London, Macmillan Press, 1981; XVIII-473 p.

Gasteyger, Curt. *Europa zwischen Spaltung und Einigung 1945-1990*. Bonn, Bundeszentrale für politische Bildung. 1990; 446 p.

General Agreement on Tariffs and Trade. *GATT, What it is, What it Does?* Geneva, GATT Information and Media Relations Division, 1989; 21 p.

Gianaris, Nicholas V. *The European Community and the United States*. New York, Praeger, 1991; XII-240 p.

Ginsberg, Roy H. *Foreign Policy Actions of the European Community: The Politics of Scale*. Boulder, Lynne Rienner, 1989; XIII-203 p.

Grieco, Joseph. *Cooperation Among Nations. Europe, America, and Non-Tariff Barriers to Trade*. Ithaca and London, Cornell University Press, 1990; 255 p.

Grosser, Alfred. *Les Occidentaux. Les pays d'Europe et les Etats-Unis depuis la guerre*. Paris, Fayard, 1981; 437 p.

Haas, Ernst B. *The Uniting of Europe: Political, Social, and Economic Forces, 1950-1957*. Stanford, Stanford University Press, 1958; XX-552 p.

Haas, Ernst B. *Beyond the Nation-State, Functionalism and International Organization*, Stanford,Standford University Press, 1964; X-595 p.

Harrison, Michael M. *The Reluctant Ally: France and Atlantic Security.* Baltimore, Johns Hopkins University Press, 1981; XIII-304 p.

Henderson, David. *1992: The External Dimension.* New York and London, Group of Thirty, 1989; 19 p.

Hinshaw, Randall. *The European Community and American Trade.* New York, Praeger/Concil on Foreign Relations, 1964; 188 p.

Hoffmann, Stanley. *Gulliver's Troubles, Or the Setting of American Foreign Policy.* New York, McGraw-Hill, 1968; 556 p.

Hufbauer, Gary C. (ed.) *Europe 1992. An American Perspective.* Washington, D.C., The Brookings Institution, 1990; 406 p.

Hunter, Robert E. and John Yochelson. *Beyond 1992: U.S. Strategy Toward the European Community.* Washington, D.C., The Center for Strategic and International Studies, September 1990;

Jouanneau, Daniel. *Le GATT.* Paris, Presses universitaires de France, 1987; 128 p.

Kaufmann, William. *The McNamara Strategy.* New York, Harper and Row, 1964; X-339 p.

Kennedy, Paul. *The Rise and Fall of the Great Powers: Economic Change and Military Conflict from 1500 to 2000.* New York, Random House, 1987; XXV-667p.

Keohane, Robert. *After Hegemony. Cooperation and Discord in the World Political Economy.* Princeton, Princeton University Press, 1984; IX, 290 p.

Krause, Lawrence. *European Economic Integration and the United States.* Washington, D.C., The Brookings Institution, 1968; 265 p.

Küsters, Hanns, Jürgen. *Fondements de la Communauté économique européenne.* Luxembourg/Brussels, Office des publications officielles des Communautés européennes/Editions Labor, 1990; 379 p.

Leimbacher, Urs. *The European Defence Pillar. Myth and Reality.* Geneva, Programme for Strategic and International Security Studies, Occasional Paper 2/1990; 67 p.

Ludlow, Peter. *Beyond 1992. Europe and Its Western Partners.* Brussels, Center for European Policy Studies, Paper No 38, 1989; 91 p.

Macchiarola, Frank (ed). *International Trade. The Changing Role of the United States.* New York, The Academy of Political Science, 1990; XIV-206 p.

Melandri, Pierre. *Les Etats-Unis face à l'unification de l'Europe, 1945-1954.* Paris, Pedone, 1980; 534 p.

Melandri, Pierre. *Les Etats-Unis et le "défi" européen, 1955-1958.* Paris, Presses universitaires de France, 1975; 220 p.

Melandri, Pierre. *Une incertaine alliance. Les Etats-Unis et l'Europe, 1973-1983.* Paris, Publications de la Sorbonne, 1988; 431 p.

Messerlin, Patrick and Karl Sauvant (ed). *The Uruguay Round. Services in the World Economy.* Washington, D.C., World Bank/ UN Centre on Transnational Corporations, 1990; 220 p.

Moodie, Michael. *Defense Implications of Europe 92.* Washington, D.C., The Center for Strategic and International Studies, 1990; 36 p.

Moyer, Wayne H. and Timothy E. Josling. *Agricultural Policy Reform: Politics and Process in the EC and the USA.* Ames, Iowa State University Press, 1990; XX, 235 p.

Murphy, Anna. *The European Community and the International Trading System. Volume II. The European Community and the Uruguay Round.* Brussels, Centre for European Policy Studies, 1990; 140 p.

Nye, Joseph *Bound to Lead: the Changing Nature of American Power.* New York, Basic Books, 1990; XII-307 p.

Palmer, John. *Europe Without America? The Crisis in Atlantic Relations.* Oxford, Oxford University Press, 1988; 219 p.

Pelkmans, Jacques, Alan Winters and Helen Wallace. *Europe's Domestic Market.* London, Royal Institute of International Affairs, 1988; X, 149 p. Chatham House Papers 43.

Pelkmans, Jacques and Marc Vankeukelen. *The Internal Market of North America: Fragmentation and Integration in the US and Canada.* Luxembourg, Commission of the European Communities, 1988; 121 p. Volume 16 of the Research on the "Cost of Non-Europe."

Pérez-Lopez, Jorge (ed). *EC 1992: Implications for U.S. Workers.* Washington, D.C., Center for Strategic and International Studies, 1990; X-149 p.

Quantock, Paul (ed.) *Opportunities in European Financial Services. 1992 and Beyond.* New York, 1990, John Wiley & Sons, XIV-245 p. Raghavan, Chakravarthi. *Recolonization. GATT, the Uruguay Round & the Third World.* Penang, Third World Network, 1990; 319 p.

Rubin, Seymour J. and Mark, L. Jones (ed). *Conflict and Resolution in US-EC Trade Relations at the Opening of the Uruguay Round.* New York, Oceana, 1989; 531 p.

Schaetzel, Robert J. *The Unhinged Alliance. America and the European Community.* New York, Harper & Row, 1975; 184 p.

Schott, Jeffrey J. (ed.). *Completing the Uruguay Round. A results-Oriented Approach to the GATT Trade Negotiations.* Washington, D.C., Institute for International Economics, 1990, 224 p.

Schwartz, Thomas Alan,. *America's Germany: John J. McCloy and the Federal Republic of Germany.* Cambridge, Harvard University Press, 1991; XIII-404 p.

Schwarze, Jürgen (ed.). *The External Relations of the European Community.* Baden-Baden, Nomos Verlag, 1989; 148 p.

Seidelmann, Reimund (ed.) *Auf dem Weg zu einer westeuropäischen Sicherheitspolitik.* Baden-Baden, Nomos Verlag, 1989; 384 p.

Serra, Enrico (ed). *Il rilancio dell'Europa e i trattati di Roma, actes du colloque de Rome, 25-28 March 1987.* Milano, Giuffrè, 1989; X-729 p.

Soldatos, Panayotis. *Le système institutionnel et politique des Communautés européennes dans un monde en mutation.* Brussels, Bruylant, 1989; 305 p.

Stoeckel Andrew, David Pearce and Gary Banks. *Western Trade Blocs.* Canberra, Centre for International Economics, 1990; 119 p. Tsakaloyannis, Panos. *Western European Security in a Changing World: From the Reactivation of the WEU to the Single European Act.* Maastricht, European Institute of Public Administration Publications, 1988; 159 p.

Tsoukalis, Loukas (ed.) *Europe, America and the World Economy.* Oxford, Blackwell, 1986; 279 p.

Twitchett, Kenneth Joseph (ed.). *Europe and the World: The External Relations of the Common Market.* London, St Martin, 1976; 210 p.

Wallace, William (ed.) *The Dynamics of European Integration.* London, Pinter for the Royal Institute of International Affairs, 1990; 315 p.

Webb, Simon. *NATO and 1992: Defence Acquisition and Free Markets.* Santa Monica, Rand Corp., July 1989; I-XV, 127 p.

Woolcock, Stephen. *The Uruguay Round: Issues for the European Community and the United States.* London, Royal Institute of International Affairs, 1990; 40 p. (RIIA Discussion Paper 31).

Articles

Bacot, Michèle and Marie-Claude Plantin. "La réactivation de l'UEO: éléments d'un rééquilibrage dans les rapports Communauté européenne Etats-Unis" in Jacques Bourrinet (ed.) *Les relations Communauté européenne-Etats-Unis.* Paris, Economica, 1987; pp. 579-592.

Berger Claude. "Crise du Golfe, embargo et après-crise," *Revue du Marché Commun.* no341, November 1990; pp. 615-620.

Bonvicini, Gianni. "La coopération politique européenne et la politique de sécurité dans les rapports Europe-Amérique," in Jacques Bourrinet (ed.) *Les relations Communauté européenne-Etats-Unis.* Paris, Economica, 1987; pp. 461-479.

Bressand, Albert and Kalypso Nicolaïdis. "Regional Integration in a Networked World Economy in William Wallace (ed.) *The Dynamics of European Integration.* London, Pinter for the Royal Institute of International Affairs, 1990; pp. 27-49.

Charpentier, Jean. "L'Europe face à la proposition américaine de participation à l'IDS" in Jacques Bourrinet (ed.) *Les relations Communauté européenne-Etats-Unis.* Paris, Economica, 1987; pp. 519-530.

Deker, Wisse. "The American Response to Europe 1992," *European Affairs 2/89.* Summer 1989; pp. 105-110.

Devuyst, Youri. "European Commmunity Integration and the United States: Toward a New Transatlantic Relationship?" *Revue d'intégration européenne/Journal of European Integration,* Fall 1990; pp. 5-29.

Di Nolfo, Enrico. "Gli Stati Uniti e le origini della Comunita economica europea", in Enrico SERRA (ed). *Il rilancio dell' Europa e i trattati di Roma, actes du colloque de Rome, 25-28 March 1987.* Milano, Giuffrè, 1989; pp. 339-351.

Falke, Andreas. "Veränderte amerikanische Einstellungen zur EG. Der Binnenmarkt und die GATT-Verhandlungen", *Europa Archiv,* March 1991; pp. 191-200.

Froment-Meurice, Henri and Peter Ludlow. "Towards a European Foreign Policy", *Governing Europe, 1989 Annual Conference Proceedings,* Brussels, Centre for European Policy Studies, 1990, Paper No. 45, pp. 1-36.

Geier, Karsten D. *The European Community in the 1982 Siberian Gas Pipeline Conflict.* Washington, George Mason University, 24-25 May 1989; 32 p. Paper presented at the Inaugural Conference of the European Community Studies Association.

Gerner, Michael. "Die WEU als Forum der Sicherheitspolitischen Zusammenarbeit in Westeuropa" in Reimund Seidelmann (ed.) *Auf dem Weg zu einer westeuropäischen Sicherheitspolitik* Baden-Baden, Nomos Verlag, 1989; pp. 181-256.

Ginsberg, Roy H. "The Political and Economic Implications of the European Community's 1992 Plan for United States-European Community Relations" in *Europe 1992 and its Effects on U.S. Science, Technology and Competitiveness.* Washington D.C., U.S. House of Representatives, Hearings before the Committee on Science, Space, and Technology, 16 May 1989; pp. 30-54.

Grapin, Jacqueline. "George Bush et l'Europe," *Politique étrangère.* 1/89; pp. 37-44.

Heisenberg, Wolfgang. "European Defence Collaboration", *Governing Europe, 1989 Annual Conference Proceedings,* Brussels, Centre for European Policy Studies, Paper No. 45, pp. 1-36.

Hoffmann, Stanley. "Europe's Identity Crisis," *Daedalus.* Fall 1964); pp. 1279-1282.

Hoffmann, Stanley. "The European Community and 1992," *Foreign Affairs.* Fall 1989; pp. 26-47.

Hoffmann, Stanley. "La France dans le nouvel ordre européen," *Politique étrangère,* Fall 1990; pp. 503-512.

Hoffmann, Stanley. "A New World and its Troubles," *Foreign Affairs,* Fall 1990; pp.115-122.

Hoffmann, Stanley. "The Case for Leadership," *Foreign Policy,* No 81, Winter 1990-1991; pp. 20-38.

Imperiali, Claude. "Coopération politique et conflit du Moyen-Orient. Divergences Europe-Etats-Unis" in Jacques Bourrinet, (ed.) *Les relations Communauté européenne-Etats-Unis.* Paris, Economica, 1987; pp. 509-517.

Inoguchi, Takashi, "Japan and Europe: Wary Partners," *European Affairs,* February-March 1991, pp. 54-58.

Katzman, Julie E. "The Euro-Siberian Pipeline Row: A Study in Community Development," *Millennium* 17, 1988; pp. 25-40.

Layne, Christopher. "Atlanticism without NATO", *Foreign Policy.* No 67, Summer 1987, pp. 22-45.

Magee, John F. "1992: "Moves Americans Must Make," *Harvard Business Review.* May-June 1989; pp. 78-87.

Meesen, Karl M. *Europe en Route to 1992: the Completion of the Internal Market and Its Impact on Non-Europeans, International Lawyer.* Vol. 23, Summer 1989; pp. 359-371.

Messerlin, Patrick. "The European Community," in Messerlin, Patrick and Karl Sauvant (ed). *The Uruguay Round. Services in the World Economy.* Washington, D.C., World Bank/UN Centre on Transnational Corporations, 1990; pp. 132-149.

Moreau-Defarges, Philippe. "La politique européenne face aux Etats-Unis," *Cadmos.* Spring 1989; pp. 45-55.

Nicolaidis, Kalypso. "Mutual Recognition: The New Frontier of Multilateralism?" *Project Promethee Perspectives,* June 1989; pp. 21-34.

Nicolaidis, Kalypso. "Learning while Negotiating: How Services Got on the Uruguay Round Agenda" in Albert Bressand and Kalypso Nicolaïdis (eds.) *Strategic Trends in Services.* New York, Harper & Row, 1989; pp. 161-180.

O'Cleireacain, Seamus. "Europe 1992 and Gaps in the EC's Common Commercial Policy", *ECSA Inaugural Conference at George Mason University.* May 1989; 22 p. (Draft).

O'Cleireacain, Seamus. "Long-Term Implications of Europe 1992 for the US Economy", *Testimony before the Joint Economic Committee, Congress of the United States.* 26 April 1989; 21 p.

Pardalis, Anastasia. "Europen Political Cooperation and the United States," *Journal of Common Market Studies.* Volume XXV, No. 4, June 1987; pp. 271-294.

Pentland, Charles. "L'évolution de la politique étrangère de la Communauté européenne : le contexte transatlantique," *Etudes internationales.* no1, 1978, pp. 106-126.

Prestowitz, Clyde V., Alan Tonelson, and Robert W. Jerome. "The Last Gasp of GATTism," *Harvard Business Review.* March-April 1991; pp. 130-138.

Rao, Venkateshwar. "The European Community and EuroAmerican Relations", *International Studies.* 25, 2, 1988; pp. 161-179.

Rummel, Reinhardt. "West European Security Cooperation and the Reaction in the United States", *ECSA Inaugural Conference at George Mason University.* May 1989; 15 p. (Not published).

Sandholtz, Wayne and John Zysman. "1992: Recasting the European Bargain". *World Politics XLII.* October 1989; pp. 95-128.

Schwok, René. "Fortress or Strainer? The External Economic Policy of the Commission of the European Communities" in *Western Europe: Contemporary Society and Future Prospects.* Institute on Western Europe at Columbia University, 1989; pp. 46-68.

Scott, Hal S. "La notion de réciprocité dans la propostion de deuxième directive de coordination bancaire", *Revue du marché commun*. No 323, January 1989; pp. 45-56.

Ullman, Richard H., "The Covert French Connection", *Foreign Policy*. Summer 1989; pp. 3-33.

Vernon, Raymond. "European Community 1992: Can the U.S. Negotiate for Trade Equality? in Frank Macchiarola,(ed). *International Trade. The Changing Role of the United States*. New York, The Academy of Political Science, 1990; pp. 9-16.

Wall, Irwin. "Jean Monnet, les Etats-Unis et le plan français," *Vingtième siècle*, April-June 1991; pp. 3-21.

Wallace, Helen. "Political Reform in the European Community," *The World Today*. January 1991; pp. 1-3.

Yannopoulos, George N. "A Comparative Analysis of the External Trade Effect From the Elimination of Non-Tariff and Tariff Barriers in Preferential Trading Blocs: Implications for the EC's Internal Market Programme", *ECSA Inaugural Conference at George Mason University*. May 1989; 39 p. (Draft).

Yaremtchouk, Romain. "L'Europe face aux Etats-Unis, *Studia Diplomatica*. 29/1986, N0 4-5; pp. 331-629.

Yochelson, John and Robert Hunter. "1992 Will Change the Trans-Atlantic Relationship", *Europe (EC Mission in Washington)*. April 1989, pp. 14-15 & 47.

Zupnik, Elliot. "EC-US and 1992: A Prelude to Trade Wars?" *European Affairs 2/89*. Summer 1989; pp. 111-119.

Zurcher, Arnold. "Coudenhove-Kalergi et les Etats-Unis," in Henri Rieben (ed.) *Coudenhove-Kalergi. Le Pionnier de l'Europe Unie*. Lausanne, Centre de recherches européennes, 1971; pp. 81-90.

INDEX

Acheson, Dean, 11
ACP. *See* African, Caribbean and
    Pacific Countries
Action Committee for the United
    States of Europe", 16
Adenauer, Konrad, 17-18, 44-45, 184
Afganistan War, 47, 226
Africa, 174
African, Caribbean and Pacific
    Countries (ACP), 146
    145-147
Aggregate Measure of Support
    See also Common Agriculture
    Policy
Agriculture, 19, 26, 52, 127, 130,
    133,139-149, 210
Airbus, 35
American Council of Independent
    Laboratories, 78, 82n
American National Standards
    Institute (ANSI), 70
AMS. *See* Aggregate Measure of
    Support
ANSI. *See* American National
    Standards Institute
Atlantic Alliance, 1
Atlantic Partnership, 24-25, 50
Atlantic solidarity, 24
Austria, 201
Automobile, 66-67, 69, 104-105
    bibliography on, 108n
    See also Rules of origin
Aziz, Tariq, 202

Bahtia, Joe, 82n
Baker, James, 170, 202
Ball, George, 16
Bank Holding Company Act,
    116-117, 118
    See also Financial
    services
Barre Plan, 30
BC-NET. *See* Business
    Cooperation Network (AMS),
Belgium, 9, 12, 176n,
    180, 190, 200-202
BENELUX. *See* individual
    countries
BERD. *See* European Bank
    of Reconstruction and
    Development
Bowie, Robert, 15
Bretton Woods System, 30,
    37
Brezhnev, Leonid, 46
Briand, Aristide, 7
Bush administration, 37,
    164-174, 209, 211
Bush George, 164
Bush, Milton, 82n
Cairns Group, 147
Calleo, David, 49n
Canada, 25, 68, 70, 91-92,
    95, 154
CAP. *See* Common Agriculture
    Policy
Capital investments